LE TOUR

Also by Geoffrey Nicholson
THE GREAT BIKE RACE

LE TOUR

The rise and rise of the
Tour de France

GEOFFREY NICHOLSON

Hodder & Stoughton
LONDON SYDNEY AUCKLAND TORONTO

British Library Cataloguing-in-Publication Data

Nicholson, Geoffrey
   Le Tour: The rise and rise of the Tour de France.
   I. Title
   796.60944.

   ISBN 0-340-54268-3

Published by Hodder and Stoughton,
a division of Hodder and Stoughton Ltd,
Mill Road, Dunton Green, Sevenoaks, Kent TN13 2YA
Editorial Office: 47 Bedford Square, London WC1B 3DP

Photoset by E.P.L. BookSet, Norwood, London

Printed in Great Britain by St Edmundsbury Press Ltd
Bury St Edmunds, Suffolk

To Stephen Bierley, Graham Jones
and Samuel Abt, my genial companions
on the 1990 Tour.

CONTENTS

TOUR DE FRANCE 1990   TOTAL DISTANCE 3400 Km

Prologue Saturday 30 June	FUTUROSCOPE individual time trial	6.3 km	Stage 11 Wednesday 11 July	ST-GERVAIS MONT-BLANC L'ALPE-D'HUEZ	182.5 km
Stage 1 Sunday 1 July a.m.	FUTUROSCOPE	138.5 km	Stage 12 Thursday 12 July	FONTAINE VILLARD-DE-LANS individual time trial	33.5 km
Stage 2 Sunday 1 July p.m.	FUTUROSCOPE team time trial	44.5 km		REST DAY	
Stage 3 Monday 2 July	POITIERS NANTES	228 km	Stage 13 Saturday 14 July	VILLARD-DE-LANS ST-ETIENNE	149 km
Stage 4 Tuesday 3 July	NANTES LE MONT-ST-MICHEL	203 km	Stage 14 Sunday 15 July	LE PUY-EN-VELAY MILLAU Causse Noir	205 km
Stage 5 Wednesday 4 July	AVRANCHES ROUEN	301 km	Stage 15 Monday 16 July	MILLAU REVEL	170 km
	AIR TRANSFER		Stage 16 Tuesday 17 July	BLAGNAC LUZ-ARDIDEN	215 km
Stage 6 Friday 6 July	SARREBOURG VITTEL	202.5 km	Stage 17 Wednesday 18 July	LOURDES PAU	150 km
Stage 7 Saturday 7 July	VITTEL EPINAL individual time trial	61.5 km	Stage 18 Thursday 19 July	PAU BORDEAUX	202 km
Stage 8 Sunday 8 July	EPINAL BESANÇON	181.5 km	Stage 19 Friday 20 July	CASTILLON la BATAILLE LIMOGES	182.5 km
Stage 9 Monday 9 July	BESANÇON GENEVA	196 km	Stage 20 Saturday 21 July	Lac de VASSIVIERE en LIMOUSIN individual time trial	45.5 km
Stage 10 Tuesday 10 July	GENEVA ST-GERVAIS MONT-BLANC	118.5 km	Stage 21 Sunday 22 July	BRETIGNY-sur-ORGE PARIS Champs-Elysées	182.5 km

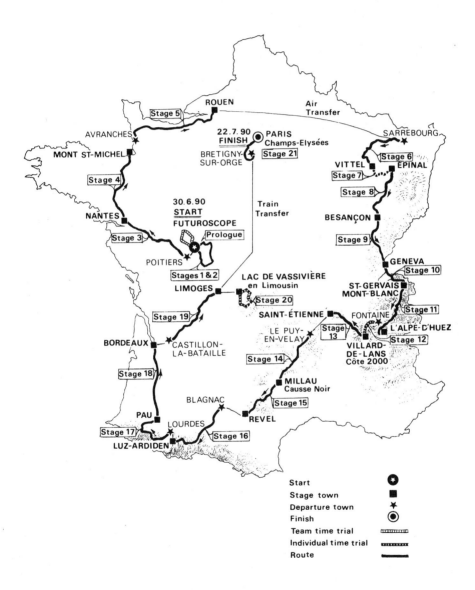

LE TOUR 1990

ROUEN
Stage 5
Air Transfer
AVRANCHES
SARREBOURG
22.7.90 FINISH
PARIS Champs-Elysées
MONT ST-MICHEL
BRETIGNY-SUR-ORGE
Stage 21
VITTEL
ÉPINAL
Stage 6
Stage 4
Stage 7
Stage 8
Train Transfer
NANTES
30.6.90 START
FUTUROSCOPE
BESANÇON
Stage 3
Prologue
Stage 9
POITIERS
Stages 1 & 2
GENEVA
LAC DE VASSIVIÈRE en Limousin
Stage 10
LIMOGES
Stage 20
ST-GERVAIS MONT-BLANC
SAINT-ÉTIENNE
FONTAINE
Stage 11
Stage 19
LE PUY-EN-VELAY
Stage 13
L'ALPE-D'HUEZ
BORDEAUX
CASTILLON-LA-BATAILLE
Stage 12
VILLARD-DE-LANS Côte 2000
Stage 14
Stage 18
MILLAU Causse Noir
BLAGNAC
Stage 15
PAU
Stage 17
LOURDES
REVEL
LUZ-ARDIDEN
Stage 16

Start
Stage town
Departure town
Finish
Team time trial
Individual time trial
Route

PHOTOGRAPHIC ACKNOWLEDGMENTS

COLOUR
Photosport International: Jacket photograph; second page: Frans Maassen, Steve Bauer and Claudio Chiappucci; eighth page: the Champs-Elysées and Podium picture.

All other pictures: **Graham Watson.**

BLACK AND WHITE
Photosport International: pp 30, 58, 71, 76, 88, 92, 97, 98, 101, 107, 114, 115, 122, 128, 131, 133, 139, 202 and 224.

Professional Sport/Presse Sport: pp 47, 49 and 185.

Graham Watson: p 151.

CHAPTER 1

The Foreign Legion

When I first encountered the Tour de France in 1965 – Félice Gimondi's year – I was astonished by its size and extravagance. Now when I look back upon it I am struck by its intimacy. In comparison, that is, with the Tour today.

This was only the third time that the Tour had started outside what the French journalists and orators like to call 'the hexagon'. In 1954 it had been at Amsterdam and in 1958 Brussels; now it was Cologne. Mercedes-Benz, one of the major sponsors, threw a splendid buck's fizz reception on a terrace overlooking the Rhine, and I remember thinking disloyally that it rubbed a little of the glitter off the Milk Race across England and Wales, until then the most glamorous cycling event I had reported.

What first impressed was the affluence of a race which could command an annual budget of nearly half a million pounds. Even then it occurred to me that its prize list of £37,000 wouldn't go far among 130 riders, and that the winner's £1,430 was a poor return on an investment of such pain and trouble over twenty-three days and 4,177 kilometres. But I knew that the big rewards for success in the Tour came later. The time the riders cashed in their fame was when they appeared at more open-handed local events all round the country or when they came to negotiate their next team contract. Making their mark in the Tour was so important to ambitious riders that they would probably have ridden it if there had been no prizes at all.

I followed the 1965 Tour for the five days which took it from Cologne to Saint-Brieuc in Brittany (this was like leaving the dinner table after the soup, but a quality British newspaper like the *Sunday Times* thought that was quite enough attention to give it). And it was when we got on the road and crossed the border into France that I began to appreciate its style and scale and, above all, its self-assurance. Nearly all the great British sporting occasions took place behind high walls and, with a little wariness, you could ignore their existence if you chose to. You could not ignore the Tour. It moved across the land like an invading army – its small, crack bicycle battalion sandwiched between two motorised divisions. The roads ahead were cleared to prevent resistance, and the population turned out to welcome it with banners and bunting.

At the end of each day's campaign it commandeered the best hotels in the district. It had a signals corps which put the various units in touch with each other through Radio Tour, and kept in contact with the outside world by means of its own mobile telephone exchange and post office. A service corps maintained the vehicles of riders and drivers and a medical corps tended the sick and wounded. The Tour had its own disciplinary body which fined any combatants who were late on parade, incorrect in their dress or found fraternising with civilians, e.g. by soliciting pushes on the hills.

Although it lived off the country at night, by day it was almost self-sufficient, carrying and distributing its own rations through its commissary, which was called Spar. On the third morning at Roubaix, Spar pinned up this menu for an army which for the next seven hours would be pedalling on its stomach: 'Three ham sandwiches, two jam sandwiches, two rice cakes, two tarts, a banana, a pear, prunes and lumps of sugar. To drink: tea, coffee, lemon juice or peppermint mineral water.' (Of course extra food-packs would be handed out at two points along the route.) It had its own banking facilities, and distributed its own honours: the Tour's Médaille de la Reconnaissance was awarded to local dignitaries and others who had rendered special service along the way. And as is the custom among invading armies, trade, represented by the publicity caravan, followed the flag.

The military analogy was further enhanced by the personal style of the Directeur Général of the Tour, Jacques Goddet, whose father, Victor, had first given the race his financial blessing. He must then have been in his mid-fifties, a fit man with a soldierly bearing and an officer's moustache. He had attended school in Oxfordshire, and though recalled home early after breaking an arm playing rugby, remained an anglophile. Brisk but courteous, he took an avuncular interest in the welfare of his riders and knew each by name.

Goddet had held the post since 1947, following the death of Henri Desgrange, 'the father of the Tour', in the early years of the war, though he had first taken over as race director midway through the 1936 race when Desgrange fell ill. A newspaperman like most of the Tour top brass, he was editor-in-chief of L'Equipe and often came into the press room to type out his daily column, which was full of battlefield oratory. But unlike most correspondents who dressed as though they had just crawled out of a foxhole, Goddet was immaculate. And once the Tour turned south to the sun, he would put on khaki drill shirt and shorts and a pith helmet, and standing with his head through the roof of the car, would direct operations like a tank commander.

Although in the past I had mainly covered sports of a Simon Pure amateurism, I was more fascinated than shocked by the degree of commercialism which surrounded the Tour. I knew that at the heart of the carnival was a contest which required greater mental concentration and physical toughness, and demanded them over longer periods, than almost any other competitive sport. Another day, another marathon of five to seven hours at 35kph or more, and the ability to recuperate overnight was in the end the most important asset a rider could possess. On the scale of danger it was roughly equal to national hunt racing (fewer fractures, perhaps, but more open wounds) and only surpassed by motor sports; and again the risks were more prolonged. Cyclists talked of pain and suffering in the matter-of-fact way that footballers refer to knocks and groin strains, and battled on with luridly exposed bruises and abrasions and hidden abscesses so severe that they would send most prudent people for a doctor's paper.

Even then I didn't see the half of it. Another two years passed before I first saw the Alps and Pyrenees with their 20km climbs to 2,000 metres and their even more fearsome 80kph descents through the hairpins. As an English rider patiently explained to me later, it wasn't so much the fear of overshooting a curve and disappearing into a chasm as the sheer effort of controlling the handlebars that left him weak and shaking by the time he reached the valley.

The cyclists, absorbed in getting round the course, were

probably not even aware of the commercial circus in which they were involved. They rarely came face to face with the caravan which laid a paper trail of sweet wrappers and special offers through the countryside for the riders to follow an hour or so later. In that era, before any association with alcohol and tobacco had been banned, it was heavily involved with both. Its main impact was made by accordionists who played continuously from their seats on top of mobile beer barrels. Not just any old café accordionists either, but World and European champions.

The teams were just as highly commercial, competing, so it seemed, for the greater public awareness of car manufacturers', brewers' and petrol companies' products. But again very little of this rubbed off on the cyclists. They were riding for themselves, and the first loyalty they owed was to each other, not to the sponsor. Nor, for that matter, did you often hear supporters shout, *'Vas-y Mercier-BP!'*

It was only since the war that companies from outside the cycle trade had begun putting money behind racing teams and advertising themselves on the riders' jerseys. The pioneers were Nivea and the man who earned the embarrassing distinction of first wearing that name across his chest was Fiorenzo Magni, a triple-winner of the Tour of Italy who was also known as the Bald Giant of Monza. However he brought it upon himself since he is credited with introducing *extrasportif* patronage into the game. And everyone was grateful to him since it got professional cycling out of a financial hole when its own industry wasn't prosperous enough to support it. Now all the riders were sandwich-board men, their jerseys and shorts plastered with logos.

Sponsorship touched every aspect of the Tour; something I take for granted now, but didn't then. 'Its arrivals and departures are timed by Longines, its results computed by IBM,' I wrote. 'Poulain chocolate rewards the best climber; Coper jams console the unfortunate; Outspan oranges offer prizes to riders with "the greatest amiability or the most agreeable humour" – though these, significantly, are worth less than the Mercedes which goes to the most aggressive rider of the Tour. And all the while the Aspro helicopter ambulance whirls overhead, ready to carry any injured to hospital.'

That degree of exploitation – which has since become the way of sporting life – was still unfamiliar in the 'sixties, and many found it disturbing. The 'events of May' 1968 – the uprising by the Sorbonne students and trade unions of the left against the apparent materialism of French society – were only three years away. And even solid citizens, not at all in sympathy with violent protest, were already questioning the right of the Tour to take over the public highways, add enormously to the duties of the police (for whose services it paid, of course) and generally disturb the peace of the nation for three weeks every July. And especially since the whole circus seemed to be run for the benefit of commercial interests.

The Tour itself saw no conflict of interest. It had been conceived in 1903 as a publicity stunt to boost the circulation of a newspaper, and its prestige had been built within an alliance of sport, journalism and business. In the sixty-odd years since then it had become not only the outstanding event in the French sports calendar but, by most measurements, the world's biggest annual competition. Its popular following was enormous, not least because the race came to the people and charged no entrance fee. There were unconfirmed though perfectly credible reports that fifteen million people watched it from the roadside, and it was evident to anyone that women were among its most ardent fans. But the criticism that the Tour was abusing its privileges had to be answered since it came from an influential minority with the power to take them away.

What the Tour did to placate the opposition in 1967 was to play the patriotic card. It scrapped trade teams in favour of national teams, a formula which it had used consistently from 1930 to 1962, since a contest between squads in French and Belgian colours would appear less blatantly commercial than one between Ford-France-Gitane and Flandria-Romeo. 'It was being done,' said *L'Equipe*, the voice of the Tour, 'in response to the noble and superior interests of the race, to the wishes of the public and the desires of the public authorities.'

The sponsors had to accept the change, but did so with ill-grace. The new arrangement, they argued, was basically unfair: they paid the riders' salaries all summer only to be denied publicity from the season's major event. They also pointed to the danger of collusion between trade-team colleagues of different nationalities, and said that the other ranks in particular would be under pressure to give foreign aid to their normal leaders.

Indeed loyalties were put under so much strain that the experiment was dropped after only two seasons. Since when nobody has seriously suggested reviving it except as an occasional variation, and the Tour has become international in a broader sense and by other means. There are still those who complain of the litter, the inconvenience and even the loss of industrial production which result from the Tour, but as a national institution it seems more secure than ever. Perhaps the turning point came after the unrest of 1968 which brought the economy and transport systems of France to a standstill. In early June, with the Tour due to set off from Vittel on the 27th, the trains were still not running and the riots were only just starting to subside. But the government insisted that the race should go ahead as a signal to the world that the country was back to normal. It did so, and has received strong political support ever since.

Despite the size and complexity of the whole operation, the Tour in 1965 was still a close, and in many ways closed, community. Only riders from a bloc of five adjoining countries in western and southern Europe were present in the Tour in any significant numbers. And within that bloc a nucleus of those same riders would cross each other's borders to turn up in one big race after another. Individual riders appeared from the fringes – from countries where cycle racing had some standing but wasn't by any means a national sport. Britain, for instance, was represented in 1965 by two English riders: the good-natured Vin Denson, who rode for Jacques Anquetil, the first man to win the Tour five times; and the ambitious Tom Simpson who rode for himself and was to win the world championship before the end of the year. But both were with French teams. Only rarely could any fringe country muster the cash or the riders to contest the Tour with their own trade team.

This became painfully obvious in 1967 when the Tour went back to international racing. In order to make up the field four countries had to be allocated nine of the thirteen teams. The

French had three: France, Bleuets and Coqs. Belgium, Italy and Spain had two, their second strings optimistically entitled Diables Rouges, Primavera and Esperanza. The Dutch, the fifth but youngest member of the inner circle, had one, as did West Germany and Great Britain. Switzerland and Luxemburg made up the final team between them. Great Britain included Simpson, Denson, Barry Hoban, a finishing sprinter of quality who had settled near Simpson's home at Ghent and would win eight Tour stages before his career was over, and Michael Wright, who had been born in Bishops Stortford but brought up in Belgium and consequently spoke scarcely any English. The other eight were stay-at-home professionals, with some talent but little experience of continental racing and none of riding anything as arduous as this. The other make-weight teams had similar weaknesses. It's true that two Swiss and one Luxemburger had won the Tour since the war; individuals could always break through. But in national terms the Tour of the 'sixties was a five-horse race.

In many ways, although the Tour today is more cosmopolitan, in the 'sixties it was more exotic. The language of the peloton was French, laced with Flemish. So it is today, officially, but at least a fifth of its members find it easier to communicate in English. It was closer to a romantic past when it didn't seem absurd for newspapers to refer to the riders simply as the Heroes or the Giants of the Road. And it was also closer to the people. It was a more frequent occurrence for riders to dismount and greet their families as they passed close to home. Weddings were timed so that the bride and groom and their guests were waiting at the roadside to watch the Tour go through, and if racing was slack, as it often was on the old long stages, the cheekier riders would stop to kiss the bride. It was thought to bring good luck on both sides.

If the riders came from fewer countries, they were also drawn from a narrower stratum of society: the working class and very often the rural society of smallholders and farm labourers, who were exchanging one form of monotonous, back-breaking toil in the sun for another. The two French heroes of the period make the point. Raymond Poulidor was the son of share-croppers on one of the great estates in the Limousin, and Jacques Anquetil, though a more subtle and sophisticated man, was raised on a Norman strawberry farm. Bernard Thévenet, who succeeded them as his country's champion, shared a similar background: a small farm near a village in Burgundy which was happily called Le Guidon, the French term for handlebar as well as for a fork in the road.

These and other successful riders became at least franc millionaires in their day (whether they frugally invested their money in land or blew it in celebration was a matter for them). But the poor bloody infantry of the peloton did well only if their leader was winning and sharing his prizes with them. Few sports had such a rigid hierarchical system or treated the members of the team so unequally. In each team there would be a leader, and one or two senior 'protected' riders; the rest were *domestiques* – servants – which was a remarkable category to find in any sport. It was their job to give up their bikes and wheels to the leader if need be, to pace him along and chase his rivals, to fetch his cold drinks from the team car and generally sacrifice their own ambitions to him.

To a degree it was an apprenticeship, but many *domestiques* burnt out whatever talents they had brought into the sport before they had a chance to display them. In compensation they ate well, dressed well and stayed in better hotels than they would ever have entered if they had stayed at home. Above all they enjoyed the reflected glory of famous events and the envy of their peers. But the financial rewards were poor – since there were always more applicants than jobs – and at the end of the season it was back to the farm to wait and see if their contract would be renewed.

Even established riders were far less independent than they are today, when if they are disgruntled they change teams readily, contract or no contract. In 1965 Tom Simpson, a Durham miner's son who was desperately anxious to earn a prosperous later life from his short career as a cyclist, was at odds with his employers, Peugeot. He was twenty-seven and already a popular figure in the sport. Even before the word had come into fashion he had created an image for himself as Mr Tommee, the English gentleman as the French imagined him, with check suit, bowler hat and rolled umbrella. More substantially he had won three classics – the Tour of Flanders, Bordeaux-Paris and Milan-San Remo – and finished sixth in the 1962 Tour de France. This was the kind of celebrity for which another team might pay highly if only Peugeot would release him, but they refused. They told him he would not be included in their team for the Tour unless he renewed his contract for a further season. He held out for a while, but appearing in the Tour was essential to his progress, so reluctantly he signed.

It was the international Tour of 1967 which enabled him to beat the system. He could compete as leader of the Great Britain team without making any commitment to his sponsor. But now, at twenty-nine years of age, he felt an almost unbearable urgency to seize what might be his last chance of persuading any would-be employers that he was worth more than Peugeot were willing to pay him. His aim, he told me, was to put aside another £50,000 and then retire. 'I have to show that I am a Tour man, prove that I can be a danger, and I have not done that yet.'

To achieve this he believed that he had either to hold the leader's yellow jersey for several stages on end, to win two or three big stages, or to finish in the first three. Nothing less would do. One of those big stages crossed Mont Ventoux to finish in Carpentras, and on its bakingly hot, bare slopes, Simpson collapsed and died before reaching hospital. In his rage to win he had taken amphetamines which, while not amounting to a fatal dose, were enough to allow him, in the words of the official medical report, 'to pass the limit of his endurance and so fall victim to excessive exhaustion'. Equally though, in his anxiety to escape through this small window of opportunity, Tom Simpson had fallen victim to a system of tied employment which still exists, as it does in most professions, but is now much more flexible.

These things I learned from speaking to Simpson and the British riders almost every day at the start and finish of the stage and visiting them in their hotels, which was more easily done then. The intimacy of the race, as I now recall it, was partly a question of numbers. There were 130 riders compared with the present 198, and 200 or so journalists, a figure which has since more than trebled. It was a comfortable ratio. There were far fewer transfers, too, between the end of one stage and the start of the next. Riders, officials and the press, instead of scattering over a radius of 100km or more, would be gathered together in the same town where, in one of the squares the nightly open-air *Spectacle de la Tour* would present Dalida accompanied by Guy Motta and his orchestra, Les Haricots Rouges and Les Majorettes (*championnes des USA*). Another free entertainment.

If you walked around the town after dinner you often found the riders doing the same. The last memory I have of Simpson was of him coming up to our table outside a restaurant in the old port of Marseilles the night before he died and, unable to resist the chance of playing to an audience, haggling with a North African hawker of carved wooden figures. It wasn't particularly significant; except for what followed I might not even have remembered it. It's just that this sort of chance encounter has become rarer.

The Tour had changed character scarcely at all by 1976 when I wrote a book called *The Great Bike Race* based on that year's events. Eddy Merckx of Belgium, probably the strongest all-rounder the sport has known, had recently completed his five Tour victories. Bernard Hinault, his equal in will-power at any rate, was shortly to begin his. That year, sandwiched between the two successes of Bernard Thévenet, it was to be the turn of another Belgian, Lucien Van Impe – a surprise winner since he had always seemed content with carrying off the crown of king of the mountains, a title he took six times. Franco-Belgian rivalry continued to rock the see-saw: that was traditional. So was second place for the tall Dutchman, Joop Zoetemelk; he managed it six times, winning only once in 1980. Jésus Manzaneque was penalised ten minutes and fined £230 for taking stimulants, and José-Luis Viejo provided a historical footnote in winning a stage by 22min 50sec (while going on to lose the race by 55min 16sec).

Any general changes to report since 1965 were more political than sporting. The Tour was the target of two separate industrial protests on consecutive days, one by printers in dispute with the *Parisien-Libéré*, co-sponsors of the race, and the other by workers from the Peugeot bicycle factory. They weren't the first of their kind, but the practice of venting frustration on the Tour seemed to be growing. The race, with its attendant reporters, provided a convenient device for attracting attention to general grievances. Perhaps, too, the protesters saw it as an arm of the establishment. And perhaps they had a point. For the second year running the Tour was allowed to finish on the Champs-Elysées. And that bore the very stamp of official approval.

If there were any other straws in the wind, I must admit I didn't notice which way they were blowing. There were changes, but they were coming slowly and began to accelerate only in the mid-'eighties. This was one of France's longer runs of success. Eight of the next nine Tours, that is all but Zoetemelk's, went their way, and in Hinault they had a rider they could depend on. Or thought they could until he suddenly disappeared from the race at Pau in 1980 when he was in the leader's yellow jersey. But the explanation he gave next day when the press tracked him down to a team-mate's home at Lourdes – that the tendons of his right knee were inflamed and he didn't want to aggravate the problem with a cold, wet ride across the Pyrenees – had to be accepted. And though they wished he had given it at the time, or at least left a farewell note, he was restored to public favour when he went on to win three more Tours.

He had familiar credentials for a French champion. He was from a small Breton country town, Yffiniac, where his father worked on the railway. But unlike Poulidor and Thévenet he seemed to have been born with a bicycle pump in one hand, a Filo-fax in the other, and ambitions and interests beyond the immediate objective of winning the next race (he is now a member of the Tour hierarchy as its technical adviser). Open to new ideas, he was very taken at one time – as was his team manager, Cyrille Guimard – with the prospect of the United States as a land of untapped resources for cycle racing. In 1982 they supported Lévitan in his ill-fated scheme for a Tour of America, having already, while with Renault the previous year, introduced the first American ever to ride the Tour. He was a Californian called Jonathan (or Jacques) Boyer who excited additional interest because he was a vegetarian and read the Bible each day. That was one small step towards the future.

The Tour took another in 1981, also involving Hinault, though this time much against his will. When he attacked on a stage in the Pyrenees he failed to shake off Phil Anderson from Melbourne who dogged his rear wheel all the way up the climb to Plat d'Adet, so becoming the first Australian ever to wear the yellow jersey. (No sentimentalist, Hinault took it from him in a time trial next day). But the Tour had contained its exotics in the past, none more famous than the Algerian Abd el Kader Zaaf, the Lion of Chebli, who was included in a North African team in 1950; having been refreshed with rosé by spectators, Zaaf fell asleep under a tree, woke up and then set off again – but in the wrong direction. He became a popular attraction of the post-Tour races, the French being happy to accept the odd foreigner. But there was no good reason to interpret the presence of a solitary American, or the overnight success of an Australian as the start of a trend. And certainly there was nothing to suggest that the last five years of the decade would produce three overall victories for the United States and one for the Republic of Ireland, with only Spain recalling the old ascendancy of the continental mainland.

If there was a turning point it came the following year. The finals of the football World Cup, the Mundial, were held in Spain in 1982, and even as the Tour set off from Basle, its echoes could be heard from television sets in every bar and hotel bedroom. It dominated the sports pages, even of *L'Equipe*, and Goddet was deeply impressed not only by the scale and popularity of the event but its truly global nature. He wrote an editorial in which he set out his proposals for the evolution of 'the world's greatest cycle race' which he entitled (on the Continent journalists tend to write their own headlines), 'Towards a Tour *Mondialisé*'. Specifically most of his ideas came to little, or came into being through unforeseen events, but their drift proved irresistible. Mondialisation became the 'eighties catchword.

Goddet divided the world into traditional and new nations. The traditional were West Germany (with Luxemburg and Austria), Belgium, Spain, France, Great Britain (with the Commonwealth), the Netherlands, Italy, the Scandinavian countries and Switzerland. The new were an African grouping, Canada, Colombia, United States, Poland, Portugal, East Germany, Czechoslovakia and the USSR. And what Goddet proposed was that every fourth year, in the summer which followed the Olympic Games, these countries should ride the Tour as eighteen national teams. It would be an open race, with mainly professionals from the first group and amateurs from the second.

To make the race even more mondial, while keeping France as its heartland, it should drop in on as many countries as was practicable. For example, it might start and hold two stages in the United States, then visit Britain, the Netherlands, Belgium, Luxemburg, Germany, Switzerland, Italy, Monaco and Spain. All of which would still leave the opportunity for nine stages in France, including 'l'arrivée magistrale' on the Champs-Elysées.

This was obviously meant to be a green paper, a discussion document, and was addressed as much to Goddet's co-director, Lévitan, now responsible for organising the Tour, as to the world at large. As such it got a fairly puzzled reception; the Cook's tour aspect in particular was considered fanciful. Race followers remembered the disruption caused eight years before when the Tour was simply taken across the Channel to Plymouth. The matter was overtaken by more immediate events as the race began, but the basic idea of opening up the Tour to a wider world, especially to the Americas and eastern Europe, was adopted as Tour policy. For years there were rumours that the next Tour but one would open in Central Park, New York, or in front of the White House, with an airlift back to France by Concorde. And although these died away when Lévitan left the organisation in 1987, having just set up an even trickier start from West Berlin, the Atlantic crossing remains a possibility. And Goddet's open Tour came to pass more quickly than even he expected.

On the rest day at Cancale in Brittany Lévitan revealed to a press conference, without warning, that the 1983 Tour would be open to amateurs and professionals. The list of amateur countries he proposed to approach was similar to Goddet's, though Venezuela, Romania and Bulgaria were slightly airily added to it and no African group was mentioned. While some professional riders complained that it would cost them their place, the principle of the top amateurs and professionals riding together wasn't new – it had been applied in reverse the previous season to the Tour de l'Avenir, the amateur version of the Tour de France – and the plan was generally well received. In his autumn presentation of the route and other arrangements for 1983, Lévitan confirmed his intentions and predicted that 'five or six' amateur countries would compete.

At that point opposition from the trade teams began to build up, just as it had against the national Tours of 1967-68. But the additional objection this time was that firms would be encouraged to sponsor the amateurs for just this one showcase event, and so would get publicity on the cheap. All the same Lévitan pressed ahead and was backed by the governing body, the UCI. And the reason the 1983 Tour was an open race in token only was that every one of the amateur countries except Colombia cried off.

In the end mondialisation was reached by way of infiltration not invitation, and was a gradual process. The Colombians returned as professionals with their own sponsors, while a few were absorbed into European teams. Sean Kelly, the first of two prodigiously talented riders from Ireland – a country where lightning had never previously been known to strike twice – had already made his debut in the Tour in 1978, winning a stage, and was joined in 1983 by Stephen Roche, who would win the Tour four years later. In 1982 the Aussie, Anderson, improved on his previous year's record by holding the yellow jersey for nine days. The mountain prize went to a Scot, Robert Millar, in 1984, in which year, too, a second and far more remarkable American, Greg LeMond, arrived in the Tour and finished third. In 1986 the first US team, sponsored by the 7-Eleven chain of convenience stores, lined up at the start. And over the next few years the rusting away of the iron curtain opened up the race to riders from eastern Europe.

By 1990 the members of the Foreign Legion were too numerous for any one of them to be considered a curiosity. If a Canadian, Steve Bauer, was in the yellow jersey, then the rest had to treat him as a potential danger. The older nations – France, Belgium, Spain, Italy, Netherlands – still provided 129 men, roughly two thirds of the peloton, with 35 Frenchmen making up the biggest contingent, though none of them finished in the top dozen. Colombia had 14 riders, Switzerland 13, and Russia, seven years after declining Lévitan's invitation, were there for the first time with 10 men, all professionals. In single figures were the United States (7), Denmark (6), East Germany (5), Ireland and Australia (both 3). Like Norway, Britain had two riders, so no advance there; Mexico, Canada, West Germany and Portugal, one. Nineteen nationalities in all.

By far the most influential of the new arrivals were the Americans, whose outlook on the sport was radically different from the Europeans'. In the United States cycling isn't seen as a cheap means of going to work or getting around the neighbourhood; it's associated with fitness and leisure and belongs by and large to the middle class. In consequence so do many who go on to take up cycle racing (LeMond's father was in real estate; both parents of Andy Hampsten, first US winner of the Tour of Italy, are university teachers). And if they turn professional it is in the expectation of earning at least as much as a reasonably successful golfer or tennis player. Much to their own surprise European teams found themselves meeting those demands. And while LeMond's £3.7million contract with the Z team leads the field by some distance, riders of all grades and nationalities have felt the benefit. It has also had a knock-on effect on the prizes in the Tour, which are meant to end up in the pockets of the team-riders not the leaders. These have risen ahead of inflation from the £37,000 in 1965 to over £1 million in 1990. And all in cash. There are no longer any of those dubiously-valued prizes of motor-cars, jewellery or holiday villas.

A further effect of the mondialisation in general and the American presence in particular has been to attract world-wide press coverage. Television now puts £2-2.5 million into the Tour funds, and an even more formidable convoy of press cars and technical vehicles onto the road. It has produced what Laurent Fignon, now the leading French rider, disparagingly calls 'gigantisme', a scale of organisation which dwarfs the action.

Even in 1965 I had been surprised by how little one saw of the race. I booked a place in the car of *Le Progrès*, a Lyons paper, whose reporter would talk to the riders at the start and then hurry ahead to a quiet spot and start typing up his interviews. At the first sign that the race was approaching he would pack up and drive to the finish. But at least you got a clear view of the sprint, the riders weren't immediately hustled away to face the TV cameras, and since the press room was close to the line, you didn't have to hurry away to the phone yourself. Now the finish and the press room are often 10km apart, and you go there and watch the closing events on television like anyone at home. All you see at first hand is the course itself. And given the size of the entourage, how can it be any different?

While everything else has enlarged, only the length of the stages has shrunk, subtly altering the character of the racing. That, too, is largely to accommodate television, which has to keep to tighter schedules than the rest of the media. But at least it is one change for the better. You may regret the passing of those long-suffering mountain stages in which the heroes tested each other to destruction. But you have to accept that shorter, faster, more competitive stages in which fewer minutes are lost and gained, prolong the agony of anticipation. Once Merckx or Hinault emerged safely from the mountains the race was as good as over. Nowadays it's rare for a Tour to be decided before the last days or hours. In 1989 it was down to the last eight seconds.

CHAPTER 2

The travelling men

Golfers, cricketers, tennis and snooker players are given to grumbling that each year the season gets longer and its nomadic life more wearisome. And few sportsmen have as much right to do so as that travelling repertory company of three hundred or so professional racing cyclists who make up the cast for the one-day classics, the great three-week tours and the rest of the annual supporting features. Their work rarely takes them outside western Europe, yet few spend more time on the road getting to events, and certainly none more time on the road competing in them. Two days after winning the 3,680km Tour of Spain in 1990, Marco Giovannetti flew from Madrid to Bari in the heel of Italy to set out on the 3,464km Giro, which did not stop one newspaper depicting him as '*le play-boy*'.

The cyclists' working year runs, by and large, from the Paris-Nice, the Race to the Sun, in early March to the Tour of Lombardy, the Race of the Falling Leaves, in late October. But November and December are the only months they can call their own. And then only if they resist the money which promoters offer the more celebrated of them to pedal the boards of the six-day races, an indoor winter circus even older than the Tour. This dates back to the Agricultural Hall in Islington, London, and the penny-farthing days of the 1870s. And although it has failed to find a permanent home in Britain, it is popular enough on the Continent to afford tempting fees.

Early in the New Year the teams come together again at ski resorts in the Alps and training camps around the Mediterranean (no rider likes to start serious racing without having stored at least 5,000kms in his legs). The only breaks in the routine of riding and resting are for ritual photo-calls and open days for the press, and in some cases a return to Belgium or the Netherlands for a stage presentation – resembling nothing so much as the launch of Ford's latest model to the motor trade – in which the team shows off its new signings and new strips, and outlines its plans and ambitions for the season. By mid-February, with the mimosa scarcely in blossom, the riders are already competing in warm-up races like the Ruta del Sol in southern Spain, and the Etoile de Bessèges and Tour of the Mediterranean along the coast of Languedoc and Provence.

During the short break before the 1990 season there had been more activity than usual in the hotel dining rooms where much of the sport's business is done. Team sponsorship is rarely a long-term commitment. It costs getting on for three million pounds to assemble and run a cycle team with any prospect of winning the big races, and several sponsors had decided that their publicity budgets could be spent elsewhere with more profit and less hassle.

ADR, the Belgian car rental firm, for instance, had retired from the sport after their star, Greg LeMond, left them for Z, a French children's clothing group – who had themselves lost their co-sponsor, Peugeot. Paternina, who took over the rump of ADR's cycling interests, withdrew in their turn when the team was refused a place in the Tour of Spain. Other familiar names to disappear were Hitachi and Domex in Belgium and Superconfex in the Netherlands. The Superconfex team had happily found a new patron in the breweries. Cycle teams are not permitted to bear the name of alcoholic drinks or cigarettes; but Buckler, a subsidiary of the Heineken group, was acceptable since it produced a non-alcoholic beer.

Even Système-U, the French supermarket chain, had decided to move on, relinquishing a stake in the sport which included Laurent Fignon, its greatest household name, and Cyrille Guimard, its most astute team manager. In this case Guimard had simply moved his squad to Castorama, a DIY multiple which dressed the riders in the season's nattiest racing gear. It consisted of blue and white jerseys and shorts so printed that they looked like carpenters' aprons worn over striped shirts. All this commercial activity, combined with the usual winter migration in search of richer pickings, meant that within a few months at least 200 riders had switched their allegiance.

This year, too, the opening of the frontiers with eastern

Europe had put a number of talented amateurs, or what had passed for amateurs, on the market, and the bidding was brisk. Alfa-Lum, who already backed an all-Soviet team based in Italy, a concession they had won from the USSR sports ministry, hoped to attract the latest prize, Vatchieslaw Ekimov, an impassive prodigy from Vyborg near the Finnish border, who at twenty-four had already won the world amateur pursuit title for the third time and set a dozen world track records. Instead a two-year contract worth £400,000 secured him for Peter Post's Dutch Panasonic team, which had also taken on, for a reputed £50,000 a year, the current Olympic road race champion, Olaf Ludwig of East Germany. Two more East Germans – Uwe Ampler, winner of world and Olympic gold medals and three Peace Races, and Uwe Raab, a past world champion – went Dutch, joining PDM. And another two, Mario Kummer and Jan Schur, half the country's gold medal time trial team, were recruited by Château d'Ax of Italy.

Whether or not they could adapt to professional racing was a question for the future. For the moment the sponsors had more than enough new or newly-packaged items to show off to the public in the first big stage race, the Paris-Nice.

This is one of cycling's most potent rites of spring, the symbolic headlong rush from frosty north to warm south to greet the new season. No matter that most of the riders had already been racing in the south and would have to travel north to Paris for the start. Or that having reached the south, they would soon have to turn back north again for a series of gritty classics in and around Belgium. The Paris-Nice is the big reunion, and nobody complained when this year, for nearly all its 1,110kms, it was a race *in* the sun.

Not all the top echelon chose to ride it. Sean Kelly had won the race seven years in succession, and while he had not in so many words been asked to stay away, there was some relief when, for a second season, he elected to open his serious racing in the overlapping Tirreno-Adriatico in Italy. Phil Anderson and TVM did the same, while Panasonic, Château d'Ax and one or two others were strong enough to divide their forces between the two events. But there was no doubt that the Paris-Nice had the classier field, attracting all four past winners of the Tour de France who were still in the saddle:

Fignon, Stephen Roche, Pedro Delgado and Greg LeMond.

The race is run with a light touch by the cycling family Leulliot, and is a pleasantly relaxed event. As long as some riders are doing their best to win the prizes, nobody minds, at this early point of the season, if others simply come along for the ride. So on a brisk, bright Sunday in early March – the day after *les Bleus* had finished their Five Nations rugby programme at the Parc des Princes – 144 riders with varying degrees of ambition signed on in the Place Léon Blum for a 7km time trial through the inner suburbs which would get the show on the road.

Fignon was one who seemed anxious to ride as hard and do as well as he could, not only for its own sake but because Milan-San Remo, the opening spring classic which he had won for the past two years, was less than a fortnight away. LeMond, on the other hand, had spent most of the New Year behind a desk or in front of television cameras (he was making a commercial) and not on his bike. Having arrived a month

Laurent Fignon, after a series of injuries and misfortunes in the early part of the season, seemed only a morose parody of the rider who had won the Tours of '83 and '84 with such bravura.

before from the United States still several pounds overweight – just how many pounds was to remain a matter of urgent debate for some months – and many thousands of kilometres undertrained, he proposed to use this race to get in shape.

Delgado was ostensibly here to help his friend and team-mate, Miguel Indurain, win the race for a second year. It was generally understood that he intended to do the same in the Tour of Spain, after which their roles would be reversed, and Delgado, with Indurain's assistance, would make his big bid of the season in the Tour de France. At least that was the theory of it.

Roche's approach was more ambiguous. In 1981 he had marked his debut as a professional with victory in the Paris-Nice, and on that slender evidence had been pencilled in as a future champion. But his abounding talent began to seem at odds with a driving impatience. He scored some notable wins and finished third in the 1985 Tour de France, but his progress took the shape not of an upward curve on the graph but some particularly jagged contour cross-section of a stage in the Alps.

In November 1985 a crash in the Paris Six-Day race damaged his left knee and brought him more lasting problems. And although an unrewarding struggle next season was followed by the *annus mirabilis* of 1987 – when in less than four months he won the tours of Romandie, Italy and France, and then the world championship – that November he had to accept the need for an operation on the knee. The succeeding summers of 1988 and 1989 brought a few successes but many more false hopes, and now, after a long period of treatment from Professor Muller, 'the doctor with magic hands' who also looked after Yvan Lendl, Boris Becker, Daley Thompson and the Bayern Munich football team, Roche was setting out again in a race of more than sentimental significance to him.

He was short of competition and roadwork, and anxious not to put himself under additional pressure by making an early challenge in a race he couldn't seriously expect to win. 'This time I am determined not to come back too soon,' he repeated from the start. All the same he achieved fourth place in the Paris time trial, won by his team's young short-distance specialist, Francis Moreau, who thereby took the race-leader's white jersey. The race moved south to Nevers, and after a frosty start headed for Lyons across the Montes de Beaujolais, where men were already in the fields pruning the bare vine stumps, and Roche continued to deploy his men like a general who meant business. He demanded that there should be a Histor rider in every breakaway, and he was obeyed.

So inevitably the pressure of expectation did build up, fuelled as much by Roche's personality as by his actions. He is the most accessible of riders; flatteringly patient, cheerful, apparently unguarded; able to switch easily from English to fluent French and serviceable Italian. He would straddle his bicycle at the stage start posing for pictures and signing autographs while reporters scribbled down his words. And however often he belittled his chances, the sheer number of words from Roche which the papers quoted told another story.

By Wednesday morning at Saint-Etienne, Indurain had taken the lead but Roche was in fourth place still only seven seconds behind. That afternoon there was to be a 44.5km team time trial in the hills behind the town, the first of three unavoidable difficulties which would determine the outcome of the race. The other two were the finish at the top of Mont Faron behind Toulon on Friday, and the individual time trial up the col d'Eze at Nice at the very end.

Roche and his Histor team had already ridden over the course and found it unexpectedly demanding; its hard ascents and sudden changes of gear would make it a strain for teams to stay together without sacrificing speed. 'There's a question mark over everyone today,' said Roche when he joined a group of British journalists at the start. But though apprehensive about the trial, he was happy with his form – 'I surprise myself every day' – and with his team.

By chance this impression of confidence was confirmed by LeMond when he interrupted his warm-up to shake Roche's hand: 'I'd better say hello to you now, Stephen, because I never meet you during the race.' This was because Roche rode at the front of the peloton doing his best to control events, while LeMond stayed at the back letting matters take their course and happy enough just to get through another day.

Roche was to surprise himself once more. Histor, who set off last as the leading team, covered the course in the fastest time, 56min 11sec, to beat Fignon's Castorama by 35sec, LeMond's

Z by 43 and Indurain's Banesto by 58. Roche was the new race leader with more than half a minute in hand on his closest opponent, Fignon. When he received his bouquet, in a characteristic gesture he tore it apart and, like a bride to his bridesmaids, passed each of his team a crumpled bunch of flowers. Yet even then he wouldn't allow himself any public optimism. He said he would calculate his chances only when the race had reached the top of Mont Faron.

He was wise to wait. The ascent of Mont Faron, which looks down on the Toulon naval shipyards, showed how much ground Roche still had to make up. Though only 5.5km long, Faron is a nasty little climb with two 1-in-7 stretches, and so far that spring Roche hadn't been up a serious climb even in practice. The race approached it in close formation, and when Indurain attacked 4km from the summit only Fignon followed. Roche kept his head down and tried to hide in case the others left it to him to lead the counter-attack. And when he reached the line in tenth place he found that Indurain, over a minute ahead of him, had comfortably beaten Fignon by 35sec. The Spaniard was leading him in the race once more, this time by 15sec.

It might have been worse. The Saturday and Sunday morning stages were unlikely to change the overall positions, and the previous year, although Roche had lost the race to Indurain, he had beaten him in the col d'Eze time trial by just over half a minute. He had only to repeat that performance to take the prize. But again Roche cautiously pointed out that he was conceding six years to Indurain, not to mention many months of undisturbed racing and training.

In the event both were to be upstaged by a Frenchman, Jean-François (Jeff) Bernard, honoured for a majestic time trial victory on Mont Ventoux in the 1987 Tour de France, where he eventually came third, but remembered for precious little since then. Like Roche he was making his come-back after a knee operation and, at twenty-seven, trying to resurrect a career in which he had once been considered the natural heir to Bernard Hinault. Bernard made his point by winning on the col d'Eze by half a minute from another, younger French dauphin, Luc Leblanc. And although Roche was third he could do no more than cut Indurain's winning margin by half.

Result: Indurain beat Roche by 8sec.

Despite the final disappointment, which he wouldn't allow to weigh upon him, Roche had found it a reasonably encouraging week. 'I didn't go into the time trial expecting to lose; you can't ever do that. I gave it the form I had. But you don't get there on class alone. It has to be in your legs.' Putting it there was a task he hoped to pick up in the 294km Milan-San Remo the following Saturday. Willy Teirlinck, the Histor manager, thought otherwise. Better for Roche, he said, to recuperate a little longer. And better for Histor to put all their effort behind their finishing sprinter, Etienne de Wilde, a more likely classic winner. Stage races are won by all-rounders whose abilities in mountain climbs, time trials and long skirmishes on the flat are balanced out over many days. More often than not one-day races – unless hills or cobbles add to the element of chance – are contested in a whirl of attacks and counter-attacks over the last 30kms, and then won only in the final metres of the sprint. Roche accepted the argument.

Milan-San Remo, the Primavera, opened the twelve-race World Cup series, cycling's equivalent of the formula-one drivers' championship, which Kelly had taken in 1989. Its terrain was difficult enough – with the Turchino Pass midway and the rippling hills of Cipressa and Poggio Sanremo in the last 34km – for Fignon, essentially an all-rounder, to win it for the past two years and to start again as favourite. But he and his team made a hash of it. A cross-wind in the broad Po valley, which was not on the list of recognised *difficultés*, split the field into three within 20km of the start. And although the Italians in the second group combined to close the gap on the first, Fignon, Kelly, LeMond and Tony Rominger, the Swiss winner of the Tour of the Mediterranean and the Tirreno-Adriatico, were left high and dry in the third. Unable to make common cause they gave up the chase and soon afterwards the race itself.

Meanwhile the group in front, numbering around fifty and pushed along at a fair clip by a wind from the sea, were apparently heading for yet another mass sprint. But on the approach to the Cipressa a Swiss-born Italian, Gianni Bugno, who had little hope of success in that sort of finish, made his move. As he crossed the summit, with 26kms still to go, he had a lead of 35sec and a good deal of trouble building up behind him, most persistently from the West German rider, Rolf Golz.

On the Poggio his lead over Golz wavered between 12 and 15sec, but once over the top he did something which he couldn't have done a year before, or done without the help he had received from Wolfgang Amadeus Mozart. He came down the other side fast enough to hold off Golz and win the race by 4sec.

Descenders, men who can give the climbers two minutes at the summit and still catch them before they reach the valley, are a class apart. They are the downhill skiers of the sport. And while not particularly famous for this skill, Bugno was sufficiently adept to hold his own until he crashed in the 1988 Tour of Italy. The following year he found himself suffering bouts of vertigo, and on the Milan-Turin race, he said, 'A curé in a soutane would have descended faster that I did.' That winter he went to Milan to consult a specialist who uses ultrasonic therapy to treat disorders of the eardrum which frequently affect balance. And what she prescribed for Bugno was a course of Mozart quartets and sonatas played at different levels of frequency and volume. It seemed to do the trick, since the vertigo disappeared, equilibrium was restored, and Bugno now had the confidence to resist pulling on his brakes until the last necessary moment.

There was no such sophisticated treatment available to Fignon. He tried more direct means. A week later he compensated for his misjudgment in the Primavera – which the French press, never reluctant to punish their best rider, had greeted with derision – by taking the two-day Critérium International in Provence. Roche, who had meanwhile finished seventh in the Semaine Catalane, came sixth in this race: two circumspect results which at least were in line with his declared intentions for the start of the season. But LeMond again failed to complete the course.

Although he had set aside a week to prepare in the Vaucluse, and had even ridden up the Ventoux, LeMond could manage no more than three days' training. Once he began racing, he found himself unable to respond to any acceleration by the field, and got down from his bike after only

100kms. He complained of a sore throat and constant tired-ness, and felt sure that he was suffering from an infection. He refused to tangle verbally with Eddy Merckx, who charged him with discrediting the world champion's rainbow jersey. Instead he consoled himself with the example of another champion, Hinault, who had often suffered periods of self-doubt in the run-up to the Tour de France, and yet rebounded to win the race.

He reproached himself for having wanted to be agreeable to everyone the previous winter when, from the moment he had returned to Minneapolis, the phone hadn't stopped ringing or the fax machine chattering. And while he had tried to keep in shape with cross-country skiing, he accepted that he had spent too little time on his bike. He stuck to his proposition that now he needed to ride himself back into form through the rest of the spring classics. But clearly he felt that the trouble had a deeper source than simple lack of training, for when he went north he also submitted himself to a blood analysis.

The season is laid out like a five-act play. Act 1 Scene 1, set among the vineyards and olive groves, was now over. Scene 2 would pick up the classic theme against a different back-ground, the greyer skies, the shorter hills, the *pavé* and the largely industrial landscape of northern France and the Low Countries. By the time it was over nearly half the World Cup programme would have been completed.

Act 2 is built around the Tours of Spain (the Vuelta) and Italy (the Giro), and a series of shorter stage races leading up to Act 3, the Tour de France.

In Act 4 the scene changes to the village fetes, like the *pardons* of Brittany, and small-town fairs of late July and August where councillors and trades people put their heads and their funds together to attract stars from the Tour to the circuit races they run through their streets. For many years riders have looked on criterium contracts as their bonus for good behaviour in July. And although the second round of World Cup races has begun to encroach on these events, they help to fill the interval before Act 5 – the world road-race championship and the autumn classics which bring the season to a close.

But back to the second scene of Act 1, when most of the

professional caravan headed north in the last week of March to complete the spring campaign. The change of scene did nothing for LeMond. Still suffering from fatigue, he covered no more than 80kms of stage 2 of the La Panne Three Days – an event which many riders were using to acclimatise themselves to the cobbles and the jostling energy of Belgian racing. In other years, too, they would have had to get used to a cold rain blowing inland from the Channel and the North Sea. But this was to prove an unusually benign spring.

On 29 March, the last day of La Panne, LeMond received the result of his analysis. He had a high white corpuscle count and was suffering from a viral infection possibly contracted from his young son, Scott. Next day he left with his family for Brussels and a flight to a secret destination in the United States. With a sympathetic tolerance rare in the sport Roger Legeay, his manager at Z, described it as 'a psychological retirement'. He added that LeMond would continue training privately and resume racing in the American Tour de Trump in early May. He would then return to Europe for the start of the Giro on 18 May. But even if he kept to that schedule, by then he would have managed only twenty-eight days racing. 'LeMond, has he lost the Tour?' asked L'Equipe in a headline on 4 April.

LeMond's weren't the only blighted hopes. In the second World Cup event, the 264km Tour of Flanders at the end of the week, the Belgian fans watched disgustedly as in a wholly untypical temperature of 25 degrees, and in the absence of the usual wintry showers, their own Rudy Dhaenens was out-sprinted at the finish by Moreno Argentin, the first Italian winner of the race in twenty-three years. And on a cobbled climb at the halfway point Kelly, involved in a mass pile-up of riders, fell and broke his collar-bone. Three weeks' inactivity might not affect his prospects in the Tour but would certainly destroy any chance he had of defending his World Cup title.

Argentin was the man now threatening to succeed Kelly, for ten days later he went on to win the Flèche Wallonne. Unfortunately for him this didn't count in the World Cup, but together with a sixth and a seventeenth place in events which did, it marked him out as a serious claimant. Argentin's talent had never been in dispute or gone unrewarded. He was reputedly earning £250,000 from his new team Ariostea, had a home near Venice, a holiday house in the Maldives and – the height of financial chic – a principal residence in Monaco. However his popularity with the Italian press, who referred to him as the computer cyclist, had been dimmed by two indifferent seasons and a growing reputation as a dilettante who simply competed when he chose.

What Ariostea had persuaded him to do was train hard before the season began and commit himself to racing until it ended. During the Milan-San Remo he had played a significant role in the Italian counter-attack, and only held back from chasing Bugno for fear of recrimination if he should thereby foil an Italian victory. This season Argentin had become, if such a thing is possible on his income, a hungry cyclist.

In the absence of LeMond, the other three past Tour winners hardly distinguished themselves in the spring classics. Roche, who rode three of the six races, achieved the most, though his results were not spectacular. He was sixth in the Flèche Wallonne, and had a sixteenth and a thirty-ninth place in World Cup races. Fignon was the only one to chance his arm in the Paris-Roubaix, the bone-breaking, bike-breaking Hell of the North, with long stretches of *pavé* fit only for farm carts – and finished twenty-seventh. He was alone, too, in riding the less fashionable Ghent-Wevelgem, where he came seventy-ninth. The Tour of Flanders he abandoned, and he didn't start the other three. And Delgado rode four races for a top place of twenty-third. All you could read into these results was that on this season's inauspicious form none of them had the capacity to dominate a long, hard tour. They might come into their own in the mountains and time trials, but they didn't measure up to a Merckx or a Hinault as undisputed boss of the peloton. At best they were first among a dozen or so near-equals.

Four events went to local specialists in classics – three of them Belgian and one Dutch, with the most desirable prize, the Paris-Roubaix, going to Eddy Planckaert, points winner in the 1988 Tour de France. At thirty-one he was the youngest in his generation of the Planckaert cycling dynasty. He had taken the Tour's green jersey twenty-two years after his oldest brother, Willy, had done so. And in that same year he had also won the Tour of Flanders twelve years after his middle brother, Walter. The family wasn't finished yet. Willy's son, Jo, had already won the Belgian junior championship.

Planckaert's victory, gained on the track at Roubaix where many Tour de France stages have finished, could hardly have been closer. Evidence from the photo-timer showed that his tyre was only 15mm ahead of that of his challenger, Steve Bauer, who so nearly became the first Canadian ever to win one of the spring classics. Planckaert's success, however, came as a great relief to his team, Panasonic, whose supremacy in Dutch cycling had been put under threat both by Kelly's PDM and by Buckler, who had two deadly finishers in Eric Vanderaerden and Jelle Nijdam. And it was to be followed by another Panasonic victory at the other end of the dramatic scale when Eric Van Lancker broke away to win the Liège-Bastogne-Liège by over half a minute.

Ghent-Wevelgem went to Roche's Histor team-mate, Herman Frison, in a six-man sprint just ahead of the field. And the final race in the series, the Amstel Gold, was won by Adrie Van der Poel of Weinmann, a sprinter with a slightly clouded reputation who had won nothing of importance in the past two years except the hand of Raymond Poulidor's daughter.

There was now to be a three-month interval in the World Cup programme; its next event would be the Wincanton Classic at Brighton on 29 July. Until then, at least, one Italian, Argentin, would hold the lead by a single point over another, Bugno. This had not been anticipated. Italian cycling had become something of a sideshow in the later 'eighties as Francesco Moser, a considerable figure, withdrew from racing into record breaking and then out of the game altogether. It's true that Argentin had won the world road race championship at Colorado Springs in 1986, and Maurizio Fondriest had done so at Ronse in Belgium two years later. But the world title often proves grander in name than reputation, since it is based on a single race at the fag-end of the season. And long before LeMond came along it was noticed that world champions regularly failed to reproduce their autumn form at the start of the next season.

Measured against the more demanding standard of the great stage races, Italy had done poorly. It had seen its own tour, the Giro, slip away to an Irishman, Roche, an American, Andy

Hampsten, and a Frenchman, Fignon, in the three years since Roberto Visentini's victory in 1986 – which was also when Alvaro Pino had last captured the Vuelta for Italy. And its attitude towards the Tour de France, after pouring its commercial and emotional efforts into the Giro only three weeks before, was notoriously lukewarm. To find an Italian winner here you had to go back to 1965 and Félice Gimondi; and the best recent Tour results had been eighth for Pino in 1986 and 1988, and 11th for Bugno in 1989.

All of a sudden there was talk of an Italian renaissance, and not simply because that label lay conveniently to hand. The Italians were currently the men who, in Roche's phrase, were pinging. Argentin had decided to forgo the Giro in favour of riding the Tour for the first time, and although he claimed to be going there to win stages, not to challenge for the lead, you could make what you wished of that. And who knew what dreams Mozart had inspired in Bugno's breast?

Of course the evidence from the early part of the season might be totally misleading. From now on the character of the races would change; they would lengthen in time and distance. But what had certainly been revealed was a power vacuum waiting to be filled. Perhaps by the Italians. Perhaps by one of *les grands favoris* rediscovering his taste for competition. Or by some unsuspected character who was waiting in the wings to make his appearance in Act 2.

CHAPTER 3

Injuries and foul suspicions

If you entertain the unworthy suspicion that journalists invent their own stories, you will be pleased to know that this is literally true in the case of the Tour de France. The race was devised by a sports paper not only for self-publicity – though perhaps that was the strongest motive – but to create news and provide it with copy to fill its pages. And there it shared a common origin with most of the long-distance cycle races established around the turn of the century, and in many cases still running.

The first point-to-point cycle race on public roads, from Paris to Rouen, was organised by the *Vélocipède-Illustré* in 1869. It was won by James Moore, an English vet who practised in Paris and eighteen months before, in the first cycle race on record, had been the fastest over 1,200 metres at the parc de Saint Cloud. Moore was a friend of the Michaux family, who ran a factory which built invalid carriages and perambulators and eight years before had invented the boneshaker. This was an adaptation of the hobby horse, but instead of being paddled along with the rider's feet on the ground, it was propelled, like today's most juvenile tricycle, by turning pedals attached to the front-wheel axle. The front wheel was larger than the back – though not going to the extremes of the ordinary or penny-farthing, the next stage in the bicycle's progress – and the saddle was suspended in between. Exhibited at the Paris Exhibition of 1867, where the French army took a fancy to it, the boneshaker was an instant success and was widely copied.

Like most of the 325 starters in the race, six of them women, Moore, naturally, rode a Michaux. His had rubber-coated iron rims; many others rode on bare metal. But whether or not this made a crucial difference, Moore covered the 134km in 10hr 25min – which was roughly twice as fast as walking pace – to win by three-quarters of an hour. The ordinary which followed was the racing camel of the sport, awkward-looking but a good deal quicker than you'd expect. Certainly quicker than the boneshaker. The rider sat over the front wheel, and the size of this wheel – and thus the amount of ground covered in a single turn of the pedals – was governed, like the length of a pair of trousers, by his inside leg measurement.

It was on ordinaries that four men first rode from Land's End to John o' Groats in 1873, but these machines were difficult to handle, and within a decade their possibilities had been exhausted. Meanwhile various experiments had been made with driving velocipedes by means of treadles, cranks and levers, but they were all short-lived, and in 1879 it was a parson's son, Harry John Lawson, manager of the Ariel Works in Coventry, who introduced what he called a 'bicyclette' driven by an endless chain to the rear wheel. It was the first 'safety bicycle', in essence if not in form the one we ride today. And since in 1888 John Boyd Dunlop had perfected the inflatable tyre, by the end of the century the groundwork on man-powered travel was complete. It was only left to refine the machine and find new uses for it.

The technical development had been so varied and inventive, and the market had grown so rapidly, that now there were hundreds of French cycle and accessory makers fighting each other to the death. Velodromes had mushroomed in the suburbs of Paris and throughout the country, and the manufacturers employed teams of professional riders to compete at them and demonstrate the superiority of their products. They also supported an increasing number of road races; the Bordeaux-Paris, Paris-Roubaix and Liège-Bastogne-Liège had all been established in the 'nineties.

Though fewer in number, newspapers and periodicals like *Le Vélo, La Vie au Grand Air, Le Monde Sportif, La Revue Sportive* and the more general *Le Petit Journal*, catering for the new craze and feeding off the manufacturers' need to advertise to their special public, were locked in an equally deadly circulation war. And since it brought them publicity and cemented their relations with the trade, they often took it upon themselves to organise races of various kinds.

The most influential of this group was *Le Vélo*, a daily printed on green paper, edited by Pierre Giffard and backed by the Count de Dion. It had a semi-official status, which gave it access to information unavailable to the rest, and it organised two of the biggest events, the Bordeaux-Paris and the Paris-Brest-Paris. With a sale of 80,000 copies it was prosperous and secure, or seemed so until the Dreyfus Affair broke out. This was the scandal which followed the 1894 court-martial of Alfred Dreyfus, a Jewish captain on the French army staff, on a charge of passing military secrets to the German government. There were strong suspicions that the evidence in the case had been forged by an anti-semitic fellow officer, Capt. Esterhazy, and the issue divided the nation, even to the management of *Le Vélo*.

Giffard, who did some moonlighting for *Le Petit Journal*, wrote an article in its pages defending Dreyfus and demanding the guillotine for Esterhazy. He also criticised an anti-Dreyfus demonstration which had taken place at Auteuil racecourse, in which, unfortunately for him, De Dion had been involved. On reading this the fiercely nationalist De Dion immediately withdrew his financial support for *Le Vélo* and, taking with him several of its prominent advertisers, set off to launch a rival daily newspaper to be printed on yellow paper and entitled *L'Auto-Vélo*.

The man he persuaded to edit it was Henri Desgrange, a one-time solicitor's clerk and amateur racing cyclist who had been forced to choose between his career and his consuming passion when one day a woman client complained that she had seen him riding in public with bare calves. He left the office, turned professional, set the first world unpaced hour record of 35.325km at Neuilly in 1893, and had latterly been running a group of velodromes in Paris. He was outwardly flamboyant, privately cautious and well-connected in the cycle industry. But he was clearly no political die-hard, for as a writer he modelled himself on Emile Zola, who had been the most reviled of all defenders of Dreyfus.

As financial manager the backers chose another velodrome director, Victor Goddet (the clear intention was to match *Le Vélo* in race promotion). And the triumvirate was completed by Géo Lefèvre, a young cyclist and rugby enthusiast, who had given up his literary studies in order to become a cycling reporter on *Le Vélo*. Desgrange made him an offer; Lefèvre dutifully told his boss; and the famously irascible Giffard sacked him on the spot simply for mentioning Desgrange's name. Lefèvre hurried round to accept the offer before Desgrange learnt that, anyway, he had been dismissed.

Despite its tribulations *Le Vélo* continued to prosper while *L'Auto-Vélo* could achieve no more than a quarter of its circulation. Giffard also successfully took Desgrange to law for plagiarising his title. Desgrange was forced to rename his paper *L'Auto* and content himself with an all-embracing subtitle which read: *Motoring, Cycling, Athletics, Yachting, Aeronavigation, Skating, Weight-lifting, Horse Racing, Alpinism.* But that solved nothing. *L'Auto* had to make a name for itself in race promotion.

It was the young Lefèvre who suggested the solution at an office meeting in December 1902. Since at present there were only races from town to town, why not a race in a series of stages which would unite all the great cities – '*un veritable tour de la France*'? It would give deprived areas 'the opportunity to discover the joys and beauties of cycle racing', establish the prestige of *L'Auto*, and with daily accounts of the contest appearing in the paper, was bound to improve circulation.

Desgrange was not immediately impressed by the idea, seeing its risks and difficulties, but after further discussion over lunch at the Brasserie Zimmer, he promised to take it to Goddet, who held the purse-strings. To Desgrange's surprise, the response from Goddet was enthusiastic, and he was cornered. The plans went ahead for a race beginning in Paris on 1 June, 1903, with five stages ending in Lyons, Marseilles, Bordeaux, Nantes and Paris, which would be reached on 5 July (a sixth stage at Toulouse was inserted as an afterthought to break the journey to Bordeaux).

At first it got a cool reception from the floating population of riders, who objected to the cost and inconvenience of being on the road for so long, and Desgrange thought of aborting the plan. But *L'Auto* gave it one more chance. It reduced the race to three weeks, 1-19 July, and the entry fee from 20 to 10 francs. At the same time it increased the prize money to 20,000 francs, and offered a daily living allowance of 5 francs to anyone finishing in the first 50 who won less than 200 francs.

Within a few days 78 cyclists had enlisted.

As the start approached Desgrange's optimism grew and so did the hyperbole of his writing: 'With the broad and powerful swing of the hand which Zola in *The Earth* gave to his ploughman, *L'Auto*, journal of ideas and action, is going to fling across France today those reckless and uncouth sowers of energy who are the great professional riders of the road . . . From Paris to the blue waves of the Mediterranean, from Marseilles to Bordeaux, passing along the roseate and dreaming roads sleeping under the sun, across the calm of the fields of the Vendée, following the Loire, which flows on still and silent, our men are going to race madly, unflaggingly.' Not that he was going to follow them. Prudently he left the practical organisation to Lefèvre who was to be race director, starter, commissaire, finishing judge, time keeper and recorder.

In the evening, in a break from these duties, Lefèvre would settle at a café table to write a full-page of copy for his paper, though much of the reporting fell to Olivier Margot who had a fine grasp of the *L'Auto*'s florid house-style (still practised by other hands in colour essays to this day). In the end 60 riders came to the well-attended start outside a café, Réveil-Matin, in a south-west suburb of Paris at 3.00pm on Wednesday, 1 July, and this is how Margot described the scene. 'The men waved their hats, the ladies their umbrellas. You felt they would have liked to touch the steel muscles of the most courageous champions since Antiquity. Yes, the most courageous because – a revolution in our splendid sport of cycling – the race will be run without pacemakers except on the final stage [this was a dig at *Le Vélo*'s Bordeaux-Paris, where pacing by bicycles, tandems, triplettes, quadruplettes, by motor-driven tricycles and motor cars had all been tried]. An end to the combines and *apaches* of every stamp. Only muscles and energy will win glory and fortune. Who will carry off the first prize, entering the pantheon where only supermen may go? I do not hesitate to make Maurice Garin, "the white bulldog", my favourite.'

The combines were not entirely destroyed. At one stop Garin handed out food and drink to other members of his La Française trade team, ignoring the reproach of the hungry, thirsty, unattached Kerff who ended up angrily seizing the bowl in which they had washed themselves and drinking the dirty water. And while there was no serious trouble, there was lurking danger in the lack of supervision and in the night riding which was forced on the race by stages which averaged over 400km. Lefèvre did what he could, following his men by bicycle and then catching a train to get ahead and watch them through the next check-point. He got some help from local officials. But often, as his son has described it, 'this young man, lost all alone in the night, stood on the edge of the road, a temperamental storm lantern in his hand, searching the shadows for riders who, from time to time, surged out of the dark, shouted out their name, and immediately disappeared into the distance. He alone, this man, was "the organisation of the Tour de France".'

All the same the race passed without serious incident. The heavily-moustached Garin, more often known as the Little Chimney Sweep than the White Bulldog, arrived at an empty quai de Saône in Lyons, having ridden faster than anyone expected, at nine the following morning. He had covered the 467km from Paris at better than 26kph. The riders now had three days for rest and repairs and sightseeing in the city before setting off on the Sunday for Marseilles. There were forty-six at the line this time, not all of whom had finished at Lyons. Any who dropped out, though excluded from the Tour itself, were allowed to restart and contest the next stage for its own sake. In fact one of these, Hippolyte Aucouturier, who had earlier retired with stomach trouble, came first at both Marseilles and Toulouse, while at Bordeaux an obscure rider called Laeser won the only stage he rode. Nantes and Paris, however, fell to the favourite, Garin, as did the race itself by 2hr 49min 45sec from the butcher's boy, Louis Pothier. Garin was 2.5 kilos lighter than when he began, but otherwise unscathed. And despite the pessimistic forecasts he was the first of twenty-one riders to complete the 2,428km course. *La Vie au Grand Air* generously congratulated Desgrange for daring to undertake such a colossal task, endowing it so magnificently, and assuming the frightening task of its preparation, organisation and surveillance. No doubt Desgrange passed on these compliments to Géo Lefèvre. The first Tour de France had ended triumphantly, seeing off *Le Vélo* which very soon went

Maurice Garin, who started life as a chimney sweep, stops to take a drink from a supporter during the 1902 Bordeaux-Paris race. A year later he won the first Tour de France, leading the race from first stage to last.

into liquidation.

The second, run over the same route a year later, was a disaster. Garin had warned of trouble in 1903, recounting how, riding at night not far from Nantes, he had met a man on a bike out looking for him with no friendly intentions. Fearing something like this he had already swopped his distinctive white jersey for a black jacket. He gave another rider's name and said that Garin had dropped some way behind. The man rode back along the course to continue his search: 'Perhaps he is riding still.'

This year's troubles came so thick and fast that they were unavoidable. Now equipped with a motor car, Lefèvre was able to make more frequent spot checks, but even so he wasn't a match for the organised supporters of certain regional riders who made a practice of attacking their rivals under cover of darkness. The worst incidents occurred on the second stage when an open car drew up alongside Garin and Pothier, crowding them to the side, while the passengers, hidden behind goggles, told them what to expect if the local man, Faure of Saint-Etienne, failed to win. Next, on the col de la République, where Faure attacked, a hundred or so men armed with sticks and stones were waiting in the grey dawn light. Faure was allowed to pass, and Pothier managed to slip through, but Garin was struck on the head with a bottle and the Italian, Gerbi, was knocked to the ground and 'beaten like plaster'. He was too badly injured to continue. It was only when Lefèvre drove up, firing his pistol into the air, that the ugly mob dispersed.

On the next stage there were demonstrations on the côte d'Alès, this time against officials and in favour of the Provençal rider, Paysan, whom they had earlier disqualified. This time it was the police who drew their revolvers. But in addition to the major incidents when someone might well have been killed, there was regular, selective harassment of the riders by partisan supporters who dropped nails on the road to cause punctures or blocked it with felled trees and farm carts. Not that you would have wanted to meet some of the riders on a dark night. They were a wily bunch of itinerant mercenaries, and allegations of cheating, sharp practice and collusion were made after almost every major race. Particularly after marathon events, like the Bordeaux-Paris, which continued between dusk and dawn, and particularly pointing a finger at Garin. Rumours of dark deeds, of riders covering part of the distance by train or car and taking pace from supporters on the road, began to surface during the Tour. In one case a rider was seen being towed along by a length of wire, the front of it attached to a car and the back threaded into a cork which he held between clenched teeth. When the Tour reached Paris, with Garin leading over Pothier once more, it was clear that Desgrange had a scandal on his hands.

That did it. 'The Tour de France is over and its second edition, I very much fear, will be the last,' Desgrange fulminated. 'It will have died of success, the blind passions that it released, the injuries and foul suspicions brought upon it by the ignorant and wicked. And for all that it seemed to us, and seems to us still, that with this great race we had built the most durable and important monument to cycle sport.' In fact there was little likelihood that Desgrange would relinquish such a valuable asset. Four months later the Union Vélocipédique de France, while alas keeping their detailed findings secret, disqualified the first four riders, banning Pothier for life and Garin for two years. So the twenty-year-old Henri Cornet was promoted from fifth place to first, and remains the youngest winner of the Tour. Desgrange supported these decisions and set about planning a more disciplined Tour for 1905.

In order to eliminate night riding the race was extended to 2,975km but divided into eleven shorter stages with early morning starts, and eleven rest days. And to reduce the handicap for those who were delayed by mechanical mishaps, the race was judged not on the riders' times but on a less punishing points system, which was continued until 1913. It was perhaps as well, for though many of the old abuses were removed there was no quick cure for the spectators' unhealthy practice of scattering nails on the road. On the opening stage to Nancy one rider punctured ten times. Again Desgrange idly threatened to call off the race.

For nearly eighty years the Tour has gloried in the crowd's emotional involvement while trying to curb its active participation. Not a balance easily struck when only the last few kilometres of each stage are lined with barriers, and towards the top of the great climbs there will be thousands pressing in on the narrow roads. There are always those who want to be

Although Henri Desgrange, the founder of the Tour, was well-known as a misogynist, and the riders led an almost monastic life of the road, women have been among the most ardent race-followers since the early days.

49

part of the race, running alongside the bikes, clapping their hands, squeezing sponges, playing hoses and pouring bottles of water over the riders' bent heads. Previously it was also part of the fun to push the riders uphill, but since nowadays a push from a spectator, if seen by an official, costs the rider a fine of 20 Swiss francs and a 20sec penalty, he is more likely to lash out at anyone trying to help him. These noisy, narrow passages, when there is always the risk of a fan stumbling under their wheel, the riders detest. They are only grateful to those thoughtful spectators who stand at the summit handing out old newspapers which they push up under their jerseys to keep out the cold air on the descent.

Hostile intervention is now rare, though not unknown. Jacques Anquetil had a bucket of icy water poured over him at the top of the Grand-Saint-Bernard Pass in 1966; even then it isn't certain whether the act was malign or well-intentioned, though Anquetil, already suffering with breathing troubles, retired next day. And Eddy Merckx was struck by a middle-aged Frenchman on the Puy-de-Dôme in 1975 (when he sued he received the one-franc damages for which he had asked). Most of the deliberate interference comes from protest groups outside the sport which are looking for publicity. For all its size and strength the Tour is extremely vulnerable. Striking steel-workers at Denain had only briefly to block the road in 1982 to force the Tour to scrub a whole stage for the first time. It was a team time trial, the one type of contest which cannot be restarted or resumed. Occasionally, too, the riders themselves take their grievances out on the race. In 1966 to protest against drug tests (the use of stimulants had recently become a legal offence) the riders slowed to a stop 5km out of Bordeaux, dismounted and began to walk chanting *Merde!* at every step. And twelve years later, annoyed by the frequent transfers between stages, they got off and pushed their bicycles across the finishing line at Valence d'Agen. No prizes were awarded.

But back to 1905 when more important than the changes in the rules was the fact that Desgrange himself took personal charge of running the Tour. He was the Phineas Barnum of cycle racing, and until illness forced him to retire in 1936 he tried everything he could think of to make the Tour de France, as Barnum would have put it, the Greatest Race on Earth.

Although preoccupied with avoiding further scandals, he still managed to enlarge the Tour that year by sending the riders over its first true col, the Ballon d'Alsace, which had 12km of 1-in-10 climbing. Some changed their bikes to ride on a lower gear, but only one man, René Pottier, managed to reach the summit without getting off. He abandoned the day after with tendon trouble, won the race the following year, but six months later committed suicide as the result of 'a sentimental disappointment'.

In 1906 Desgrange took the race across the German frontier into the 'lost provinces' of Alsace-Lorraine, where the police had agreed not to prosecute any riders for exceeding the speed limit, and in 1910 extended its boundaries even further by taking it into the Pyrenees to climb the Peyresourde, Aspin, Tourmalet and Aubisque. This was seen as total folly, since bears still inhabited the mountains and the high passes were normally used only by carts. The tracks were composed of two stony ruts with a high mound in between. At the bottom the rider had to make a choice of one or other, the bank or the open side, with no chance of changing over if they had opted for the wrong one. The Aubisque was particularly rough, scarcely better than a goat track, and as Desgrange waited at the summit he began to fear that his riders might have disappeared over the edge. Finally one man arrived on foot, but when Desgrange tried to question him about the others he went on without a word. Fifteen minutes later Oscar Lapize, who was to win the Tour, came into sight, also pushing his bike. He did spare a word, but it was only *'Assassins!'*, before he, too, mounted and rode away down the other side. Desgrange was delighted with the response, and from there on the Pyrenees, the Circle of Death as the cyclists called them, featured regularly on the course.

So Desgrange established the character of the Tour as a battle against fearful odds and often fought in inhospitable regions which the readers of the newspaper reports would never see and could only imagine. Some of the writers of those reports hadn't seen them either, but they wrote of summits being conquered, of the suffering and agony of a race of Titans. Speed and skill scarcely came into it; the age of the *routier-sprinter* was decades away. The qualities to be admired were courage, strength, fortitude and perseverance. And when the riders came back to earth they certainly looked the part: spare, fierce men with curling moustaches, dust sticking to the sweat on their faces except for the circles where their goggles had been, their spare tyres strung like bandoleers in a figure eight across their shoulders.

Legends abounded of François Faber, the 1909 winner, breaking his chain a kilometre from the finish and completing the stage by running with his bicycle on his shoulder, and of Henri Alavoine trotting the last 10km to reach the Parc des Princes in Paris. Of Duboc, a rider from Rouen, who performed prodigies in the Pyrenees, winning at Perpignan and Luchon, and then collapsing on the road to Bayonne, deliberately poisoned it was said; who thereby lost the Tour and yet went on to win two more stages. And of Desgrange himself, not to be left out of the story, chasing the race in horse-drawn carriage after his car broke down.

Still, the classic folk-tale concerned Eugène Christophe, who broke the front fork of his machine descending the Tourmalet while he was leading the 1913 Tour. Maintenance was up to the rider; no service was provided at that time. There was nothing for it but for Christophe to carry his bike 14km downhill to the village of Sainte-Marie-de-Campan, open up the blacksmith's forge, light the fire and shape a piece of metal to weld to the broken stem. Since his hands were occupied he asked a small boy to work the bellows. The job completed he rode on having lost two hours and the overall lead, but he was still in the race. However, to complete the hard luck story, the incident was watched by officials who said nothing at the time but later penalised him an extra two minutes for allowing the boy to help with the repair.

The most famous and romantic piece of writing on the Tour was woven around the retirement of the Pélissier brothers, Henri and Francis, from the 1924 Tour. Henri had appeared at the cold morning start wearing two jerseys and cast one aside as the day warmed up. An official warned him, 'It is forbidden to throw anything on the road.' 'But the jersey belongs to me,' Henri protested. That evening, still furious about the incident, Henri met Albert Londres of *Le Petit Parisien* and told him, 'Before being cyclists we are men, and free.' The next day a story from Londres appeared entitled '*Les forçats de la route*' – the convicts of the road or, better perhaps, the chain gang.

In it the two brothers and their team-mate, Maurice Ville, talk of the hardship of the race:

– You've no idea what it is, the Tour de France, says Henri. It is a calvary. And beside, the road of the cross had only fourteen stations, while ours adds up to fifteen. We suffer on the road, but do you want to see how we keep going? Wait – from his bag he brings out a phial:

– It is cocaine for the eyes and chloroform for the gums.

– That, says Ville, emptying the bag, is ointment to warm the knees.

– And the pills? Do you want to see the pills?

They bring out three boxes each.

– In short, we keep going on dynamite . . .

– And one's toenails. I have lost six out of ten. They fall out little by little on each stage . . .

– The day will come when they will put lead in our pockets, because they will claim that God has made man too light.

Desgrange, who wrote of 'the divine bicycle . . . and the ineffable and precious joys that it affords', succeeded in giving a heroic stature to his mixed bag of adventurers and an epic quality to their deeds, yet remained at heart a showman. He was constantly experimenting with the format and presentation of the race, and his most fruitful idea was to identify the leader of the race to the crowds by putting him into a yellow jersey (yellow to match the pages of *L'Auto*). It came to him during the 1919 Tour, the jerseys were run up immediately, and at Grenoble the first was awarded appropriately to the immensely popular Christophe, 'le Vieux Gaulois', who was now thirty-four. The ultimate jersey, however, went to Firmin Lambot who carried it back to Belgium, and for ten of the next eleven years it was to leave its country of origin at the end of the Tour.

Desgrange felt that the fault lay in the trade team system, so in 1930 he decided to run the Tour on national lines with regional teams brought in to make up the numbers. The sponsors were outraged and withdrew their support, so the Tour itself provided all the riders' bicycles, which carried no maker's name and, for a familiar reason, were painted yellow. To meet the extra costs Desgrange introduced the publicity caravan, a fleet of rather dour advertisers' trucks which preceded the race. An official Tour de France song was composed. And for the first time spectators at the stage finish were entertained with amplified accordion music. Commercial interests unrelated to the sport had found a place in the Tour, and since they coincided with a sequence of five French victories, Desgrange had no reason to regret his experiment.

There have been constant changes since. Desgrange was succeeded by Jacques Goddet, who did his best to allow the Tour to evolve and grow while guarding its traditions. After World War Two *L'Auto* became *L'Equipe* and began to share the organisation of the race with its sister paper *Le Parisien Libéré* (now *Le Parisien*). The cyclists' lot was made easier by variable gears, lighter machines and far better roads, though what they won on that roundabout they lost in the swing to greater speed. And these in turn led to the prominence of the time trial stage, the bunch sprint, the development of more tactical team racing. Would even Eddy Merckx have stood a chance in 1903? Far more probably than that Garin could win the Tour today.

CHAPTER 4

An Italian summer

Act 2, the tours of May and June, opened to solemn music from the orchestra pit mocked by snatches of cheerful bel canto from the wings. Of our four heroes, Greg LeMond had retired to a secret address in California, where he was said to be recuperating with two hours' training a day; Stephen Roche was building up his strength with a regime of comparatively minor races; Laurent Fignon, although often described as being not just in form but in super-form, had produced no results to confirm this since the Critérium International; and Pedro Delgado, a notoriously late riser in spring, had no more than rubbed the sleep from his eyes in late March with a stage win in the Semaine Catalane. The Italians, meanwhile, ignoring these riders' past reputations and present problems, had jubilantly rifled the prizes. And by the end of the second act, we were going to find them in even better voice.

Only one of our four, Delgado, was involved in the Tour of Spain, which began among the Mediterranean palm trees and glaring white hotels of Benicasim on 24 April. And as in the Paris-Nice his projected role was as the senior pro, helping the talented young Basque, Miguel Indurain, take and keep the leader's jersey, the *maillot amarillo*. But their team, Banesto, was easily the strongest in the race and had a third protected rider, thirty-year-old Julian Gorospe. It would suit Delgado to take a back seat and save himself for the Tour de France, for he always found the Vuelta the more stressful of the two. He was so harassed by the fans that he had to enter hotels by the service door, and would leave his room at night only to go down for dinner. In France he found it relaxing to stroll around the stage town after his meal; in Spain this was impossible. On the other hand he accepted his obligations. He knew that if neither Indurain nor Gorospe was winning the race for Banesto, he would have to step in. It was expected of him.

Banesto's strength had to be taken on trust at the beginning. Ruiz-Cabestany of ONCE became the first race leader – after a curious prologue which took the form of a three-man team time trial – and was succeeded by Viktor Klimov of Alfa-Lum, the first Russian ever to wear the leader's jersey in one of the major tours. Klimov, though he had no reputation as a climber, was still ahead when the fifth stage finished with much laboured breathing at 2,400 metres in the thin atmosphere of the Sierra Nevada. But behind him Banesto had dealt a series of blows to the adversaries they feared most – Jean-François Bernard and Marino Lejaretta – and on stage 6 their third man, Gorospe, found his way into a counter-attack which took him to the head of the race.

Clearly Banesto had no great confidence in Gorospe as a long-term prospect. On stage 9 Indurain made a forceful attack to try and advance his own claims, only for ONCE to counter-mand them, and two days later the team's doubts about Gorospe were shown to be well-founded. He blew up on the second of the Tour's summit finishes at San Isidro – Banesto leaving him to his fate as a hopeless case – and the man who had been shadowing him almost unnoticed for the past five days, Marco Giovannetti, an Italian riding for the Spanish SEUR team, took over by 41sec.

Giovannetti was quite the most diffident of the new, or at any rate remodelled, faces to emerge in this Italian summer. 'It will be a miracle if I keep the jersey next Tuesday after the time trial at Valdezcaray,' he said. 'I will defend it as long as I can, but with two time trials to come I won't have it in Madrid.' He had some grounds for modesty since, apart from the low regard in which he held his own performances against the clock, he was built like a rugby flanker – 6ft 3in tall and weighing 12st 8lb – and had done well to make light of his bulk in the mountains so far. He was not even particularly ambitious. An Olympic gold medallist in the 100km team time trial at Los Angeles in 1984, he had gone to Spain for the money: a two-year contract with SEUR worth £250,000, which was more than Italy would pay a rider who had finished the Giro in the top ten on four occasions, but had few victories to his credit (and those back in 1987). He liked racing in Spain, which didn't prevent him flying home to Lucca twenty times a season. He also liked money – invested in a Tuscan restaurant, the business in which he had been brought up – but again this didn't stop him playing and losing in the casinos. He was not a man to look for trouble and he hadn't searched assiduously to become a leader.

Still, a leader he was and a leader he stayed. He almost lost the jersey in the mountains the following day, relying on his team-mate, Alvaro Pino, to lead him over the final kilometres: 'I told him to leave me, but he refused. Keep going, he kept telling me, and he was right.' It was clear that Banesto had on this occasion backed the wrong man. In the mountain time trial at Valdezcaray, ridden in hail and fog, he lost 50sec to Delgado but to everyone's surprise gained six on Indurain. And in the Pyrenees, while Delgado finished alongside Giovannetti at Cerler, Indurain, well below his best, lost another 50sec. There was no option for Delgado; he had to lead the counter-attack. But he had forfeited too many opportunities, assuming that Indurain would take them, and now he couldn't close the gap. Giovannetti won the Vuelta by a comfortable 1min 28sec, and since his contract with SEUR was coming to an end, he flew off to the Giro knowing that suddenly 'some very interesting proposals' would be coming to him from several Spanish and Italian managers.

Meanwhile the supporting racing programme was continuing to the north. Stephen Roche, whose season hinged on the Tour de France, was looking avidly for a victory which would confirm his recovery and also make a point to Histor, with whom, after the happy affair of the Paris-Nice, he had rapidly fallen out of love. He felt they had done less than they had promised to strengthen their squad for the big stage races. For these they needed climbers, but, like many other Belgian teams, they had become preoccupied with winning the classics, for which they needed sprinters. Roche found his victory in the Dunkirk Four-Day in early May, though it was at some cost.

Roche made his move on the second day when a fall left him with wounds on his shoulder and thigh and the need to pursue for 15km just to catch up with the field. But not content with regaining his place he attacked immediately the junction was made, carrying with him François Lemarchand of the Z team. Lemarchand took the stage but Roche had gained what he needed. That afternoon, in spite of his injuries, he finished fifth in the time trial at Boulogne and took the leader's pink jersey. The race was shortly heading for Cassel where, just a year before in the same event, Roche had scored his last win. 'I'm sentimental,' he said ironically.

Even before he got there, however, Roche fell heavily again only 300 metres into the first of five stretches of *pavé*. Once more he finished covered in blood, and insisted on cleaning up before going on to the platform, 'so that I look like a cyclist, not a butcher'. From there he was taken to hospital at

Stephen Roche was still trying to recuperate from injury and to rediscover the exuberant form of 1987 when, riding for Carrera, he had won the Tours of Italy and France and the world championship
58 *in the space of three months.*

Armentières where an x-ray showed that his shoulder hadn't been fractured as was feared, though two small stones and a fragment of bone had to be removed from it. He returned to take third place in the next morning's time trial and – on alternate sleeping pills and pain-killers and with his right shoulder in a splint – went on to win the race by 17sec. (On the strength of that you might have expected Histor to offer to buy him the climber of his choice; instead, a month or so later, they signed up two new sprinters).

LeMond, 9,000km away in Santa Rosa, north California, was also painfully coming to terms with his troubles. But his were less easily diagnosed and to be cured only with time and seemingly unrewarded effort. Finding himself overtaken in training by tourists just going places on their bicycles (but also showing enough faith in his future to consider some new triathlon handlebars for the time trials in the Tour) LeMond was in no real condition to resume racing on the appointed day, the start of the 1,800km Tour de Trump from Wilmington, Del. to Boston on 3 May. As a kind of personal prologue to the race he had agreed to appear in the Washington Criterium five days before, but even that undemanding commitment ended lamely with his retirement after only 70kms. It was just with gastric trouble, but LeMond's comeback seemed fated.

Roger Legeay, the Z manager, had come over to the Trump from France to lend moral support and practical help with press relations, but LeMond needed more than that. He was 36sec down after the first day, 3min 32sec down on the second, and on the third lost 26min 30sec to the stage winner at Charlottesville, an American amateur, Nate Reiss, and finished only just ahead of the broom wagon. It was humiliating to face such defeat in front of his own people, and LeMond came close to abandoning the race. But although he drew little sympathy from the crowd – if he was a champion why wasn't he winning? – he submitted to the ordeal for 11 days. He was convinced that the only way to regain his strength was to cover the miles in competition.

The race was a long battle between a nineteen-year-old Soviet amateur, Vyatcheslav Bobrik, and the experienced Mexican professional, Raul Alcala of PDM. And it was not until the Catskill mountains on stage 8 that Alcala got the upper hand. He eventually won the tour by 43sec from the Norwegian, Atle Kvalsvoll, who was to be LeMond's *domestique* in the Tour de France, and by 1min 44sec from his own PDM team-mate, Eric Breukink. LeMond finished 80th at 1hr 53min 18sec. In less than a week he would be at the start of the Giro. It didn't seem a great deal to build on, but he insisted that he wasn't dismayed. He put it to *L'Equipe*: 'I have contested four Tours de France and I have never cracked. I have confidence in myself. And you?'

Fignon was also heading for the Giro, having just completed the Tour of Romandie in western Switzerland, a race won by Charly Mottet in a lively clash with Robert Millar who took a stage and finished second. Since the Critérium International Fignon had ridden inconspicuously, and the Giro, which he had won the previous year, was mainly to be a preparation for the Tour. But whereas LeMond wanted nothing more than to build up the kilometres and finish the race, Fignon's approach was more aggressive. He was not the kind of man who would want to compete in a major tour without leaving his mark on it.

The prologue at Bari was a straightforward trial of strength over 13km, out into a headwind, home with a tailwind and devil take those who couldn't stand the pace. To the delight of the Italians, who had decided that a new Coppi, or at least a new Moser, had been born to them, Gianni Bugno beat Thierry Marie, the French specialist in these short, explosive events by 3sec and the main favourites by considerably more. Fignon and Visentini were both at 29sec, while Mottet, Rooks and Theunisse were not even in the first twenty. LeMond, on the other hand, was: to be exact, twentieth at 31sec, a result from which, in his straitened circumstances, he took some comfort.

The next day Fignon made a brief and rare appearance as a sprinter, only to be beaten into second place by Bugno's man, Giovanni Fidanza. And the effort of his Castorama team-mate, Marie, to take the pink jersey from Bugno with the aid of a bonus in the mid-way sprint was equally foiled by the Château d'Ax team. His third place, worth two seconds, left him a single second behind Bugno overall. But that was as near as he would come to the jersey, for on stage 2 he dropped from sight as Bugno attacked strongly with the Spaniard, Eduardo

Chozas, on the slopes of Mount Vesuvius. Fignon fell a minute behind, LeMond lost quarter of an hour – but then he was practically riding a different race – and even so early in the Tour Bugno had established himself as a solid favourite, not only in Italian eyes.

Three events occurred in the next few days which were to bear directly on the Tour de France. The first was a stage win at Sora for the Australian Phil Anderson, who made one of his noted and often successful attacks a kilometre from the line to avoid any sprinters getting in his way. This was more than another agreeable landmark in his long career. His team, sponsored by the Dutch insurance group, TVM, had not qualified on FICP points for one of the first sixteen places in the Tour de France. It would have to rely on being drawn as one of the six wild cards, and it hadn't been conspicuous enough this season to count on that. Relations between the thirty-one-year-old Anderson and his manager, Cees Priem, had been strained. This was (to quote the French expression) the *kangourou*'s reply. One up to Anderson, though he said that before considering the Tour, 'I want to show that I am not finished as some try to make me believe.' Two up to Anderson was that his American companion, Shelly Verses, a *soigneuse* with TVM, joined the race. Priem hadn't wanted her on the Giro, but the return home of another *soigneur* forced a change of plan, and her arrival coincided with a burst of activity from Anderson who continually turned up in the first four at the stage finish. It was then that the Tour must have begun to mark TVM on its racecard.

The second incident was a crash involving Fignon on stage 5. It was one of several as the riders passed through unlighted tunnels cut into the Abruzzo massif north of Naples, but it was all the worse for coming on a fast descent from the Paso di Campanelle. Someone touched his brakes in alarm, another crashed in to him, and a score of riders came down, with Fignon, who slid along the ground on the seat of his disintegrating shorts, most seriously hurt. Bugno called off a counterattack which was in progress, and Fignon was able to regain the peloton with, as a reporter expressed it succinctly, if unfeelingly, a bottom like a baboon. He struggled on for another three days, but the pain in his back was getting more severe and since he could manage only a small gear he could no longer compete. On stage 9, having lost five minutes on the first col of the day, he retired; and after returning to Paris he was advised that there was some displacement of his pelvis. The Tour was still a month away, and Fignon hoped to make his come-back in the Route du Sud on June 6, but his manager, Cyrille Guimard, was concerned that the time for serious preparation was running out.

On the same day as Fignon's crash, it was also announced that the Dutch climber, Gert-Jan Theunisse, had failed a dope test after the Flèche Wallonne. This was his second positive result within two years – in each case testosterone had been identified as the forbidden substance – and it should have meant instant disqualification. Instead on technical grounds this was deemed a first offence by the UCI (we'll return to this in Chapter 13), and he was free to ride on. Reacting with unusual anger and solidarity, the other riders and managers staged a strike in protest at the decision before the start of stage 6. But Panasonic refused to withdraw their man, a reluctant compromise was reached, and without taking a significant part in the race, Theunisse brazened it out to finish the Giro in 15th place. All the same it appeared inconceivable that Theunisse would be back to defend his mountain title in the Tour.

Bugno, whose previous best result in any major tour had been his 11th place in the 1989 Tour de France, now had this one by the collar. He rode it as Eddy Merckx might have done. He made his own race, exploiting the opportunities of each stage as they presented themselves and refusing to shape his tactics to the strength of other riders. He led; he didn't shadow. And if one of his rivals followed when he attacked, at least he knew he was seeing off the rest of the opposition.

After having won the prologue and come second on Vesuvius, he won stage 7 with its 10km climb to the finish at Vallambrosa. He was second to another Italian, Luca Gelfi, in the 68km time trial; and second to both the Z rider, Eric Boyer, and to Mottet in mountain stages. Finally he won the uphill time trial at Varese to take the Giro by 3min 33sec from Mottet and 9min 1sec from the irrepressible Giovannetti. This was the widest winning margin since that of Merckx in 1973, and

Bugno was only the fourth man to lead the Giro from start to finish. In three months the unexpected winner of the Milan-San Remo had become – along with LeMond and Fignon, and you couldn't be quite sure of them at this moment – the strongest rider in the professional field.

Would he now ride the Tour? He was told not to, in particular by his regular adviser, the past Tour winner Félice Gimondi, who felt he had more to lose than to gain by tackling another marathon so soon. It could only damage his reputation if he cracked. Bugno said he'd leave it to Château d'Ax, and not surprisingly they took a more commercial view of gains and losses and said yes.

LeMond finished 107th, nearly three hours down on Bugno, but he did finish, which had been his main objective. And on stage 11 he had even blown the spark of his old spirit into life, persisting for 120kms in an attack with the Italian veteran, Bruno Leali, before getting caught 23km from the finish. 'I have never made so important an escape in all my career,' he said afterwards. 'It was the first time this year I have felt really good in the hills, and I only made one mistake, which was to believe I was tougher than, in reality, I was.' He didn't repeat that experiment, but in the second test he had set himself – the final time trial which proved disagreeably wet and foggy – he came a fairly noncommittal twelfth.

The Tour de France was now only three weeks away. After some pessimistic speculation in the press, Fignon made his return in the Route du Sud, the pain in his back still troublesome but more dispersed than it had been. He said he'd see how he went from day to day, but was sufficiently encouraged to go on to the Tour of Luxemburg where Anderson, still fighting TVM's battle, led the race for a while but finally conceded victory to Fignon's *équipier*, Christophe Lavainne. There was now little doubt that, unless his troubles flared up again, Fignon would be at the Futuroscope for the start of the Tour.

LeMond's last public engagement was the Tour of Switzerland, a country in which he would remain for five days afterwards to round off his private training. And for the first time in that race he finished a heavy mountain stage in ninth place and in the company of his peers. Again he said: 'It was the finest day of my season,' though he added, 'there is still a lot to do, for I can't yet manage the very big gears.' Was there enough time left to do it?

The Z team, largely in his absence, had enjoyed a highly successful season. While the Giro was going on Millar had won his first stage race, the Dauphiné, coming second to Thierry Claveyrolat on a day which included the cols de Porte and du Coq, and then beating him in the final time trial to win overall with a minute and a half to spare. And in the Tour of Switzerland he had finished second to Sean Kelly. Boyer had taken two fine stages in the Giro, and Kvalsvoll his second place in the Tour de Trump. The morale of the team couldn't have been higher. Now all that Z needed was a leader.

CHAPTER 5

The American connection

It is a good deal less surprising to find Americans riding the Tour de France than to think of the United States staging the 1994 World Cup (winning the Tour three years out of five, as Greg LeMond has done, is another matter; it is remarkable for anyone but the French or Belgians to do that). Soccer has never existed there on a popular level, but track racing was strong at the turn of the century, producing a number of world champions, including a sprinter who competed as Maj. Taylor. And six-day cycle racing, run indoors on a steeply-raked wooden circuit, was introduced into New York from England in the 1890s, and refined there before being reimported by Europe.

It was the Americans who invented the perpetual relay race at the heart of the Six – a wild chase in which one member of each two-man team flies around the inside of the track trying to steal a lap, and is then relieved by his partner who has been slowly circling the top of the banking. This type of relay, in which the partners swop roles with a hand-sling into the fray just whenever they wish, is still known as the madison, after Madison Square Garden, or in France, as *l'Americaine*. Sixes were put on regularly between the wars in Chicago, Cleveland, Milwaukee, Minneapolis and San Francisco, as well as New York, and finally went the way of marathon dancing and the pogo stick only in the late 'fifties. Road racing never took off; roads were for automobiles.

Britain's experience (which essentially meant England's) was rather different. In the later years of the nineteenth century, it yielded nothing to France in its enthusiasm for cycle racing. Quite apart from the feats of James Moore, related in chapter 3, English amateurs took the first three places in the inaugural Bordeaux-Paris race in 1891, and later in the decade the professionals won the world middle-distance (*demi-fond*) title on the track for five years in succession.

The early racing in England was held in parks because the public roads were so badly maintained, but later special ash, shale, gravel and grass circuits were laid out in most big towns, and at the Putney velodrome in 1891 the first concrete track was built. Races in which the contestants were paced around the track by tandems – or later by triplets, quads, quints and so on up to ten-seaters – attracted crowds of 10,000 and more and there was heavy betting on the results.

By 1886 the country had sixty-eight bicycle factories. Ten years later there were 700, turning out 750,000 machines a year for largely middle-class customers (even with mass production a machine cost upward of fifteen guineas). And although the earliest off-track sport was setting place-to-place and other long-distance records, road racing had already begun and would probably have developed as it did on the continent if it had not been for intervention by the police. In 1883 they defined the bicycle as a 'carriage', and so subject to a speed limit of 12mph. And after a series of prosecutions had been brought for 'furious riding', the National Cyclists' Union decided in 1888 to confine their future racing to the track.

When racing cyclists came back on the road in 1895 it was to take up a form of the sport designed to avoid antagonising the authorities. This was the time trial, in which the cyclists rode singly at intervals along the road. As an extra precaution events were held at dawn, on courses denoted only by a code number, and for riders who were obliged to wear 'inconspicuous clothing'. This consisted of dark jacket and tights and was scarcely a foolproof disguise. But since the organisers of these trials without witnesses were clearly people of the utmost probity, the police generally turned a blind eye to them.

So, for more than half a century, two of the world's pioneer cycling nations were divorced from the most exciting and fastest-growing area of the sport, massed-start racing. In Britain's case the divorce was never made absolute. Time trialing kept competitive cycling alive, and when the restrictions on road-racing were lifted – within limits – after world war two, many of the more adventurous riders who did well in it at home were drawn to the continent in the hope of doing even better. The first British national team, sponsored by Hercules, appeared in the 1955 Tour de France, and was followed at intervals by three more; and in 1987 the first British trade team, ANC-Halfords, was accepted. But the best results have generally come from those who crossed the Channel as individuals and went native, attaching themselves to an amateur club in France or Belgium, learning the language and then earning a contract with a continental team.

If Britain had been insular up to the war, the United States had been positively isolationist; with a few exceptions even their Six Day men preferred to ride at home rather than chance their arm on the European circuit. So when young Americans began to take up cycling for home-spun ecological reasons in the 'sixties, only their grandparents might vaguely have remembered a time when their country had any international status in cycle sport. If they wanted to race, they had to start from scratch.

It was women who made the initial breach. In heavy rain at Brno in 1969 Audrey McElmury reached the line alone to become the first American women's world road-race champion. But it was not until 1982 that Beth Heiden added her name to McElmury's, by which time their countrywomen had made an even greater impact on the track. In 1973 at San Sebastian, Sheila Young, bronze medallist the year before, took the world title in the sprint, an event which Soviet riders had monopolised for fifteen years, only once failing to take silver as well as gold. And over the next eleven years, through Young (twice more), Sue Novarra (2) and Connie Paraskevin (3), the United States became the dominant power. Coming through rather later, the American pursuiter Rebecca Twigg won four gold medals between 1982 and 1987, and Connie Carpenter, the first women's Olympic road-race champion (1984) took another.

One curious explanation for this sudden but prolonged success was that many of these young women had come into cycling from speed skating, another formidable test of nerve and balance, and were able to adapt their temperament, as well as some of their skills and physical training, from one to the other (just as many of the great descenders on the Tour de France have learned from downhill skiing). Also, it has to be said, women's track racing was probably a softer target than road-racing was for the men, since the Catholic countries of western Europe did little to encourage it. The Soviets had it much their own way, with their stately sprinter, Galina Ermolaeva, sailing through the opposition like a galleon until the United States sent in their sleeker, faster and surprisingly hostile craft.

The men had to serve a longer apprenticeship just to be accepted in races, but more than any of the other 'new' nations they applied themselves, built up experience and refused to be discouraged. They rode their first Milk Race in 1974 and finished bottom of the team classification; nine years later their leader, Mike Eaton, won the event. This was a surprise but no sensation. By then the American amateurs had picked up more experience of continental racing than many of the British cyclists they rode against. In 1979 a team of eight had turned up in France, as *L'Equipe* sniffily reported it, 'dressed in cowboy clothes with broad-brimmed hats and rodeo trousers'. But they gained respect when George Mount won the opening stage of the Circuit de la Sarthe, in which professionals were also engaged, and Mark Pringle, who had long, fair hair, 'and seemed to be enjoying himself in the pelotons', finished second in the Tour of Loir-et-Cher in the same time as the French winner, Michel Larpe. The Americans also took fourth and fifth place and the team competition. 'On that level of performance,' conceded *L'Equipe*, 'the "cow-boys" have shown a collective strength rich in promise for the future.'

Jonathan Boyer was the down-payment on that promise: the first American to ride the Tour. He was twenty-five when he arrived for the 1981 start in Nice as a member of Bernard Hinault's Renault team, having finished fifth behind his new leader in the previous summer's world championships. An elegant, slightly dandified young man, he, too, affected a stetson in which he would sometimes be photographed before the stage although it was seven years since he had first come to France. He had been born in Utah, raised in California and, having first intended studying at the University of Colorado to qualify as a veterinarian, instead came to Europe to try his luck as a racing cyclist (Laurent Fignon, another aspiring vet, later trod the same primrose path). He arrived in France before he was eighteen, was spotted in junior races by ACBB – the Association Cycliste de Boulogne-Billancourt, a celebrated nursery for would-be professionals – and graduated to the Lejeune trade team. Each winter he would return to the United States to keep himself going with casual work, but his career was interrupted by a longer stay there, lasting nearly two years, recuperating from a virus apparently picked up in the 1977 world championships in Venezuela.

On his full return in 1980 he was with the Puch-Sem team when, in the world championships at Sallanches, not far from the rented house in the Haute-Savoie where he lived with his wife, Elizabeth, he achieved his most publicised result so far. Now here he was in Renault's crack team. He was an approachable person who answered questions with candour and possessed a great deal of charm, but the French couldn't really make him out. It was not simply his religion; but he had newly become an adventist, and although he didn't parade the fact, it was perhaps a more conspicuous choice than the unspoken Catholicism of much of the peloton. Nor was it his diet, though he ate no red meat and no food with colouring or additives, having avoided them since his illness. He relied heavily on dried fruit, in particular the Californian dates with which he filled his pockets before the stage, and kept in almost daily touch with doctors at the Hinsdale hospital in Illinois who were monitoring his progress. (Two years later a reporter who went to interview him during the Tour was also taken aback to find him receiving acupuncture from Dr Kim Wha Ja, a Korean family friend with a clinic in California, who had treated other members of the team).

What made it hard to place Boyer, too, was not just that his career had been disrupted, but that it was now split between cycle racing and his business interests as the European agent for American Grab-One accessories. That too he patiently explained. While he rode he did so with all his effort and concentration, but not simply to make money; he could earn more back home. He raced because he enjoyed it, and because it furthered his other ambition to take professional cycling to the United States where he hoped to be involved in its promotion and maybe in television and journalism. He was both friendly and reserved, a detached participant; Cyrille Guimard, his *directeur-sportif* at Renault, described him as a *marginal*. And those who couldn't quite see what he was doing at Hinault's side assumed that it was to act as chaperone to a higher-flying American who had joined the team but was still far too young to ride the Tour – Greg LeMond, about whom there had been a buzz in Europe ever since he had won the world junior road race title in 1979.

The role suited neither of them; they were both too independent. Boyer was the more experienced and a fluent French speaker whereas LeMond was just picking up the language, but he was not the senior in racing terms. By his twentieth birthday LeMond had already won the top American race, the Coors Classic. And then in 1982 the coolness between them dropped to several degrees of frost following their clash in the world championship road race at Goodwood. Both were nominally riding for the United States, but since the team had no manager, masseur, expense allowance or common cause, in reality they were riding as individuals. And both were still up with the leaders after more than six hours' racing over the downs when the race neared the end of its final 10-mile lap. In the last half-mile Boyer attacked and went clear; LeMond counter-attacked, drawing along the Italian, Giuseppe Saronni, and Sean Kelly in his wake; Boyer was caught, Saronni drove on to take the gold medal, with LeMond holding off Kelly to secure the silver; and Boyer finished tenth.

Convinced that he would have won the title but for LeMond's intervention, Boyer was furious, LeMond unrepentant. 'I don't think Boyer could or should be a world champion,' he said to reporters afterwards. 'He has never even won a professional race, and his Tour rides were not impressive. But the real truth is that this US team was not a team at all. I did not stay with the other riders, or spend time with them, and I paid my own way to the World's . . . If Saronni and I had been the only ones to pass Jock [at that time it was usually Jock or Jacques not Jonathan], that would have been one thing; actually the field was completely capable of pulling him back, which is how all those other riders went by . . . I was definitely not going to give up my chances for someone who would never do the same for me.'

LeMond was twenty-one at the time, a slightly-built and slightly elfin young man, his teeth bound in a network of corrective braces, a monument to American orthodontics. He no longer speaks so abrasively of opponents, at least not to the press, but his estimate of his own worth has changed very little.

I had arranged to phone him next day to get some additional information for *Sports Illustrated*, *Time-Life*'s weekly magazine, one of whose staff writers had spent several weeks preparing a feature on him. Instead I got a call from his father, Bob, courteously explaining that Renault had sent for LeMond to ride the pro-am Tour de l'Avenir. Modelled on the Tour de France, it was the biggest race of its kind, and LeMond won it by a record 10 minutes. Despite that, *Sports-Illustrated*, who were to make him their Sportsman of the Year in 1989, didn't run the piece. Europe was a faraway place and cycling a sport about which they still knew very little.

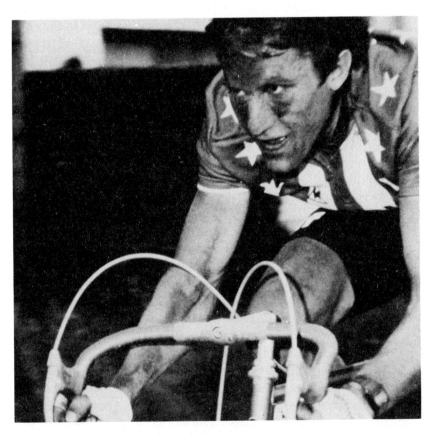

Star-spangled jersey and, when in mufti, a stetson hat: Jonathan Boyer left no-one in any doubt that he was the first American to ride the Tour. This was in 1981, three years before LeMond came to the start.

Having moved from Renault back to Sem, Boyer joined 7-Eleven in 1986 when they became the first US team to enter the Tour, acting as what's now known as an *équipier-de-luxe*, reading the race and advising the younger riders. At the end of 1987 he retired from racing, but was back in 1990 attached to the PDM team for whom he acted as *directeur-sportif* when they raced in the United States. He was a consultant for the CBS network, had many other business interests, and though he was now literally, in Guimard's expression, a marginal figure, he was in a more enviable position than many riders who had made a greater name for themselves in competition.

LeMond was to build his first fortune on the bike, and only then to multiply it by extending into business through Team LeMond – which markets cycles and accessories in the United States – endorsements, commercials and a restaurant. When he joined La Vie Claire in 1985 it was to exchange Renault's 100,000 dollars a year for a million-dollar three-year contract. Its last year, 1987, brought a change of team name since the sponsor wanted to stress his Toshiba connection, but in any case LeMond rode only briefly in its colours, for in April he was gravely injured in a hunting accident.

His next move, to the Dutch-based PDM in 1988, had less to do with money than with the opportunities a stronger team could offer; but again these were curtailed by his slow recovery and he still wasn't strong enough to ride the Tour de France. He did not renew his contract with PDM at the end of the season, but this time for direct commercial reasons. It was two years since he had won the Tour, Team LeMond had bicycles to shift – 350,000 dollars' worth, it was said – and to promote those sales LeMond, and his father, thought he should ride part of the season in the United States. PDM, wanting LeMond to advertise their sound and video tapes in Europe, wouldn't agree to share their rider's time. There was also the complication that an associate of PDM was exporting bicycles into the US market and there was a clear conflict of interest. So the LeMonds negotiated a more favourable deal with the Belgian team, ADR, who would pay 250,000 dollars for the rider's services in Europe, leaving him free to make a 350,000 dollar agreement with the Coors brewery to ride the American races for them.

The commercial equation had worked out neatly, and ADR got not only a Tour de France victory but a world title for their money. But LeMond had to achieve both with little help from the team, and at the end of 1989 he made his best and, since he was now twenty-eight, possibly his final major transfer. He joined Z, sponsored by Roger Zannier, the French children's clothing manufacturer, for 5.5 million dollars (£3.7 million) over three years with an agreement that the team would ride Greg LeMond cycles. Z were sympathetic to LeMond's US interests, showed an almost saintly forebearance over his health problems in the first half of the 1990 season, and provided him with a team for whom he ended up feeling gratitude and affection. LeMond could hardly ask for anything more.

Some of his earlier employers were unhappy about the sums of money that he – or his father, who represented him – asked for. But unlike many previous champions, who accepted whatever they were offered, LeMond always had a firm idea of his commercial value and of the money that comparable sportsmen were earning in the United States. And if he raised the stakes for himself, he helped to do the same for the others. There is little evident jealousy of his position, and certainly not among his own team who share the profit of his victories. Beside which, LeMond is famously generous towards his riders and the various team workers behind the scenes.

His candidly businesslike approach to money and ambition – as something you should not be ashamed of or try to hide – strikes the French as particularly American. So does his attitude to his family. By tradition in the world of professional cycling mothers stay at home, have stage wins dedicated to them and are sent the winner's bouquet. Fathers work in the fields and have nothing to say in the matter. And wives and girl friends keep their distance except on rest days when conjugal rights may be permitted at the management's discretion. The aim of the *directeur-sportif*, like that of the old boxing coach, has been to protect his riders from emotional distractions even of the most innocent and familial kind. LeMond is rare in having his father as his business partner and liking to know that his wife and children are not too far away. He shares his profession with his family in a way that wouldn't occur to most continental riders who believe in keeping separate the two sides of their life.

All the same it is not being American that allows LeMond to live by his own rules, it is being a phenomenon. He is not the best climber on the circuit, though day after day he is among the top half-dozen. He is not essentially a sprinter, though if need be he can pull out a faster finish than most *rouleurs*. He is not even the quickest time-trialist at the moment, though that has been his strength in the past and you feel he still has something in reserve. He is not even, as American sports writers put it, the winningest rider around, but he is a formidable competitor in any race he has targeted. These qualities, plus a gift for quick recovery from his efforts (he has off-months but rarely off-days) would be enough in themselves to make him successful. What puts him in another category is a stubborn belief in himself and in the benefits of perseverance.

LeMond saw his first cycle-race when he was fourteen and his family had moved from California, where he was born in 1961, to the Washoe Valley, Nevada. It brought an instant conversion from downhill skiing, in which he had shown some promise, to cycling in which he made even faster progress. Encouraged and trained by his father, he rose through the amateur grades, and was eighteen when he won his world junior title in Buenos Aires. Next on his schedule was an appearance at the Moscow Olympics, and in the early summer of 1980 he went with the US team for a series of preparation races in Europe during which he won the Circuit de la Sarthe. But at this point his appointment book was rewritten for him; Cyrille Guimard came to watch him race and later in Paris offered him a professional contract with Renault for the following season. And then LeMond returned home to win the Olympic selection race only for the US government to declare a boycott of the Games. He closed the deal with Renault even more quickly than he expected, and still only nineteen – young even by continental standards – he turned professional, setting up home in France with his newly-wed Kathy at the start of the 1981 season.

He was still several years away from riding the Tour; there are no age limits, but by general consent twenty-three has come to be regarded as the age of suitable maturity. Meanwhile LeMond took the Coors Classic and two stages in the

Tour de l'Oise in his opening year, and in 1982, beside the world silver medal and the l'Avenir with three of its stages, he was hardly ever out of the first five in other races. By the autumn of 1983 he had won the Dauphiné Libéré, again with three stages; he had taken the world title at Altenrhein, coming in alone with more than a minute to spare; and he was top of the Super Prestige Pernod, the professional riders' championship. He could hardly have proved more conclusively that he was now ready for the Tour, which in 1984 would start three days after his twenty-third birthday.

Hinault had recently left Renault for La Vie Claire, and the new team leader was Laurent Fignon, winner of the previous year's Tour. Fignon's tenure was not that secure, for he had won in the absence of Hinault, who was having a knee operation, and partly through the mischance of the race leader, Pascal Simon, who broke his collar-bone in a fall. So it was understood that the position might be reviewed if after some days LeMond was more favourably placed than Fignon in the order. Fignon never allowed this to become a remote possibility. He won both the early time trials, dominated the racing in the Alps, and won his second Tour by over ten and a half minutes with Hinault in second place and LeMond third, a further minute behind. It was another moon walk for LeMond: the first American to stand on the podium in Paris. But now Fignon was unassailably Renault's leader; LeMond's chances of rapid promotion were blocked, so that autumn he joined Hinault, an older man who might be nearing the end of his career, at La Vie Claire.

The pact between them was that LeMond would work for Hinault in the first year, so helping him to gain a third Giro d'Italia and, more important, the fifth Tour de France which would equal the record of Jacques Anquetil and Merckx. The second year Hinault would return the compliment, so passing on his mantle to his young American protégé. So it worked out: Hinault first and LeMond third behind Francesco Moser in the Giro; Hinault first and LeMond second, at 1min 42sec, in the Tour. But a certain ambiguity entered into the arrangement during the Tour when Hinault found LeMond uncomfortably close behind him at the end of the first week. He asserted himself in the long time trial between Sarrebourg and

Strasbourg, and again, in the company of Luis Herrera, on the climb to Avoriaz in the Alps. But three days later he crashed as he sprinted for second place behind Herrera at Saint-Etienne, and next morning he had trouble with his breathing.

There is some question whether LeMond could now have won the Tour if he had tried, and also whether or not he did try. The opportunity came when he outdistanced Hinault on the climb to Luz Ardiden in the Pyrenees but was ordered by his team officials to slacken off since he was also aiding their mutual rival, Stephen Roche. Reluctantly he did so, forfeiting his chance of a stage win and possibly the yellow jersey (which he might or might not have allowed Hinault to regain). Despite his anger LeMond's only further revolt was purely symbolic: he beat Hinault in the time trial at the lac de Vassivière to win his first Tour stage. Hinault expressed pleasure with his young ward, and for the time being nothing more was said, at least in public.

The tensions between the two men surfaced again, however, during the 1986 Tour. Hinault said he was there only to aid LeMond, and yet openly played with the idea of a sixth win which would seal his place in the history of the Tour. And while protesting his good intentions, he seemed to make life as difficult as possible for LeMond. When pressed on the subject he would only say that he was doing it for the American's benefit. At the Nantes time trial he beat LeMond by 44sec, and

Bernard Hinault might be wearing the red and white mountain jersey but, during the ambiguous contest of 1986, LeMond could never be certain that his old leader might not want to change his spots for the yellow jersey.

at Pau, after breaking away with Pedro Delgado he was leading the race by over four and a half minutes. LeMond was in torment, uncertain whether he could trust his ally and convinced that the Frenchmen in his team were working for a Hinault victory. The next day Hinault attacked again, alone, on the descent from the Tourmalet, but this time wasn't equal to the task. He was caught on the Peyresourde and beaten on the climb to Superbagnères where LeMond won his second Tour stage and recouped nearly all his losses. Four days later at Serre-Chevalier in the Alps LeMond took the yellow jersey, relegating Hinault to third place.

The second alpine stage, over the Galibier to finish at l'Alpe d'Huez, was the most extraordinary of all. Again Hinault led the charge down the Galibier, drawing off five other riders plus LeMond, and gradually shedding them on the Croix-de-Fer until only Hinault and LeMond were left. They climbed the hairpins of l'Alpe d'Huez together, chatting and sharing food from their pockets, and came to the line with their arms across each other's shoulders, LeMond giving Hinault the honour of the stage. A truce had been declared, or so LeMond believed.

But had it? Despite the fact that all the team's enemies had been routed, the following morning at a press conference Hinault declared that still the Tour wasn't over. He would only concede the victory if LeMond stayed ahead after next day's stage at Saint-Etienne. This was a time trial, the last of Hinault's career, and he won it. But despite crashing as he over-eagerly hit a corner LeMond was only 25sec slower. This time the crisis really was over. There was no further aggression from Hinault, and LeMond reached Paris with over three minutes to spare. None of LeMond's Tour victories has been easy, but none has been so bewildering or has put him under so much psychological pressure as the first.

LeMond's defence of his crown in 1987 might not have been simple, but with Hinault absent from the scene it would certainly have been more straightforward. Unfortunately he wasn't there to make it. He had gone to Europe in the February, riding the Tour of Valencia in Spain and Het Volk in Belgium before moving on to Italy for the Tirreno-Adriatica, where early in the race he broke his wrist and collar-bone in a mass pile-up of riders. This wasn't a serious injury, but it would take time to mend and meanwhile he went home to rest and train in California. It was a few days before he was due to rejoin his team that he had the accident which almost cost his life and was to have lasting consequences.

A country boy, he was used to shooting quail and pheasant, but this time he agreed to go turkey hunting in a party of four on his uncle's land nearby. Turkey are warier birds, rarely breaking cover, which can encourage a certain trigger-happiness in inexperienced hunters. This seemed to be the case this day. One of the party, a cousin, shot at a movement in the bushes and hit LeMond in the back, breaking two ribs, and a little finger, and leaving pellets in his body, arms and legs. Some had entered his small intestine, liver and diaphragm. He was unconscious, losing blood and his lung had partially collapsed. All that saved his life was the chance presence in the area of a Highway Patrol helicopter, responding to a minor emergency on the road, and a quick airlift to the Davis Medical Centre at Sacramento, which had a trauma unit. Had he been taken by ambulance to a local general hospital he would almost certainly have died.

As it was, his recovery was slow and painful, and many in his situation would have abandoned any thought of picking up a career with such heavy physical demands. LeMond was determined to do so. The rest of the 1987 season was devoted to healing and building up his wasted muscles. In 1988 he made a partial return to Europe but abandoned the Dunkirk Four-Day when it became clear to him that he would not be fit to ride the Tour de France. The one encouragement from the season was that he managed to finish fourth in the Tour of the Americas.

The next year was to mark his come-back, although he was still unsure how his body would respond to the pressure. He went through a heavy programme of classics and short stage races early in the season, achieving some reasonable results, and in May set out on the Giro, his first major Tour in three years. He finished 39th, but more important he finished, and was ready for the ultimate test of his stamina, the Tour.

It was a remarkable race, a protracted and finely balanced struggle between Fignon, Delgado and himself, in which

LeMond took the yellow jersey in the Dinard-Rennes time trial, lost it to Fignon at Superbagnères, regained it at Orcières-Merlette and lost it once more at l'Alpe d'Huez. And it had an even more remarkable conclusion: a 24.5km time trial from Versaille to the Champs-Elysées in which LeMond gained 58sec on Fignon to win by the narrowest margin ever, eight seconds. The headline on *L'Equipe* was the one word INOUBLIABLE! – and unforgettable it was. Nor did it end there. Before the end of the summer LeMond, winning a six-man sprint at Chambéry, became world champion once again.

Despite the ringing triumph of 1989, there are still two charges made against LeMond. The first is Fignon's: that he is no longer an attacking rider. He allows his opponents to make the running and then strikes when they overreach themselves. LeMond's reply is that he will and does attack whenever he needs to, but that races are won with the head as much as the legs. And when finally provoked he invites Fignon to compare their two records in the Tour. The other charge, from Eddy Merckx, has more substance (though LeMond suggests that it might just be influenced by their rivalry as cycle-makers). It is that nowadays LeMond's season is hinged on two events, the Tour de France and the World Championship, and that he doesn't do justice to the classics and the other stage races.

In his day, of course, the voracious Merckx would try to win practically everything. LeMond doesn't pretend that the Tour and the World are not the most important events to him, as they are to his sponsors (though he would dearly like to win that hard man's classic, the Paris-Roubaix). And generally the cyclists who have any choice in the matter are becoming, like other athletes, more selective in their efforts. Is that altogether a bad thing? The trend has certainly encouraged the others, and made for more open, exciting races in which one favourite has been replaced by a dozen possible winners. Admirable as Merckx was, he and his Red Guard did smother the competition.

In any case Fignon and Merckx – and Hinault with his constant complaint that the peloton has been without a strong leader since his own day – cannot press their criticism too far. It is an article of their faith that there is no such thing as an unworthy Tour de France winner.

CHAPTER 6

Into the Futuroscope

The points of departure for the Tour seem to become increasingly remote from everyday French life. Not simply foreign, like Luxemburg in 1989, or West Berlin two years before. Or even obscure, though Pontchâteau (1988), an inland village in southern Brittany, was quiet enough to make Clochemerle look like Sin City, and so short of facilities that all the serious preparatory business had to be conducted down the road at Nantes. The thing is, they're becoming more abstract.

If you imagined a suitable starting place, it might be somewhere like Poitiers. A pre-Roman settlement standing on a ridge where two rivers join and with a university at which Rabelais and Descartes studied. A market town with cafés, plane trees and *pétanque* in the squares, murky areas where the drains smell, and its own local industries. A place where families cycle to school and work and to the shops, and occasionally produce a Tour de France rider.

And Poitiers was the road sign we all followed in the last week of June 1990, though only for convenience. The Tour wasn't due to assemble at Poitiers itself, but 7km to the north at the Futuroscope, a scientific theme park dropped, apparently by space rocket, in the rolling Vienne countryside of mid-west France.

As theme parks go, the Futuroscope is higher minded than most. It was launched by the Département de la Vienne in 1984 'to make visitors more sensitive to the great social changes due to the rapid evolution in techniques of communication'. It was meant to alter French perceptions of Vienne as an agricultural area more jealous of its past than its future, and of Poitiers as a city where you simply stopped to admire the romanesque buildings on your way to somewhere else; to attract industry (out of bounds to the public is a teaching, research and development sector with its own téléport linked by satellite with the rest of the world and twinned with another at Osaka in Japan); and to bring the old province of Poitou into the New France.

To that worthy end something like an artist's impression of a lunar space station has been laid out on former fields of grain and sunflowers. One building has been put together in sloping stacks of glass to represent raw crystal. Hemispheres abound, free-standing or balanced on glass ramps. You can enter a giant ice-cream sundae or a walnut whirl. Inside, for the most part, you find cinema presentations with split-screens, 360-degree screens, the largest flat screen in Europe, three-dimensional effects ... Live a galactic adventure with Christophe Colomb and his faithful Toucan! Travel through time and space in a Lego-land of working models! And so on. With its outdoor amusement park and its gyroscopic lift revolving on a pillar, the Futuroscope attracted 800,000 visitors in 1989.

But what has that got to do with the Tour? Money and publicity are the short answer. The race first dropped in four years ago when this was still a building site provisionally called the Parc du Futur. In 1987 Stephen Roche won a time trial here on his way to winning the Tour. Two years later there was a third visit, and now, with the place a going concern, the Futuroscope were prepared to lay out £500,000 to host the time trial prologue on the Saturday, two stages beginning and ending in the park next day, and almost a week of build-up and speculation.

What the Tour would get in return, apart from the money, was not immediately clear. The only apparent connection between an eighty-seven-year-old race for men on pedal-cycles and the electronic gadgetry of the Futuroscope was that the Tour – as it would now be the first to acknowledge – was also in the communications business. But if this appears far-fetched, the Tour looked like moving still farther towards self-parody. According to a story slipped into L'Equipe, who usually know a thing or two before the rest of us, the 1992 Tour was expected to open at the new Eurodisneyland (sic) in Marne-la-Vallée, a new town development to the east of Paris. Greg LeMond, meet your fellow American, Mickey Mouse. But whether through a hitch or second thoughts, the Tour has now announced its 1992 start as San Sebastian, Spain.

The drawback with the Futuroscope is that, except for the

residents and staff at the hotels and certain maintenance workers, the place is uninhabited. Even for the Tour it is little more than an accommodation address to be used during visiting hours. Only Castorama are staying on site at the three-star Hotel d'Angleterre; most of the other teams have been put up in Poitiers.

Setting off from a ghost town, however scintillating, is a break with tradition (to be temporarily repaired at Lyons, France's third city, already named as the 1991 race start), but does it really matter? Assuming that the fans find their way to the course in respectable numbers over the weekend (as they will), what has the Tour lost? A decade ago, the Tour's chief distinction was that it took the race to the nation's front doors, and provided the world's most generous allowance of free sporting entertainment. And at that time it lived from hand to mouth. Now it increasingly took the race into people's front rooms by means of television, and it had achieved an annual income of £10 million. A million of that was profit.

The crowds at the roadside hadn't noticeably diminished (though they fluctuated both with the weather and the likely success or failure of French riders). But the television audience had increased out of all proportion. In the words of Jean-Claude Hérault, the commercial director of the Société du Tour de France, 'The Tour has become a worldwide media event.' To exploit that trend, the surface glamour of the Futuroscope, with floodlights and fireworks reflecting from the crystalline Kinémax and the fountains in the small lake before it, provided a suitably spectacular television setting. And not simply to present the teams on the eve of the Tour. The last of a highly popular series of variety programmes, the Paris-based *Champs-Elysées* on Antenne-2, was also to be presented by Michel Drucker from the Futuroscope. This combination of the Tour and the *Champs* was, according to a reporter in the *Nouvelle République du Centre-Ouest*, a p.r. triumph for the local authorities: 'It is hard to imagine a prettier *coup de pub*.' That man will go far in provincial journalism.

The changing nature of the Tour was also reflected in the size and composition of the party who gathered at the Futuroscope for the 3,400km race. There were 198 riders in twenty-two nine-man teams. This was below both the record 210 in 1986 and the current limit of 200 imposed by the UCI, but rather than the possible 20 x 10, the Tour preferred to have two more teams and two fewer riders. As it was the Spanish team, B-H, and more surprisingly Café de Colombia with Luis Herrera, sixth in the 1988 Tour and twice winner of the mountain prize, had failed to qualify. Accompanying these teams was a regiment of 264 managers, mechanics, soigneurs, soigneuses, drivers and publicists, and twenty officials from the UCI and the French Cycling Federation. Between them they had 140 vehicles.

The organisation had grown to forty-six regular and 217 temporary staff running 312 vehicles from saloons to the huge, articulated mobile press centre. It was noticeable, too, that many of the younger ones nowadays spoke English, which may be explained by the even more significant increase in the numbers and nationalities of the third group: the press.

Not so long ago you knew practically all the reporters by sight, and at the end of the stage they could be fitted into a schoolroom. This year a record 659 journalists and photographers from twenty-three countries, 305 newspapers, twenty-nine television channels and forty-three radio stations had applied for accreditation. And since it takes eight people to ask a simple question on television and record the answer, even they were outnumbered by 745 technicians and drivers. These again were behind the wheels of the largest number of cars and trucks: 574 in all.

There was the regular escort of forty-two members of the Motorcycle Squadron of the 1st Infantry Regiment of the Garde Républicaine, whose normal duties are to protect the President and visiting heads of state. And finally the 1,362 workers and 489 painted wagons, newspaper vans and go-karts with plastic apple pies on top which comprised the publicity caravan.

This seemed to be the one area of shrinkage. Even regulars were missing. No giant dead flies struck down by Catch insecticide this year. Sadder still, no Michelin men (Bibendum is the name), standing on the seat of a motorbike or waving from the top of a vintage fire engine – fat men dressed in white spare tyres inside which there is always a thin man longing to get out for a breather or a smoke.

All the same, where in 1976 I reckoned that the Tour had 2,000 camp followers, now it had over 3,500, borne along by a fleet of 1,550 motors. And the near doubling in the size of the operation had been matched by as great a change in its style and content. But, as with the increase in riders from the New Nations, this had been a gradual process. As we sat in the press room at the Futuroscope, housed not in a globe or a flying wedge but in the disappointingly straight-sided Palais des Congrès, I had to turn back to *The Great Bike Race* to get precise bearings.

By 1976 the absolute ban on women travelling in the convoy had been dropped, but still there were only two in the press corps: a French colour writer, sitting in for a few days, and a reporter from a progressive Spanish daily who was chaperoned by her journalist husband. Now there were a dozen or more women correspondents, including Mme Fignon, who was writing a daily column, simply called Nathalie, for *Le Parisien*.

In 1976 television was the junior partner in the media, recording the Tour for consumption at home and that handful of countries in western Europe directly involved in it. Newspapermen had conceived the Tour, and the analysis of the racing and weaving of the romance which surrounded it were still very largely in the hands of writers. But if this was now a media event, the particular medium which led the way was television. Nowadays people from New Zealand to Japan and Mexico were gathering their first impressions of the Tour not through what they read but what they saw in their homes. And although the edited highlights on the screen might be as 'real' as the partly-observed, partly-imagined stories on the page, it was not the same Tour they were depicting. It was an exciting, all-action struggle which lost some of that sense of place and that element of long, often languid travel which were also essential aspects of the race, and which writers could convey in their indulgent essays. The need to fill the page on an uneventful day has encouraged an awful lot of windy prose, but on the credit side, also some racking of brains for telling detail and digging around for stories.

If the two rival Colombian radio stations provided the noisiest, fastest-talking broadcasters, in sheer numbers the most conspicuous crew was from ABC television who were deploying a staff of seventy and feeding their reports into *Good Morning, America*, the station's daytime flagship programme. As you'd expect from a US company, they had also helped to increase the proportion of women involved in the race – as well, of course, as the number of English speakers.

This was another shift in emphasis. In 1976 there were only three British journalists on the Tour: the late David Saunders of the *Daily Telegraph*, who was also covering radio and television; Phil Liggett of *The Guardian*; and myself, from *The Observer*. Having the only air-conditioned car in the convoy, a large Japanese saloon, we travelled along in splendid isolation with the windows wound up. The only people we could talk to in our own language were the Dutch and the odd Dane and Belgian. Now there were ten reporters from British papers or news agencies, the Tour having recently become the mid-summer darling of the heavy press, though it was still largely ignored by the tabloids. Three Irish papers and RTE radio had sent their correspondents. To these were added three American reporters, an Australian, a French-Canadian, a Mexican – plus half-a-dozen English-speaking press photographers.

The cantankerous Louis Lapeyre, still press officer in 1976, had been so convinced that journalists from Britain were unable to drive on the right, follow simple instructions or fit in with the conventions of the Tour – in short were unsuited to be there at all – that at first he would only deal with them through an interpreter, the veteran English Tourist, J. B. Wadley. Even then he would have to be convinced they spoke French before he issued them with certain standard press kit items like the race regulations and the prize list. Today the young head of the press office, Philippe Sudres, spoke fluent, colloquial English, and *les Britanniques*, as they tend to be called without discrimination, had no need to apologise for their considerable presence.

Another smaller but also indicative change was in the atmosphere of the press room. I had written of cycling reporters who belonged 'to the denim not the creaseless cotton school of roving correspondent ... one-time athletes whose jeans and shorts and tee-shirts ripple with fat but who still engage their typewriters in prolonged bouts of formidable energy.' The uniform was still that of people who lived out of suitcases and had better things to do with their evenings than search for a launderette. But whatever happened to typewriters? Though still occasionally seen, they had become objects of curiosity, made obsolete by the laptop word processors on which most reporters now picked out their stories with a delicacy they hadn't known they possessed.

The great thing about the word processor is that when it is coupled to a phone, and certain buttons are pressed, the story is instantly reproduced in the computer system of a newspaper in London, New York or Amsterdam. Or usually it is. What I described as the most evocative sound of the 1976 Tour was a burst of fury from an Italian dictating at high speed to Turin and finding his phone had gone dead. That of 1990 would be the anguished cry of one whose screen has been wiped clean without his story reaching its destination. It had simply disappeared into some purgatory of the ether from which no prayers could retrieve it.

Unchanged in fourteen years was the ritual of signing on and harvesting the freebies: the Futuroscope wristwatch, sponsors' tee-shirts, satchels, haversack, pens on string, pads and badges. And it was only when these had been safely gathered in on the Thursday afternoon that we could turn our mind to the prospects for the race.

By now the riders had begun to arrive at their hotels by car and team bus – or in the case of LeMond and the Z team, by bicycle. For reasons which were to emerge on the Saturday morning, they had got together at the home of Roger Legeay, their *directeur-sportif*, in Le Mans, and had used the remaining 160km for a final training ride. It was a characteristic piece of moral one-upmanship.

Friday was to bring medical checks and bike inspections at the Futuroscope, and a final round of press conferences and interviews in which the favourites would predict their own and their rivals' chances of winning the race. At least, if they could find anything new to say.

In fact when the French journalists met Fignon over breakfast at his hotel on Friday morning, they too seemed tongue-tied. 'No questions?' said his manager, Cyrille Guimard.

Finally, to break the ice, someone asked Fignon how things were going. It was Guimard who replied: 'Well, or so it seems. We'll see tomorrow whether they are going very well.' Asked if he would like to comment, Fignon, who doesn't waste words, said: 'You have answered very well.' But things did warm up a little after that. Fignon regretted the loss of ten days' hard racing after his injury in the Giro, but refused to play the popular French game of expressing his present condition as a percentage of his best form. He considered that the race would be between three men: Delgado, who was at the head of his list as a specialist in the great tours, a climber and an improving rider against the clock. Then LeMond and himself. And a step behind was Bugno. No mention of Roche.

He also said his defeat by LeMond the previous year no longer troubled him. He knew he shouldn't have lost, but there was nothing to be gained from self-pity. Even so he couldn't mention LeMond without criticising the cautiousness of his approach: 'He marks his most dangerous opponent without exposing himself.' His own style wasn't LeMond's; he preferred to attack and adapt to the consequences.

Earlier Delgado had produced a more generous list of contenders. His favourites were the same as Fignon's, except that he showed more confidence in LeMond – 'The American will be there, and well and truly there' – and since the Giro he also regarded Bugno as a serious candidate for the final victory. But for good measure he added Roche, the Colombian, Fabio Parra, and even Jean-François Bernard. That was based on what Delgado had seen of him in the Vuelta, though he admitted that the irregularity of Bernard's performances made him a hard man to judge.

The critics, finding more negative than positive evidence in the past four months, preferred to cast their nets wider. Delgado was acceptable as the *grand favori* since his past spoke for itself and nothing was known against him this season. He might have achieved little, but at least he had a clean medical record, and was known to prepare seriously and secretly for the Tour.

They would have liked to feel more enthusiastic about Fignon, but only three weeks ago he couldn't even climb the stairs. And LeMond, well everyone knew about LeMond – his

Left: Pedro Delgado, winner in 1988, was to remain the most fancied challenger to LeMond until the Pyrenees, where it became clear that even the loyal support of Miguel Indurain couldn't get him through his difficulties.
Right: Like Oscar Wilde at the New York Custom House, LeMond arrived at the Futuroscope with nothing to declare but his genius. The past few months had been disastrous. Yet it took only second place in the prologue to restore him to favourite. ,

mis-spent winter, his sickly spring and early summer, and his well-known ability to overcome far worse problems than these.

Yet equally there were doubts about the riders who had already proved their form in major tours this season. Nobody seriously believed that after winning the Vuelta and coming third in the Giro, Marco Giovannetti still had a Tour de France left in him. It was accepted that he was here because without him SEUR would not have qualified for the race; an early retirement would leave Alvaro Pino, a respectable eighth in the Tour of 1988, to lead the team. And Bugno, the Giro winner, while saying he wouldn't have come to the start unless he thought he had a role to play, wasn't thinking of victory. He hoped only to finish highly placed.

With such fragile guidelines to cling to, the critics could

only mutter the excuse that this was an exceptionally open Tour and rope in a few more conceivable winners. The Frenchman, Charly Mottet, for instance, runner-up in the Giro but surely without the staying power or the time-trialing skill to succeed here. The Dutchman Eric Breukink, a climber and time-trialist of considerable style, but also inclined to have one disastrously bad day during the three weeks. Miguel Indurain, though only if Delgado conceded the team lead to him . . . Raul Alcala, Steven Rooks, Andy Hampsten, Robert Millar, Sean Kelly. The lists went on and on. But as if to prove that, even for tipsters, there's no safety in numbers, none of them went so far as to mention the three men of more than middling ability who, between them, were to win all the yellow jerseys except for the first and the last.

When the others had said their piece, LeMond held his press conference, mid-way through Friday afternoon, in the icecream sundae building. It was, in what might well have been dispiriting circumstances, a remarkable performance: relaxed, self-assured, good-humoured and astute. By chance he had recently told *Le Parisien*, 'I am not an intellectual. I would never have been brilliant enough to make a doctor, for example. If I hadn't been a professional cyclist I think I would have been most suited to business.' But now he was standing alone on the platform in a steeply-raked and well-attended lecture hall, a screen behind him, a blue baize-covered table in front of him, and in his white shirt looking every inch the popular, gifted young surgeon taking a seminar in an American carbolic opera.

His message was the one he had been repeating ever since he returned to France: 'I feel great, really strong – better than last year at this time. I'm confident, very confident. Last year was harder because I didn't know where I was. But this year I know there's nothing wrong with me. Just a lack of training and fitness. I didn't like being where I was, the World Championship and Tour de France winner – and struggling. I started at zero again at the Tour de Trump. But' – he repeated – 'I knew there was nothing wrong.'

All the same he was grateful for Legeay's and Z's forebearance. 'Any other team, considering what they pay me, would have panicked. He knows my possibilities. For myself, I don't have to be told to do that, that and that, which is what happened in other teams before. Athletes aren't robots.'

Speaking mainly in French, in which he has become far more fluent over the years, he assessed the opposition. He praised the regularity of Delgado: 'He is stronger than me in the cols, but I believe I am better in the time trials.' He found Bugno difficult to assess, since he was out to win the Giro while others were simply using it as preparation: 'But he will be dangerous in the future.' Alcala was riding better than ever before.

It was only when someone mentioned Fignon's criticism of him that morning that LeMond went on the attack. 'I prefer to race with my legs not my words. Besides, Fignon is hard to judge this year. When he is on form he is strong all round, but that's all there is to say. I have ridden the Tours four times: two wins, a second and a third place. He should review his own record before criticising me. The race isn't won only with the legs but with the head. I am not bluffing, and I don't want a war with Fignon. Criticism gets to me, especially when it is justified. But since I won last year I have been criticised for finishing ahead of Fignon. In 1985 I finished behind Bernard Hinault; he bluffed us, and I could have won the Tour. But I accepted it, unhappy as I was. I am American; that's my character. I have come here to win.'

It was not that he assumed he would: 'I will wait for the Alps to know where I stand . . . but I think I have as good a chance as anyone.' And while he added, in answer to another question, that 'no sport taxes you as physically and mentally as the Tour de France,' LeMond looked as though he had just received a rebate. An initially sceptical audience was disarmed, and next morning the local paper asked in its headline whether Z now stood for Zorro.

L'Equipe also gave up their front page to an exclusive photograph of 'LeMond's secret weapon'. This was a revolutionary triathlete handlebar which he had decided to use in the prologue and in other suitable time trials during the race. He had come across it in Santa Rosa, California, during the winter, and had since experimented with it there and at home in Courtrai. He had put it through a final test on the Bugatti motor racing circuit at Le Mans on Wednesday, and the next day Legeay had sought approval for it from Nicolas Ledent, president of the jury on the Tour. Ledent found in its favour since whatever their form – and the new one, the LeMond Extreme, was certainly a stopper – the use of tri-bars had already been authorised.

These bars had been developed in the triathlon, a combination of cycling, swimming and running first practised on the US west coast – the original home, too, of the mountain bike and the hang-glider. They consisted of a delta-shaped tube attached to the centre of the normal handlebar and tilting forward and upward at an angle of 40-45 degrees. Projecting backward were pads on which the rider rested his arms just below the elbow. And in use together these reduced his wind resistance. The act of holding the bar on either side drew the rider's body forward and downward, tucking his arms into his sides, in the compact posture of a downhill skier. In fact it was the aerodynamics of skiing which first encouraged American bike and accessory builders in their tri-bar experiments.

LeMond, who is fascinated by technical innovations, introduced the tri-bar into the 1989 Tour in sensational fashion, employing it for a winning ride in the 73km time trial from Dinard to Rennes which brought him the yellow jersey (in fact the American 7-Eleven team used it too, though that went largely unremarked). Hackles and eyebrows rose and there were cries of foul, but use of the attachment had been sanctioned that very morning, and within months it had become, like the disc rear wheel, *de rigueur* for all serious trialists.

Wind tunnel tests showed, to LeMond's satisfaction, that it was probably worth 15sec to him in the final 24.5km time trial into Paris and, since that was almost double the margin by which he had beaten Fignon, his faith in the tri-bar was confirmed. There was another theory which held that Fignon's blond ponytail bobbing in the air, instead of being tucked into an aerodynamic helmet, had cost him just as dearly. But that wasn't capable of being put to any scientific tests.

LeMond's 1990 tri-bar was far more outlandish, and he could hardly have improved on the Futuroscope as the setting for its European launch. This was not an attachment but a bar in itself, created by the American designer, Scott. It swung out to the sides, where the brake-levers were attached, then swept

The prologue at the Futuroscope: LeMond, a dedicated gadget fancier, tries out his new Scott tri-bar, the LeMond Extreme, for the first time in competition. Only the French prologue specialist, Thierry Marie, will beat him.

inward and upward to form a single arm tilted only a little forward from the perpendicular. In short it was like a unicorn's horn. By gripping the arm in both hands, with fingers overlapping at the front, the rider was forced into an even more pronounced head-down crouch. And that, LeMond was convinced, not only allowed him to pull harder on the bar while he pedalled, but gave him better penetration through the air. 'As for comfort, I feel at least as good,' LeMond said.

Fignon's manager, Cyrille Guimard, would not have agreed since he argued that the use of tri-bars compressed the rider's thoracic cage. But at the same time he was trying, with less success, to get official clearance for an innovation which he believed would benefit his man. This was a saddle with a hard, vertical cushion at the back serving as a dorsal support. A similar saddle had been used by Jean-François Bernard in the Vuelta. But in this case M. Ledent was not to be persuaded by a precedent. The regulations said that the saddle should be flat, and even if, as Guimard pointed out, there was no such thing as a truly flat saddle, he was not prepared to authorise the use of a saddle as un-flat as that one. Things simply weren't running Fignon's way.

Prologue, Futuroscope, 6.3km (individual time trial)
Saturday, 30 June was overcast and blustery, the wind blowing up dust from the bare earth where the new grass hadn't yet spread out between the buildings, and snapping one of the ropes which kept the DEPART banner unfurled. It wasn't a pleasant day for hanging about, but the race officials had no choice. Even starting at one-minute intervals it would take over three and a quarter hours for all 198 riders to plunge in turn down the ramp from the starting platform and out onto the course.

Nobody would forget the dreadful lesson of Delgado. The previous year in Luxemburg he had turned up in good time for the prologue, wearing his yellow jersey as the 1988 Tour winner, and then in a fit of inattention had ridden off down a side street for a final warm-up. By the time he returned he had missed his start by 2min 40sec, and having begun the day in yellow ended it carrying the *lanterne rouge*. Even *L'Equipe* this morning headlined their list of start times: 'Pedro, attention: 16h 30!'

Not to be similarly caught out, riders milled around the platform like messengers from space, all streamlined helmets and kaleidoscopic disc wheels, waiting for their names to be called out. Then they took their place on the stool at the back of the platform while the man ahead was given his countdown. Not a moment was lost. The scene had its attractions. In particular watching the Colombian broadcasters trap each of their countrymen with a microphone as he came to the stool. Try that on with Fignon – or even Robert Millar. But it was ten minutes entertainment at best, and most spectators preferred to be out on the course which, with its two hills and its mixture of tailwinds, crosswinds and headwinds, was more difficult and 'technical' than the old style of drag-strip prologue.

The first serious figure on the leader board, and first to break eight minutes, was the young Francis Moreau, winner of the Paris-Nice prologue. His 7min 59sec was three seconds too fast for the fancied Russian record-holder, Vatchieslaw Ekimov. Moreau was succeeded by Alcala with 7min 53sec. And then came the fair-haired Thierry Marie – 'the Viking with eyes of porcelain', as the Castorama advertisement put it – covering the distance at better than 48kph in 7min 49sec. Nobody could beat that, and Marie, as in 1986, took the first yellow jersey. But the man who came closest, a split-second faster than Alcala, was LeMond. His 15sec on Fignon and 20sec on Delgado were nothing. But although, as he said at his press conference, 6km was not his sort of distance, he had promised to 'tackle it all out'. And this he had done for the first time since he won the rainbow jersey the previous summer.

Prologue result: 1. Marie (Castorama): 7'49"; 2. LeMond (Z) at 4"; 3. Alcala (PDM) at 4"; 4. Moreau (Histor) at 10"; 5. Vanderaerden (Buckler) at 12"; 6. Ekimov (Panasonic) at 13" ... 10. Roche (Histor) at 18"; 15. Fignon (Castorama) at 19"; 22. Breukink (PDM) at 23"; 26. Delgado (Banesto) at 24".

CHAPTER 7

English spoken here

Against the odds, not to say propinquity, it's American English that is heard most often in the peloton, shading off to the Canadian accent of Steve Bauer, a man who frequently features in the yellow jersey early in the Tour, and in the south to the Spanish of the Mexican, Raul Alcala, winner of his country's first stage in the 1990 Vittel-Epinal time trial.

The Aussies, coming from even further away but born travellers, also had their regular star that year, Phil Anderson, leader of TVM, plus two senior team-riders, Alan Peiper of Panasonic and Stephen Hodge who had joined the Spanish team, ONCE. The Brits were down to two, though both of them riders of considerable quality: Robert Millar from Glasgow, and Sean Yates who was born in Ewell, Surrey. There was a third who certainly deserved to be there: Malcolm Elliott of Sheffield, a prolifically successful sprinter and points winner in the 1989 Tour of Spain. Unfortunately his Spanish team, Teka, failed to qualify on their overall record. Last the Irish: two of the great names of the past decade, Sean Kelly and Stephen Roche, and Kelly's lieutenant and a stage winner in his own right, Martin Earley. All had done their countries proud, though the Irish were probably the only ones to be honoured as highly at home as they were on the continent.

Anderson, born in London in 1959 but brought up in the Melbourne suburbs, had been talked of for several years as a possible Tour winner after making an explosive start to his career. He was nineteen when he won the Commonwealth title at Edmonton, twenty when he came to France to ride for ACBB, the same Peugeot-sponsored amateur academy that Jonathan Boyer had enrolled in, and twenty-one when he turned professional with Peugeot. Only one year older, having won the Tour de l'Aude and scored a number of smaller victories by cheerfully and cussedly doing his own thing – the French put this down to the fact that he didn't really understand their language or their conventions – Anderson rode the 1981 Tour. And there he took the yellow jersey by following Hinault's wheel in the Pyrenees. This was a form of *lèse-majesté* which few Frenchmen would have risked, and Hinault took his revenge next day. But Anderson had made his mark, finishing tenth as the Best Young Rider. And in the following year he not only won the yellow jersey again but held it for nine days.

Some great riders, like Gimondi, Merckx and Hinault, win the Tour at the first attempt, and most eventual winners declare their intentions early on. Few work their way gradually to the top; the caste system doesn't allow it. Anderson, then, had made the kind of start that attracts attention among the team managers, but although in the next few years he twice finished fifth and once ninth, he didn't develop the strength as a climber or the consistency in time trials to go further. The opportunities slipped away, so did his place among the top favourites, but not his popularity. To the French he remains Skippy, after the cartoon kangaroo in a television series: a cheerful, competitive Aussie with a smile like a croissant, a combative and often reckless opportunist with a string of victories in the Amstel Gold and Frankfurt Grand Prix and shorter stage races like the Tours of Switzerland and Romandie and the Dauphiné-Libéré.

Unlike Anderson, who has a word for everyone, Millar, the first Briton to win the mountain prize in the Tour, is not the most sociable of riders. 'The banality of the questions people ask me I find insupportable,' he told a *L'Equipe* journalist (curious how often riders become more eloquent in French than in their own language). Like Anderson and Fignon he has long hair pulled back into an elastic band, which seems to be the slightly dated badge of the nonconformist in the peloton nowadays, and in his case, as in Fignon's, it's matched by an independent and often abrasive manner. Precociously talented he was already British champion when he left Glasgow at the age of twenty to join the ACBB club, and has only infrequently been back. 'I go there two or three days a year, to see my father. I have no need, like Greg, to get back to my country as soon as possible. It is three years since I have seen my brother, and I don't even know where my sister lives.' He is married to Sylvie, lives near her family in Troyes and admits to having just a few close friends. But for all that, the small, birdlike Millar is well liked in the peloton, for he is a rider's rider: loyal, hard-working, correct. He too was considered a potential Tour winner; in 1984, when he was King of the Mountains he also finished fourth overall. The following year, too, he would have won the Tour of Spain if on the next-to-last stage the Spanish teams hadn't formed an alliance against him and in favour of Delgado. He had many stage wins in high, inhospitable places, but it was not until 1990 that he won his first important stage-race, the Dauphiné Libéré. And ironically he won it in that sector of the sport that had generally been his fatal weakness, the time trial.

It has been the strength of the far more gregarious Yates, however. For all the national devotion to time trialing, British riders have rarely done particularly well in these events on the continent. This is because the courses involve more changes of

Left: Phil Anderson, the first Australian to wear the yellow jersey in the Tour and one of three riders – Fignon and Millar are the others – to wear his hair in a pig-tail. At thirty-one still a thrillingly reckless rider.
Right: Winner of the 1990 Dauphiné, second in the Tour of Switzerland, Pensec's devoted minder in the Alps – Robert Millar of Glasgow is riding as effectively now as he did in 1984 when he was King of the Mountains in the Tour.   97

Sean Yates, the sole Englishman left in the race, and at his best in those English specialities, the pursuit and the time trial. Became the fifth British stage-winner when he took the Liévin-Wasquehal time trial in 1988.

pace and direction, a finer choice of gear and line than is usual at home; they test skill as much as speed. Yates, who had won the twenty-five-mile championship and set a ten-mile record as an amateur, and on the track had twice won the national pro pursuit title, was the exception. A powerful rider who was used to manual labour in the family's landscape gardening firm, he modestly accepted his role as *domestique* and willing workhorse for seven years before suddenly breaking out of his shell in 1988. Well prepared for the start of the season he won stages in the Paris-Nice (where he also wore the leader's jersey), the Tour of Spain and Midi-Libre. So, when he set off on the first time trial of the Tour, a 52km zig-zag from Liévin to Wasquehal, he felt reasonably confident of improving on fifteenth place, his previous best. In fact, since he was one of the earlier starters from the bottom half of the field, his time of 1hr 3min 22sec stood at the head of the leader board for two hours before the favourites like Eric Breukink, Charly Mottet and the specialist Jelle Nijdam even started. All that time Yates endured the water-drip torture of hearing a new result announced each alternate minute. But when everyone else had been counted in, he was still there at the top. He had added his name below Brian Robinson, Michael Wright, Barry Hoban and Millar as only the fifth British rider to win a stage in the Tour.

Altogether the British presence in the Tour has been pretty consistent since the 'fifties and, when you add Tom Simpson's name to that list, of real significance to the racing. All the same in the last decade the Brits have been regularly outclassed and often outnumbered by the Irish who, with far smaller resources of money and manpower in their sport at home, have managed to produce two riders of outstanding achievement: Sean Kelly, who topped the world ranking for wins and places from March 1984 to the end of 1989, and Stephen Roche who in 1987 equalled Merckx in his clean sweep of the Tours of Italy and France and the world title.

Just as the British had Robinson as a lone pioneer, so in the late 'fifties and 'sixties, the Irish had Shay Elliott, a hero not unsung exactly, but certainly underplayed. He won the Het Volk classic, and a stage, plus the yellow jersey, in the Tour de France; he came third in the 1962 Tour of Spain, and second later that year in the world championship. In fact he achieved more in continental road racing than any English-speaking rider before him. But his career ended in disillusion and he died by his own hand a few years later, his example giving little direct encouragement to other Irish riders. So Kelly and, three years later, Roche, seemed to come from nowhere – or as far as the French were concerned, from somewhere better known for its rain and rugby than for its cycle racing. And when, in spite of this, they were instantly successful, it created the same kind of shock as the Americans were to do in a few years' time.

Yet in many ways Kelly, coming from Catholic farming stock, had more in common with the traditional figures of the Tour – the Poulidors and Thévenets, the hungry riders with a peasant's fortitude and a peasant's cunning – than with the new wave from across the Atlantic. He is now a man of substance in his birthplace, Carrick-on-Suir, a small, rural, stone-built town of 6,000 people and nearly twenty per cent unemployment on the Tipperary county boundary (to be strict his old home is just over the other side in Co. Waterford). Near the town centre a widened area of Greystone Street between Bennett's Cash & Carry and Kehoe's Bar has been renamed Sean Kelly Square (which is more than the council have done for Anne Boleyn, their only other famous, if dubious, connection). As Kelly said several years ago: 'If I stopped cycling tomorrow, I'd be secure for the rest of my life.' But Carrick and the countryside is where he feels he belongs, and it's more than likely when he retires, in the next two or three years, that he will follow his money back to the land – 'depending', he added with habitual caution, 'on the state of Irish agriculture at the time'.

You might guess at Kelly's background even if you first met him on the Champs Elysées, but you couldn't easily imagine the esteem in which Carrick holds him. In 1985 the second stage of the first Nissan International Classic, now the annual pro tour of the Republic, finished by no great coincidence at Carrick. That year Irish Telecom offered stage-winners a free phone call home from the rostrum, and Kelly was the first to exercise that privilege (though true to his laconic nature he spoke to his mother for exactly fifteen seconds). Once the news reached Carrick, however, that Kelly had won at Wexford and would be riding home next day in the leader's yellow jersey, Dan Grant, his more vociferous father-in-law and president of the Carrick Wheelers, swung into action. Within the hour he was driving round the streets with the club loudspeaker on the top of the car, broadcasting the good news.

Schools were closed, the population of the town was at least quadrupled, Leahy's, Leaders Nationwide in School/Wedding/Office Stationery, offered a commemorative discount on all supplies, and Kelly came back amid Irish tricolor bunting and banners which read SEAN YOU LOOK GOOD IN YELLOW and HOME IS THE HERO. 'Carrick is very proud of you, Sean,' said the UDC chairman. 'You have given the town fame and prestige in Europe and beyond.' The hoopla went on to midnight and beyond – the bars had an extension – and there was Irish dancing on a platform in the main street where a male-voice trio led the audience in:

All the world is mad about Kelly,
He's Ireland's number one.
All the word is mad about Kelly,
He's Ireland's famous son.

The house where Kelly was raised is everyone's picture of a farm on the Celtic fringes: tin-roofed cottage, ducks and chickens filing through the yard, cattle noises coming through the open top doors. It is on a typical forty-five-acre smallholding, a third of it wetland, and when he took me to see it, with a photographer, in the winter of 1985-86, his parents, John and Nelly Kelly, were still working it. Kelly and his wife, Linda – a lively, capable young woman – weren't staying there. Nor were they at the house he had bought in the town, and which they were renting out. They were in the modern home of a cousin on the outskirts. But it is one of the likeable things about Kelly that he didn't hesitate to show us the much humbler farm from which he had come, or to introduce his parents, whose stubborn refusal to modernise he regarded with tolerant affection.

Although Roche stole some of his thunder in 1987, Sean Kelly has proved by far the most durable of the Irish exiles. Sprinters generally burn out quickly, but Kelly's record four green jerseys cover eight seasons.

101

The farm wouldn't support an extra adult, so when Kelly left school at fourteen he served his time as a bricklayer and at the weekends rode with the Wheelers. There he showed a precocious talent for reaching the finish with the leaders and leaving them for dead in the sprint. By the age of eighteen he was an amateur international and a member of the Irish international squad.

He might have remained an amateur but for a political indiscretion a year later. During the summer of 1975 he accepted an invitation to ride in an international road-race in South Africa. Competing like other guest riders under a false name, he might have got away with it. But unfortunately for him his success in the race caught the eye of a freelance journalist who happened to be in the area on the trail of the honeymooning Richard Burton and Elizabeth Taylor. Photographs were sent back to a London newspaper, the riders were identified, and Kelly was banned from the sport for three months.

On his reinstatement he won an important Irish race, the Tour of the North, which should have clinched his place for the Montreal Games. Instead he was told that the ban would still rule him out of the Olympics. Apart from the sense of grievance he felt, he was at a loss to find somewhere to race. And it was at this point that he remembered about Metz. In Sheffield the previous summer he had won his first stage in the Milk Race, and among the crowd were a family of visitors connected with the Metz cycle club. This was one of many in France, apart from ACBB, which like to recruit, for a season or two, promising young 'British' riders, and they offered Kelly a place whenever he liked to take it up. He thought little of it at the time, expecting to be in Montreal, but now it offered an escape.

Kelly knew no French, indeed was not exactly eloquent in English. He is a reserved man with a strong jaw and a shyly taciturn manner; he talks freely once he gets going, but he is celebrated for having nodded in reply to a question on radio. But this was of no account in Metz; his strength as a cyclist spoke for him. In what remained of the season Kelly won twenty events, including the amateur Tour of Lombardy, at which point team managers began to wave contracts at the other end of the telephone.

He turned them all down, mainly out of his attachment for cycle racing. If he failed as a professional he would have to wait two years before he could get back his amateur licence. He didn't want a second spell out of competition. But one manager persisted: the wealthy, independent Jean de Gribaldy, an ex-rider who had made his fortune in the furniture business and then returned to the sport as a passionate entrepreneur. He was now running the Belgian-based Flandria team. After Kelly returned home for the winter, de Gribaldy flew into Dublin airport in his private plane, asked a taxi driver to take him to Carrick, ninety-five miles away, and arrived at the farm unannounced bringing with him an interpreter to spell out his terms. Kelly didn't volunteer what they were, but certainly they were better than a brickie's wages. Even so he didn't accept them on the spot; with no-one to turn to for advice, he thought it over for a week before he agreed to turn professional with Flandria in the new year.

Metz had given him a taste of continental racing, and two New Zealanders with the clubs had helped him through the language problem. At Flandria the riders were either Belgian or French, and though some spoke a few words of English it was up to Kelly to learn to communicate (French and Flemish come easily to him now, though when I first met him a couple of years later, he was still in a linguistic limbo, even to speaking a kind of pidgin English when he had been a long time from home). But his talent on a bicycle broke the barriers and even in his first year he pulled off four victories, one of which, the Circuit de l'Indre, gave him special satisfaction since he held the great Eddy Merckx in second place and Willy Tierlinck, the Belgian champion, in third.

Even so Kelly, recruited by de Gribaldy as a potential winner not a water-carrier, had to play second fiddle to Freddy Maertens, a nervy, restless Flemish rider who was easily the fastest and most deadly finishing sprinter of his day. It became Kelly's job to act as Maertens' path-finder, taking him up through the bunch, hitting the front, moving to one side and so launching him with a flying start to the line. There's no doubt that this gave Kelly an intensive education in sprinting tactics. And there were times when their roles were reversed. In the

1978 Tour of Holland, when Kelly was better placed overall, Maertens would lead Kelly out in the sprints so that he could pick up any time bonuses which were going. But those occasions were rare, and although at Poitiers that year Kelly had the chance to win his first stage in the Tour de France – Maertens winning three to take the green jersey for the second time – he was impatient for his freedom. In 1979 he left Flandria for Splendor. There was no personal rift with de Gribaldy, who understood Kelly's feelings, and three years later they were reunited in the Sem team. But by that time Kelly was the man to be protected.

In fourteen seasons – and his career is not yet over – he has won the Paris-Nice seven times (he is invariably one of the first out of hibernation), the green jersey in the Tour de France a record four, the Critérium International and Tour de Pays Basque three, the Tour of Switzerland and Tour of Lombardy twice, the Tour of Spain (1988) and every major classic except the Tour of Flanders.

· What he hasn't won is the world championships – it is his kind of hard man's race, but he has usually ridden too many criteriums in August to prepare for it as he should have done – or the Tour de France, although he has finished fourth and fifth and worn the yellow jersey.

Sprinting skill, which is essential for a rider who wants to win the classics, has a limited value in stage-races. It's all very well as an optional extra; a stage-win is good for the ego and small bonuses can be earned by being first across various lines. But it's a means of gaining seconds rather than minutes. The big strides are made by the *rouleurs* who stay with the leaders, *are* the leaders, day after day, by the time trialists and the climbers. To be a specialist sprinter can even be a positive disadvantage.

Kelly on his day had all these attributes. He was a *rouleur*, powerfully built and indefatigable. By the same token he rode well, if need be, very well, against the clock. He was not an effective climber when he began, but improved steadily as he matured; no rider could have won the Tours of Spain and Switzerland or finished as highly placed in the Tour de France without being able at least to hold his own in the mountains. But what made him a star was his sprinting. He never quite achieved the demonic pace of Maertens, but in the mid-'eighties his strength often put him first among such equals as Vanderaerden, Planckaert, Bontempi and Argentin. As a result he was overworked and never had the chance to shape his season around the Tour, allowing himself spells of rest and mountain training. For publicity's sake his team constantly needed him in their lineout to win races and stages; he was their banker. And while the tourists could treat many of the season's preliminary events as preparation, Kelly always had to work at them so that he would be in at the kill.

The other disadvantage for Kelly was that he had to nurture his gift. He admitted in 1985 that though his time-trialing had improved over the years, he had been afraid of working on his technique, which depends on control and regularity: 'I thought it might knock the edge off my sprint.' For the same reason during the Tours, once he had decided that the points prize was his objective he had to concentrate on his daily placings at the expense of his overall time. Kelly has come close to fulfilling the ideal of the complete rider, but only a Merckx or a Hinault could win the Tour and, almost as an afterthought, pick up the green jersey on the way.

Kelly and Roche have little in common except their nationality and their highly competitive friendship. Sometimes, although in different teams (which seems to have been a matter of choice), they are in alliance, two against the world. And generally they try not to rub against each other; if one attacks, the other won't lead the counter-attack, though he will certainly join it when somebody else does. But there are times when they can't avoid confrontation, as in the 1987 Paris-Nice. Roche was leading the race when he punctured on the col de Vence; Kelly hammered away at the front of the bunch with the result that Roche did not regain his place after his wheel-change; Roche lost the race, and Kelly won it. At the time Roche was furious at what he saw as Kelly's treachery. But the two men went out training together a few days later, and in his autobiography he has put a friendlier gloss on Kelly's behaviour. It is that since Kelly was already forcing the pace before the puncture, trying to dislodge a rival Spanish sprinter, he was under no obligation to modify his tactics.

If Kelly, the countryman, has nothing to say he says nothing;

Roche, the Dubliner, is never stuck for words. Kelly is retiring; Roche has the friendly charm of a good Irish barman. Kelly looks severe; Roche in his early thirties, with a French wife, Lydia, and two children, still looks like a choirboy. But it would be a mistake to assume that because Roche appears easy-going he hasn't the successful sportsman's usual streak of hard self-interest, as the later events of 1987 proved.

The little that the two Irishmen do have in common is that Roche also left school early, at fifteen, to serve an apprenticeship as a fitter in the workshop of the dairy where his father was a milkman. He too felt he had exhausted the possibilities of Irish racing early on. He did ride the 1980 Olympics in Moscow four years after Kelly had missed the trip to Montreal. But by then he was on the brink of turning professional with Peugeot, having already spent a season in France with, once again, ACBB. There he had won two amateur classics, the Paris-Roubaix and Paris-Reims, as well as the Route de France, so that he already had a name as a coming rider before he made his return in the new year of 1981.

His professional debut was dangerously successful. Within a few weeks of leaving the Peugeot training camp he had won the Tour of Corsica, not a major race but big enough to attract Bernard Hinault who had been expected to take it in the final time trial. Next Peugeot moved on to the Paris-Nice, which had never gone to a first-year pro, and Roche won that too, also coming first in the time trial on the col d'Eze. May brought another stage-race victory in the Circuit de l'Indre-et-Loire, at which point Peugeot thought of putting Roche, though still only twenty-one and with just a few months' experience of professional racing, into the Tour de France. He was saved from that thoughtless piece of infanticide by a tired performance in the Dauphiné-Libéré, but still finished the season second in the time-trial classic, the Grand Prix des Nations. After that precocious display of talent Roche was talked of as the new Hinault, even though the old Hinault had another five good years of racing ahead of him.

The talk was premature in Roche's case too. That winter he did too little training, the next season was a dreadful let-down, and it was not until 1983 that he embarked on the Tour at the conventional age of twenty-three. The race produced one notable entry in the history of Irish cycle-racing: the day at Pau when Kelly went up to the platform to receive the yellow jersey as well as the green, and was joined by Roche who put on the white as the Leading Young Rider. Before the end Roche was to lose that to another young prodigy, the winner, Laurent Fignon, but he finished a satisfactory thirteenth. He also won four good races that summer, as well as coming third in the world championships.

From this point, however, the lean and fat years seemed to alternate: 1984, unremarkable, though he won his second successive Tour of Romandie early on; 1985, a great improvement, finishing third in the Tour behind Hinault and LeMond, and first in one of the great stages on the summit of the Aubisque; 1986, pretty much a washout after damaging his knee in the Paris Six; 1987, a revival due, though after the previous season nobody expected anything on this scale.

After his disappointment in the Paris-Nice, Roche made a mess of the finish of the Liège-Bastogne-Liège and was beaten into second place by Moreno Argentin. But he then won his third Romandie by taking both stages on the final day and went to the start of his next assignment, the Tour of Italy, considerably cheered. He was now riding for an Italian team, Carrera, for whom Roberto Visentini had won the race the year

Two genial talkers from the Celtic fringes of Europe who always had something quotable to say to the press: the ever-optimistic Breton, Ronan Pensec (left) and the disappointed but undismayed Dubliner, Stephen Roche.

before. It was never explicitly stated that Visentini was to be their man again; it was implied that the team would support the better-placed rider. But Roche was aware that the management and riders would prefer an Italian to an Irish winner.

In effect the two men rode the race as rivals. Visentini won the prologue; Roche beat him in the first long time trial; and after the team time trial Roche was in the leader's pink jersey. The tension increased over the first fortnight, Visentini refusing to co-operate with Roche, and once attacking when he had mechanical trouble. After ten days leading the race, Roche, who had been under constant pressure all the while, rode untypically badly in the second time trial, and Visentini rode well, winning the stage and regaining the jersey. Carrera assumed that that was that, and the nine remaining days would see a united team riding for Visentini. But Roche had no intention of giving up the prize.

He chose his moment on the mountain stage to Sappada, breaking away recklessly on a twisting descent and detonating the field behind him. On the flat he was instructed by his manager to ease up, which he ignored, and was perhaps naively outraged to find that it was not the opposing teams but Carrera who were leading the chase. He was joined by two small counter-attacking groups, which included Millar and Anderson, and on the final climb by Visentini and what was left of the chasers. But this at least ensured that Roche now had the help of his one ally and the only other non-Italian in the Carrera team, the Belgian, Eddy Schepers. With his encouragement Roche kept going at the front of the group unaware that Visentini had cracked on the ascent. When Visentini finished nearly six minutes down, Roche was already back in the pink jersey which he was to keep to the end.

Carrera were furious and talked of sending Roche home, but it was a *fait accompli*. With Visentini out of the running, they had either to support Roche or lose the race. The fans were not as forgiving, and for the remainder of the Tour Roche was spat at and shouted at wherever he went. In the mountains in particular, when the race slowed to jogging pace, he needed police protection. Nor was Visentini reconciled to losing; after trying to ride Roche and Schepers off the road, he was fined by the governing body for threatening to use his fists next time. But if Roche was distressed by these reactions, he didn't let it affect his performance. The conventions, paper-thin at the best of times, had been torn to shreds on both sides, and as usual the stronger-muscled and stronger-minded rider had won. Typically, too, by the end of the race the Carrera team had begun to rally round the man who was going to collect – and distribute – the prize money.

At any rate, when it came to the Tour de France scarcely a fortnight later Roche was less concerned with the loyalty of his riders, Visentini being absent, than with his own state of fitness. It was the interregnum. Hinault had retired; LeMond had been shot; the only previous winner around was Fignon, but his form was suspect. So the French looked to Jean-François Bernard, Hinault's nominated heir, or perhaps Mottet to fill the vacuum, while those who had weighed up the mountain course rather fancied the climbers: the Colombian, Herrera, the Spaniard, Delgado, and the Scot, Millar. Roche also had his backers, but opinion was divided over whether the Giro victory had given him an edge or blunted it.

The Tour began in West Berlin, and by the time it was safely back in France, three different riders had worn the yellow jersey, and the third was one of Roche's *équipiers*, Eric Maechler of Switzerland. This was a slight embarrassment since the team would have to expend its energy on Maechler's behalf instead of saving it to serve Roche, and as the leaderless race developed an anarchic life of its own, Roche had to wait until stage 10 to assert himself. This was the 87km time trial from Saumur to the dreaded Futuroscope and Roche, now thoroughly ridden in, won it in a masterly fashion to take second place overall behind Mottet, who owed his rise to an earlier attack in Germany.

The Pyrenees caused no significant changes in the lead, but the 36.5km time trial on the 2,000-metre Mont Ventoux brought a transformation. Here 'Jeff' Bernard had his finest 1hr 39min, winning the trial and taking the jersey 2min 34sec ahead of Roche. It was agreed that Carrera should counter-attack at once before Bernard could recover from his effort, and chance played into their hands on the next day's pre-alpine stage from Valréas to Villard-de-Lans. Near the top of a mid-way climb Bernard punctured and got a slow wheel-change. The others took no immediate advantage of his misfortune, but when he failed to regain his place on the narrow descent, the voluntary neutralisation came to an end. His rivals gave it all they had and by the summit of the final climb just two of them were together in the lead: Pedro Delgado, who would win the stage, and Roche, who would take the yellow jersey.

Roche still wasn't sanguine about his chances, since in advancing his own cause he had also promoted Delgado: 'Getting to Paris is one thing; getting there in yellow is something else.' Sure enough, the Spaniards and Colombians scaled l'Alpe-d'Huez as though they were swarming up the rigging, and though Delgado wasn't in the first wave he took enough time out of Roche to seize the race lead by 25sec. Roche could accept that. On all known form he would beat Delgado by more than half a minute in the final time trial at Dijon. But there were still two more days in the Alps and he could not afford any more concessions.

On another uphill finish at La Plagne it again looked as though Delgado had eluded him. But with a ride of conspicuous courage over the last 5km, Roche limited his losses to 4sec, collapsing on the line and needing oxygen to bring him round. And even though he was fined 10sec for taking food from his team car outside the permitted limits, he did not let it upset him. Next day, again supported by the faithful Schepers, he reached the top of the Joux-Plane alongside Delgado, and then took off on one of his perilous descents to recoup at Morzine what he had lost at La Plagne, and with a little to spare. The battle was over and mopping up at Dijon a formality. Although his winning margin of 40sec was the second-smallest since the war, the final circuits of the Champs-Elysées were simply laps of honour. The Irish prime minister, Charles Haughey, was in Paris to welcome him; the president, Dr Patrick Hillery, sent a message expressing the nation's pride in his achievement; a civic reception was waiting for him on his return to Dublin, and for the first time ever, to honour his success, the staid *Irish Times* ran a colour picture on its front page.

CHAPTER 8

Roads to Rouen

Stage 1, Futuroscope, 138.5km
Sunday, 1 July: The early stages of the Tour, circling clockwise
for the first time since 1985, would take the riders north to the
Channel then eastward as far as Rouen. From there they would
fly to Sarrebourg on the German border to begin their approach to the Alps. But first, under grey, unsummery skies,
they had to settle their account at the Futuroscope with a
double bill: an early morning stage looping through the rippling Vienne countryside; and then, after lunch and a few
hours' rest, a team time trial beginning at 3.30pm.

Less than a decade ago the early stages would, for the most
part, have been treated as steady, uneventful journeys to the
next sprint finish. But the autocrats of the peloton who used to
set the tempo and lay down the orders of precedence have
passed on. Democracy has broken out – anarchy some would
say. There are so many unconsidered riders who feel they are
in with a shout that life is made very difficult for the favourites.

Nowadays it's a mistake to assume that even the opening
stage will be treated as a warm-up. Perhaps especially the
opening stage – and more especially when it is the curtain-
raiser to a team time trial. The opportunists know the last
thing the leaders want is to spend a tiring morning chasing
breaks. By exploiting this nervousness in Berlin in 1987, Lech
Piasecki became the first ever Polish race leader, and it was
not until the end of stage 10 that a recognised favourite,
Stephen Roche, put on the yellow jersey. In Brittany a year
later, Steve Bauer of Canada did the same by industrious
foraging for bonuses in the morning sprints. And although he
lost the jersey that afternoon, he stayed in contention to regain
it on stage 8. In Luxemburg in 1989, it was the Portuguese,
Acacio da Silva, who seized the lead and kept it for the next
three days.

The 1990 leaders should have been warned. Instead they rode open-eyed into the trap. It was set after only 6km as the race, leaving the cornfields, reached the oak forest of la Molière. First to detach himself was the admirable Claudio Chiappucci. He had been with Carrera all his professional life, serving under Visentini and Roche, and now, at the age of twenty-seven, Buggin's turn had brought him to the leadership. A vigorous rider, he took his responsibilities seriously indeed. He had so far been King of the Mountains in the Paris-Nice and the Giro, and had come to the Tour in search of a third crown.

Despite his impressive record he was not a climber in the class of Miguel Indurain or Steven Rooks; he was more an uphill sprinter, a man for the short côtes not the high cols. So his tactics were to gather sufficient points in the lower-category climbs to insure against losses in the Alps. This explained his early break: two 4th-cats would be rising gently out of the plain in the first 24km.

The 7-Eleven team had agreed among themselves to get one rider into every break that morning. This was not in fact the first. Earlier Andy Hampsten had marked one tentative attack (and had it succeeded the Tour might have taken a very different course). Now it was Bauer's turn. Z had the same plan, and the Breton, Ronan Pensec, also followed the Italian's rear wheel up the road as LeMond's representative. The fourth rider to enlist in the enterprise, Frans Maassen, a twenty-five-year-old Dutchman from the Buckler team, seems to have done so spontaneously. He saw his chance and, as the only recognised sprinter in the escape, knew that the odds were on his winning the stage if it succeeded.

At the côtes de Bonneuil and d'Archigny, Chiappucci duly won his mountain points, and from his point of view the main purpose of the attack had been achieved. But although the quartet's lead was no more than 30sec it was not diminishing. At La Puye, 10km further on, were the first of two bonus sprints, and Bauer suggested that they should at least press on that far at tempo and see whether the field reacted. The ayes had it. An extra spice of adventure was added to the enterprise by the straw bales, tree branches and diesel oil strewn on the road by sheepfarmers up in arms against foreign competition –

obstacles which a small group could easily avoid. And the time checks showed that they were gaining. By the time they reached Montmorillon, just past halfway, they had stretched out their lead to over eight minutes. The leaders, whatever they were up to, had left them with no option but to carry on to the finish.

Back at the bunch, only the veteran Sean Kelly seemed to appreciate the danger and absurdity of the situation. He ordered his PDM team to force the pace at the front and tried to rally support for a counter-attack. But LeMond said it wasn't up to him to lead the chase since it was his own man, Pensec, up ahead. Fignon, who might have been expected to try and defend Thierry Marie's yellow jersey, also declined. He felt that in the previous year he had worked to close too many gaps – to his cost and LeMond's benefit. Roche also turned down his countryman, reportedly saying that nobody was likely to chase for him in the mountains. The fact was that no team wanted to commit itself to an exhausting pursuit now. In the afternoon's trial minutes could be lost to more immediate rivals. That was when the big collective effort would be needed.

If Delgado had been consulted he would probably have voted with the rest, but he had other preoccupations. First a puncture, then mechanical problems, and finally at 77km a crash, along with a dozen or so others, on a patch of diesel. He wasn't hurt, but he and his Banesto team-mates had their work cut out regaining the peloton. Another chase was not on their schedule. Kelly, too, eventually decided that the struggle was pointless if it wasn't to be shared, and after 30km, when the course turned into a headwind, he called off his men.

Z belatedly stirred into action to limit the damage when the stately pleasure domes of the Futuroscope were almost in sight once more. But this had little effect. The four fugitives finished on the same time, Maassen very properly taking the sprint and Bauer the yellow jersey. Having come nineteenth in the prologue, Bauer had needed only a 22sec lead on Marie to accomplish that. What he and the other three gained was of another order. The arrival of the Dane, John Carlsen, and the Swiss, Guido Winterberg, pursuing at a considerable distance, did a little to keep the spectators at the finish entertained. But before the East German, Olaf Ludwig, led the main field over the line, they had to wait a preposterous 10min 35sec. What did the leaders think they were playing at?

Of course it often suits them to give a few riders their head. It acts as a safety valve and has a calming influence on the wilder spirits. There is little point in breaking out of jail if you know that others have already picked up the loot at the sprints and mountain primes. But normally this freedom is only granted to selected riders: men so far down in the table that they can't conceivably tip the balance of the race. Even then they are given only so much rope.

Two things were remarkable about today's unchallenged escape. First the extravagance of the quartet's profit: ten and a half minutes when the race had scarcely begun and still only 91sec separated the yellow jersey from the *lanterne rouge*. Second the quality of the profiteers.

Only Maassen could be disregarded as a possible Tour winner, unless he suddenly developed unsuspected gifts as a

While the favourites refuse to lead the chase, Maassen, Pensec, Chiappucci and Bauer return to the Futuroscope at the end of the opening stage with a preposterous lead of over 8min. In-croy-able!

This wasn't the first time the Canadian, Steve Bauer, had taken the yellow jersey on the opening stage. He also did so in 1988, losing then regaining it, and finishing fourth, his best Tour result.

climber and time-trialist. Bauer had finished the 1988 Tour in fourth place, and since established himself as a solid second-ranking professional. He had probably made the best-paid career move of the close season, leaving Helvetia to join 7-Eleven where his estimated salary was £50,000 a month and he shared the team leadership with Hampsten. He climbed efficiently, rode well against the clock and could also sprint; in April he had come within less than a tyre's width of winning the toughest of the classics, the Paris-Roubaix.

Pensec was also a man to watch: sixth in his first Tour de France in 1986, seventh two years later, a strong man over long mountainous courses, though inconsistent in time trials. Since those early successes his concentration had wavered, but LeMond's arrival in the Z team seemed to have revived his interest. Asked if he was now the Z leader, he modestly replied, 'Let us say that Greg and I are privileged in the team.' As for Chiappucci, nine seconds behind Bauer, he certainly had more successes to his credit than Marco Giovannetti, the man who found himself leading the Vuelta almost by chance and then day by day grew into the role.

Bauer, a friend and near-neighbour of the LeMonds at Courtrai in Belgium, wasn't bowled over by his good fortune. 'You know, ten minutes between Greg LeMond and me is a great deal,' he said. 'But ten minutes between me and Greg is very little.' Maybe, but Bauer, Pensec and Chiappucci were none of them riders to whom you'd want to give a 10min start before the Tour had even moved from its starting place.

That the leaders had done this apparently without a thought for the consequences outraged the past winners of the Tour. And as usual there were several of them employed on the race. 'In my day an Eddy Merckx would not have let such an escape get away,' said Roger Pingeon, the 1967 winner who was working as a consultant with a Swiss television station.

Luis Ocana (1973), a radio consultant with the Spanish Antenna 3, described the affair as a first-class funeral. 'There is only one leader in Z, that's LeMond. He showed it in the prologue. If I had been LeMond I would have ended the attack as soon as it reached two minutes, Pensec or no Pensec.' Ocana said that in his winning year one of his team-mates, Jacques Catieau, had attacked with an opponent, Van Springel, on the opening day in order to wear the yellow jersey as he passed through his home district. That night Ocana had taken down his case as if to pack, and told his manager: 'You choose, it's him or me.' That was how things were done. 'Do they want to play havoc with the Tour?'

Stage 1 result: 1. Maassen (Buckler) 3hr19'1"; 2. Pensec (Z) same time; 3. Chiappucci (Carrera) s.t.; 4. Bauer (7-Eleven) s.t.;

5. Carlsen (Toshiba) at 8'36"; 6. Winterberg (Helvetia) at 9'24".

Overall placings: 1. Bauer (7-Eleven) 3hr.27'1"; 2. Maassen (Buckler) at 2"; 3. Chiappucci (Carrera) at 9"; 4. Pensec (Z) at 21"; 5. Carlsen (Toshiba) at 9'3"; 6. Winterberg (Helvetia) 9'41".

Stage 2, Futuroscope, 44.5km (team time trial)
The leaders' refusal to answer the morning's escape with a show of force may have built up problems for the future but at least it took account of those they faced after lunch. Here the teams would set off at 4min intervals to cover an exposed, uneven circuit to the north of the Futuroscope. Provided that the riders finished together, each team would take the time of the fifth man to cross the line. That collective time would also be added on to each rider's individual total on general classification. If for any reason a rider failed to keep up with his team, he would receive, in effect, a 5min penalty. And if his personal finishing time fell outside the time limit he faced elimination from the race.

So teams had to solve a delicate equation: balancing the wish to go fast with the need to stay together. They might have to sacrifice the odd laggard or puncture victim, trusting that he would limp home within the limit. But only in extremis would they drop a protected rider who was in difficulty; there was no 'You go on, just leave me my gun and one bullet.' They might curse, but they would adjust their pace to his. By the same token, even if a leader was full of running, he could not improve on the time of his fifth-fastest man.

Some teams get these sums right; others make a dreadful botch of it, shedding riders and still producing poor times. But the event has so much effect on individual placings nowadays that most teams with any pretensions to winning the Tour have worked on the techniques of formation riding, the vortex which smoothly takes one man after another forward to set the pace at the front. Peter Post's teams have always specialised in it, and what the French press call the Panasonic TGV won again at the Futuroscope with all men accounted for.

All the same PDM, their Dutch rivals, were only 7sec

slower. And since PDM alone had done the chasing that morning, this put some perspective on the others' refusal to join them. Justified at the time as a perfectly natural care for their health, it now began to look more like hypochondria. But whatever the rights and wrongs of that, PDM's close second place put Alcala, Kelly and Breukink into the top twelve overall with a gain of 15sec on Roche, 26sec on Fignon, 41sec on Bauer, 46sec on LeMond and 1min 51sec on Delgado (having earlier spent some effort helping Julian Gorospe through a rough patch, Delgado himself was struggling 4km from home).

The other live issue of the stage was whether Pensec could snatch the yellow jersey from Bauer and wear it through his native Brittany over the next two days. A gain of 22sec would be enough to do it. But Z's teamwork was unremarkable, and they finished one place and 5sec behind Bauer's 7-Eleven. Pensec would have to soldier on in the strip cartoon symbols of the Z jersey. LeMond would have to recoup the 20sec he had just lost on Fignon. And at some point someone would have to go out and look for Bauer and company. But on the face of it there would be no clear-cut opportunity to do that before the Vittel-Epinal time trial in another six days' time.

Stage 2 result: 1. Panasonic 53'24"; 2. PDM at 7"; 3. ONCE at 22"; 4. Histor at 22"; 5. Castorama at 33"; 6. 7-Eleven at 48"; 7. Z at 53" . . . 16. Banesto at 1'58".

Overall placings: 1. Bauer (7-Eleven) 4hr21'13"; 2. Maassen (Buckler) at 10"; 3. Pensec (Z) at 26"; 4. Chiappucci (Carrera) at 50"; 5. Alcala (PDM) at 9'47"; 6. Ekimov (Panasonic) at 9'49".

Stage 3, Poitiers – Nantes, 233km
After two days of racing which finished where it started, the Tour was at last on the move. The weather was much the same, patchy cloud and a watery sun, but at least we were in a city inhabited by people not geometric objects. And there, before the riders lined up beneath the banner, the Union Paysanne, as promised, presented a live, beribboned lamb to the team which had come last in the previous day's time trial.

Fabio Parra accepted it for Kelme and held it up for the cameras. What happened to it afterwards we never learned. Nothing good I imagine. But the Union had already denied responsibility for obstructing the course on stage 1, and the gift was taken as a gesture of goodwill.

News had reached the Tour, however, that this goodwill might not extend all the way from Poitiers to Nantes. Further along the road there were thought to be groups of more militant sheepfarmers. Angry at the quota system and the import of mutton from eastern Europe, they intended to bring the race to a stop just as in 1982 the steel workers of Denain had done when they barricaded the road and forced the cancellation of the team time trial. Not out of hostility to the Tour, simply to publicise their grievances.

Knowing nothing of this, the riders moved off rapidly, Roche testing out Bauer in an immediate attack which drew in fifteen or so more riders, including LeMond and his adjutant, Duclos-Lassalle.

But Bauer was watchful enough to enlist too, and before the peloton, led by Delgado and Indurain, caught them at 10km the leader put to most inconvenience was Fignon whose pursuit was interrupted by a puncture. At one point he was half-a-minute behind, and he did not regain his place until km 28.

After that the riders settled down, breaking ranks only for Olaf Ludwig to win the bonus sprint at Loudun (km 49), and they were still together when they faced their next crisis another 36km on at Saint-Gemme. This in fact was not so much sheep as beef and dairy country. Ahead were the commune of Geay where a third of the population was involved in raising cattle for meat and milk, and the town of Bressure where France's principal abattoir annually slaughters and processes over 30,000 tonnes of fat cattle. But presumably there was solidarity between the ovine and bovine sections of the peasants' movement, and it suited the shepherds to make their protest along this stretch of road for other reasons.

As they well knew, between Geay and Bressure, at km 92, was, well, Kilometre 92. This was the well-attended roadside buffet which the General Council of Hauts-de-Seine (which also happened to be Département 92) daily laid on for the press at this distance into the stage. If the protesters made any trouble, then the reporters would be conveniently at hand to report their grievances.

The Tour organisers were now convinced that there would be an attempt to stop the race. Word had come back from their motorcycle escort that four newly-felled trees were lying close to the road with a group of men playing *pétanque* beside them, and that a tractor stood by to drag this barricade onto the route. There were straw bales for the same purpose, and black smoke rose from a pile of old tyres. Demonstrators carried banners which read, '*Liberté, Moutoniers, Fraternité*' and '*Miterant* [sic] – *ruine des paysans et de la France.*'

Rather than allow the riders to run this gauntlet, Jean-Marie Leblanc, the race director, brought them to a halt at km 86 while a detour was worked out. At which moment a local youth on a *vélomoteur* – a power-assisted bike – stopped and offered to guide them through the side lanes. It seems unlikely that the race direction and the gendarmerie didn't have a map between them and couldn't have found their own way. But the popular version – the press know a good legend in the making when they see one – was that the Tour accepted his offer. Most papers were content to describe him as 'a mysterious saviour', but one managed to establish that he was sixteen, came from Pierrefitte and was called Michaël, 'without whom the riders might have been ensnared by branches and manure'.

For 25km the race was neutralised, some compensation for the 5km added to the journey, but once the way was clear the attacks built up again. Hampsten, Anderson and Bernard tried repeatedly to get away. Another break was aborted only when LeMond joined it. But by now the rain was falling hard, the riders were in their racing capes, and it looked as though the stage would end in a mass sprint.

That was not how Moreno Argentin, the World Cup leader and classics specialist, saw it. He had passed up the Giro and was making his belated debut in the Tour at the age of thirty with the idea of winning stages, not achieving a high place overall ('though the idea of taking the green jersey doesn't displease me'). In his mind it was a series of one-day races, some worth contesting, some not. This one, with a wet, snaky and slightly undulating finish looked a possibility. Having ridden inconspicuously all day, he suddenly slipped away

46km from home. The field reacted too sluggishly to stop him; he was not a threat to the leaders anyway. And the sprinters, at least those who noticed him slip away and saw themselves deprived of their grandstand finish, organised their pursuit too late. Argentin took the second bonus sprint at Monnières by over 2min, and a little further on had a lead of over 4.

The slippery roads produced two crashes. At Clisson, 35km from the finish, Fignon came down with a dozen others, and though he regained the bunch he felt some pain in his right calf. And on the run-in to Nantes Argentin came off on a corner, also hurting his leg. Neither injury seemed important at the time. Argentin remounted to take the stage, and almost 2.5min passed before Christophe Lavainne led in the main field. He, poor chap, raised his arms in a victory salute as he crossed the line, unaware that Argentin had got there before him. One of the hardest things for a rider is to keep up with the movements of the others. As he said: 'There are 200 lads in the race and you can't keep a watch on them all.'

It had been an uncomfortable, frustrating day for everyone, though Argentin had no complaints. Before going off to get his wounds attended to, the late convert was full of enthusiasm for the race: 'Everyone should contest it once in his career. The Giro is the nursery school; the Tour de France is the university.'

Stage 3 result: 1. Argentin (Ariostea) 5hr46'13"; 2. Lavainne (Castorama) at 2'29"; 3. Raab (PDM), s.t.; 4. Ludwig (Panasonic) s.t. 5. Capiot (TVM) s.t.; 6. Kelly (PDM) s.t.

Overall placings: 1. Bauer (7-Eleven) 10hr9'55"; 2. Maassen (Buckler) at 8"; 3. Pensec (Z) at 26"; 4. Chiappucci (Carrera) at 50"; 5. Argentin (Ariostea) at 8'23"; 6. Alcala (PDM) at 9'47".

Stage 4, Nantes – Le Mont-St-Michel, 203km
Things seemed more cheerful the following morning. The sun shone on the place St-Pierre in front of the cathedral where the stage was to start. And beside it in the Village Départ, the little white-trellised oasis where riders and reporters mixed or avoided each other according to taste, a second breakfast of

oysters and Muscadet was served. But as so often in the opening week, and much of the second, the weather didn't hold, and the luck of some riders showed no improvement either, Fignon's in particular. He had woken with the pain in his calf still troubling him.

There was to be sporadic rather than determined racing, and the atmosphere was sufficiently relaxed for the regional rider, Gérard Rué, to dismount and greet his family beside the road at Bédée. It was clearly one of those days when some of the lesser riders sensed that the leaders might like to see the back of them and quietly get on with the business of marking each other.

Roche's young lieutenant, Francis Moreau, was the first to attack, but stayed away for only 6km. Next, at 130km, Gilles Delion of Helvetia made his escape, followed into the distance by Edwin Van Hooydonck of Buckler. Both were twenty-four and already successful: Van Hooydonck, older by just one day, was leader of his team, Delion one of the (it was hoped)

The Village Départ, pitched near the start of each stage, where the press can collect their newspapers, take a late breakfast or early brunch of local delicacies and, if they still have time, interview the

riders.

coming Frenchmen. Any other time the would-be leaders of the race might have tried to stop them. Today they didn't have to worry. Panasonic were doing all the necessary chasing.

The evening before, Peter Post's East German acquisition, Olaf Ludwig, had taken the lead in the points competition, and in order to protect his green jersey Panasonic would do everything to give him a privileged position at the second bonus sprint (he had been runner-up at the first) and at the stage finish. Team-work is what Panasonic are noted for. No sooner had Van Hooydonck caught Delion than Panasonic, at the head of the peloton, caught them both. And although they gave Soren Lilholt, one of the two Danes in Roche's Histor team, his freedom for 40km, they never allowed him to gain more than 45sec. When they judged the time was right they pounced on him and on his newly-arrived companion, Kurt Steinmann.

That was at 14km from home. At 11km was the village of Villechèrel where the streets were too narrow to allow free passage to 197 riders (one had abandoned) in full career, and the peloton was torn apart. And at 9km was Pontorson and the second of the day's sprints, which Ludwig won to show his gratitude. By now the front-runners could sniff the sea from the bay of le Mont-Saint-Michel where the tide comes in across the grey sands at the speed of a galloping horse. And what with the riders' attempts to do much the same in the other direction, and the buffeting of the wind from the Channel, it was almost impossible even for those in the front group to hold each other's wheels and stay together.

The finish was on what has been described, no doubt by Bretons, as the most beautiful kilometre in France: the causeway which crosses the bay to the pinnacled fantasy of Mont-Saint-Michel. There Ludwig made the mistake of starting his final effort too soon. It was suggested that he was confused by the placing of the Coca-Cola van in front of the finish, not behind it, but Ludwig didn't offer that excuse. He said he followed the wheel of a Helvetia rider who died on him, leaving him stranded 400 metres from the line. The Belgian, Johan Museeuw, and the Italian, Guido Bontempi, came past, leaving Ludwig in third place, still good enough to keep a firm grasp on the green jersey.

The leading group was so strung out that the first fifty riders, who included LeMond and Pensec, were given the same time as the winner. The next twenty-four, with Roche and Alcala unlucky to find themselves in fifty-first and fifty-second place and in company with Chiappucci – had 7sec added to their time. Then at various intervals came the remaining 123 who had been delayed by the incidents at Villechèrel. At first it was thought that there had been a crash there, when all it had been was an impenetrable bottleneck. Some may have fallen as they stopped suddenly to put their foot to the ground, but once the road was blocked it was simply the problem of getting through and getting going again which produced the unexpectedly wide gaps at the finish.

Delgado, Breukink, Indurain, Hampsten, Bugno and Maassen, the last of the stage 1 gang of four, lost 21sec, after coming up to the front group but then losing contact in the strong head-wind. Bernard was among a dozen at 33sec. And Fignon, Lejaretta, Parra and Millar were with fifty-eight men at 44sec. All this on a stage which, under Panasonic's command, had promised a bunch finish.

Afterwards LeMond was asked if he had known about the crash (as it was then thought to be) which had impeded Fignon. He said he hadn't, though he was aware of Fignon's absence, and then observed sharply that the way to avoid getting blocked was to ride at the front of the peloton. End of moral discussion.

With Fignon there was no discussion at all. Millions of viewers saw him brush past the Antenne-2 interviewer, Jean-Paul Olivier, careless of the impression he made and wanting only to reach his team car. Things looked ominous.

Stage 4 result: 1. Museeuw (Lotto) 5hr23'33"; 2. Bontempi (Carrera) s.t.; 3. Ludwig (Panasonic) s.t.; 4. Phinney (7-Eleven) s.t.; 5. Baffi (Ariostea) s.t.; 6. Capiot (TVM) s.t.

Overall placings: 1. Bauer (7-Eleven) 15hr33'24"; 2. Pensec (Z) at 30"; 3. Maassen (Buckler) at 33"; 4. Chiappucci (Carrera) at 1'1"; 5. Argentin (Ariostea) at 8'27"; 6. Alcala (PDM) at 9'58".

Stage 5, Avranches – Rouen, 301km

When Louison Bobet abandoned his final Tour in 1959, he climbed to the summit of the Iseran before climbing off his bike. Laurent Fignon had no such grandiose option. The longest stage of 1990 ran through Normandy, and though the province is nowhere near as flat as it's made out to be, the course took the northern route across the undulating Caen plain rather than plunging through the hills and valleys of the Suisse normande around Bagnoles-de-l'Orne. But even allowing for its prosaic setting, Fignon's departure from the Tour seemed remarkably low key – somewhere on the scale between discreet and furtive, and in much the same class as Bernard Hinault's mysterious disappearance at Pau in 1983, which cleared the way for Fignon's first Tour victory.

The newspapers that morning had been sounding warning notes. Cyrille Guimard was worried: Fignon felt unwell, he was in pain, and he had just lost 44sec. Guimard didn't believe that in itself the calf injury was all that serious, but there was an 80 per cent chance that Fignon's earlier fall in the Giro would cost him the Tour de France, leaving only a 20 per cent margin for optimism. After the time trial next Saturday they would know if he could win, but who knew what might happen meanwhile. The Rouen stage was long, it would probably be wet and the racing would be highly strung.

Fignon had come to the Tour needing to ride himself steadily back into form. Instead any progress had been undermined by a series of set-backs which left him in forty-seventh place overall, 11min 16sec down on Bauer and 39sec on LeMond. Understandably, his morale was low, and today's conditions, just as Guimard had predicted them, were not designed to lift it. In heavy drizzle seven riders of modest means made away as the course turned inland from the coast at Granville (35km), and although, this early in the stage, the break had no apparent significance, the peloton accelerated to stop it getting out of hand. This was too much for Fignon as he rode along morosely in his white rainproof. He drifted back, and having already warned Guimard that he might not complete the stage, prepared to quit the race at Villers-Bocage, the first feeding station.

It was not a dignified exit; the persistence of the press and his own stubborn nature saw to that. He went through the line of stationary team cars looking for a place where he could stop in privacy. There was none. He turned in the road and cycled back, still trying but failing to avoid the photographers. Then he dismounted and, holding a newspaper up to his face, sat in the back seat of a car belonging to one of the helicopter pilots with the Tour. He was next sighted at Castorama's hotel at Rouen, where he kept to his resolve not to speak to reporters, and from there returned home to Paris. It was no surprise, but it was a little melancholy to see a rider who had ridden with such panache in his time retire from the race with so little.

The marathon stage continued relentlessly. The seven were caught 2km beyond the feed, and after a period of calm an experienced Dutchman, Gerrit Solleveld, broke away and rode the last 95km alone to take the stage by four and a half minutes. It was an enterprise which brought him rapid promotion from 110th to fifth overall, but perhaps less public attention than he might have expected. Fignon was still the main story, even if its punch-line had been signalled.

LeMond was unimpressed. 'I also had troubles at the start of the season. And although he wasn't very polite about me at that time I don't want to criticise him. It changes nothing very much for me. I was already the man to beat at the start. From the first day I knew he wasn't going very well. He was never at the front.'

It happened to be the US Independence Day. But even the French, with their attachment to birthdays, anniversaries and happy coincidences, couldn't read much into that.

Stage 5 result: 1. Solleveld (Buckler) 7hr43'7"; 2. Museeuw (Lotto) at 4'27"; 3. De Wilde (Histor) s.t.; 4. Ludwig (Panasonic) at 4'30"; 5. Vanderaerden (Buckler) s.t.; 6. Baffi (Ariostea) s.t.

Overall placings: 1. Bauer (7-Eleven) 23hr20'57"; 2. Pensec (Z) at 34"; 3. Maassen (Buckler) at 37"; 4. Chiappucci (Carrera) at 1'5"; 5. Solleveld (Buckler) at 7'26"; 6. Alcala (PDM) at 10'2".

CHAPTER 9

Search for a Superman

At the beginning of July 1982, Bernard Hinault had already won the Tour de France three times in four attempts, and had just won his second Giro. His previous success in Italy had come in 1980, the year when inflammation of the tendons in his right knee forced him to abandon the Tour. So this was his second chance to bring off the double which would bracket him in the records with Fausto Coppi, Jacques Anquetil and Eddy Merckx, and to win a fourth Tour, a feat which only the last two had achieved. It was, in short, his chance to create a legend, a concept close to the spirit of the Tour and to the hearts of the French journalists who wrote about it. The cycling magazine, *Vélo*, had no doubt that Hinault would triumph. That month they happened to change their format and on the cover, instead of running the usual action photograph or portraits, they got an artist to paint a strip-cartoon illustration of Hinault soaring upward from the peloton. A red silk cloak flowed from his shoulders. A red H was printed on a yellow shield covering the chest of his blue jersey. His clenched right fist was thrust in front of him, and below was spread out the landscape of his native Brittany. 'Super Hinault', for whom all things were possible, was on his way.

Coppi, Louison Bobet, Anquetil, Merckx and Hinault – five riders who won twenty Tours between them – in turn filled the role of Superman in the post-war years. Whether or not they were 'better' cyclists than those who rode between the wars, they certainly took more honours. They were dominant individuals who shaped the race and controlled the peloton, the kind of *patrons* whose absence nowadays is ritually deplored by the critics every July.

Because the war severed his career, Coppi was thirty before he first rode the Tour, and thirty-three when he won it for the second and last time. Seven years later, still postponing his retirement, he went to the Upper Volta in French West Africa with a small group of celebrities from the sport – Géminiani, Anquetil, Rivière, Anglade, Hassenforder – to appear in the Grand Prix d'Ouagadougou, and then travel on for a few days' hunting in the Porga game reserve before returning home. Within a month, on 2 January, 1960, he died of malaria. At Castellania, the hillside village in Piedmont where he was

But for the war – which meant that Fausto Coppi was thirty before he rode his first Tour – he, the Campionissimo, rather than Merckx, the
Cannibal, might have been cycling's most prodigious winner.

born, 10,000 people attended his funeral. And in France the news of his death was received with the same emotional shock. Coppi's racing there may have been limited but it had been so brutally decisive and dramatic that few disputed his Italian title, *Il Campionissimo*, the champion of champions. Later French cyclists from Briançon put a marble urn at the foot of his grave containing bags of earth from the peaks of the Galibier, the Izoard and other great cols of the Tour.

Castellania had a population of 300, most of them Coppis and employed on the land. Fausto, too, was born on a farm and, when he left school at thirteen, worked in the fields before getting a job as a butcher's errand boy in Novi-Ligure. What lifted him out of obscurity was a gift of money from his uncle – the head of the Coppi clan who had gone to sea and risen to ship's captain – to buy a hand-built racing frame. That same uncle later managed his considerable fortune, which, as with Sean Kelly, mostly went to buy land in his region.

Coppi remained amateur only long enough to gain a professional contract, and in 1940 was twenty when he scored the first of his five Giro victories in the last edition of the race before Italy entered the war. Round-shouldered and heron-like, he looked anything but an athlete, yet his physique perfectly suited his purpose: long slender legs, short body, the large thorax of an opera singer and a slow pulse-rate of 44 in repose. He had two weaknesses: the first was brittle bones which converted minor spills into costly accidents. The other was the lack of a convincing sprint, which he turned to advantage by attacking alone long before the finish or by setting such a punishing pace that the others hadn't the strength left to turn on him. He won the 1946 Milan-San Remo by 14min, the 1950 Flèche Wallonne by 6, and the hardest alpine stage of the 1952 Tour from l'Alpe-d'Huez to Sestrière by nearly 8.

His first Tour victory in 1949 was all the more piquant because his only serious rival was his own team-mate, Gino Bartali, who had won the race the year before. They were the best of enemies. Together they rode across the Izoard to arrive with over 5min lead at Briançon where Bartali took the sprint and the yellow jersey. Next day they broke away in tandem once more until Bartali punctured on the Petit Saint Bernard and Coppi, without a flicker of hesitation, sped away alone to take over the lead, which he enhanced by 7min in the time trial from Colmar to Nancy. In 1952 he met no such opposition, and finished in Paris with a lead of almost half an hour.

Coppi's victories were balm to Italian egos bruised by defeat in the war. He took one world championship on the road and two in the professional pursuit on the track; he won twelve classic races (including five Tours of Lombardy); and he set a world hour record. The slogans *Forza Fausto* and *Forza Coppi* were daubed on walls and roads from the toe to the thigh of Italy, and he was mobbed, and paid, like a film star. He was also involved in the type of scandal which seemed more appropriate to that style of life. Leaving his wife and, unable to get a divorce, he moved in with 'the Woman in White' as the gossip writers called her, by whom he had a son. The *tifosi*, never the most dependable of fans, would not forgive him until his early death wiped out the offence. The French, who couldn't see what all the fuss was about, went on regarding Coppi as one of their own.

Victory in the Tour also came late to Louison Bobet, a baker's son from a small Breton village outside Rennes, though it was not for want of trying. He was twenty-eight before he succeeded at the sixth attempt in 1953 – and then went on to become the first rider to win three Tours in succession, combining this with the world title in 1954. Not a natural rider, Bobet got there by application after many black periods when he thought of giving up the sport. 'He didn't look too good on the bike and had to improve his position,' according to a contemporary critic, René de Latour. 'His legs were more those of a footballer than a real pedaller.' Yet he won his first Tour in the manner, if not with the style of Coppi, climbing the Vars and the Izoard to win by nearly six minutes at Briançon, and then forcefully extending his lead in the final time trial. Bobet was also the first of the Supermen to convert his winnings into a fortune after he retired by setting up a sea-cure centre at Quiberon, the Institute of Thalassotherapy, and flying his own plane some years before that became a standard executive toy.

Anquetil, the next in line, was totally different from his two predecessors in relying on his gifts as a time-trialist to destroy the opposition. It was not that he couldn't climb. The most celebrated film sequence of the Tour, included in almost every

The first man to win the Tour five times, largely due to his mastery of the time trial sections,'Maitre' Jacques Anquetil remained a familiar figure as a journalist on the race until his death in 1987 at the age of fifty-three.

retrospective feature on the race, shows him on 12 July, 1964, riding shoulder-to-shoulder with Raymond Poulidor up the Puy-de-Dôme near Clermont-Ferrand, a winding, conical climb on an extinct volcano where 500,000 spectators had gathered. He was too tenacious to allow the yellow jersey to slip from his shoulders, but also too proud to tuck in behind Poulidor and let the stronger climber be seen to tow him. It didn't matter that the two great Spanish climbers, Julio Jimenez, who was to win the stage, and Federico Bahamontes, were ahead of them. The Anquetil-Poulidor duel was the centrepiece of the stage. It was only in the last kilometres that Poulidor was able to ease away and gain 42sec, while Anquetil, sticking to the task, plodded after him to save his race lead by 14sec. That was ample. In the time trial to the finish in Paris, Anquetil typically extended it to 55sec to win his fifth Tour and his fourth in succession, both records.

Dismissed as a climber, Anquetil was also under-rated as a *rouleur* and sprinter. Again unfairly. Even as a twenty-three-year-old debutant in the 1957 Tour Anquetil refused to ride for France if Bobet was to be the leader. Never one to sell himself short, he said he'd rather be number one in a provincial team. Bobet withdrew, 'rather than come to blows with pens and microphones', and Anquetil was promoted. He now had to take the first chance to justify his arrogance, which he did by winning the third stage in a twelve-man sprint in his native Rouen.

Again in 1961, on the morning of the opening day he was active in a breakaway by sixteen riders which took 5min out of the field. This time it was his team-mate, André Darrigade, who won this first sprint, as he made a habit of doing, but it was this attack before lunch, even more than his afternoon victory in the time trial, which enabled Anquetil to win the yellow jersey which he kept from the first day to the last. And not content with an 8min lead on his principal rivals, which virtually ended the race before it had gone 200km, Anquetil continued to nag away at them, extending his final lead to more than 12min.

Yet although Anquetil was a more accomplished all-rounder than the public cared to acknowledge, it was his disciplined riding against the clock which gave him the edge, and on which he increasingly relied. He was precociously talented. At eighteen he won the French amateur road-race title and an Olympic bronze medal in the team time trial. A year later came the first of six consecutive victories in the time trial classic, the Grand Prix des Nations (which he was to win a record nine times). And by now he was able to earn more in a day's racing than his father did in six months from his strawberry farm. So it went on: five wins in the Paris-Nice, four in the Critérium National, two in the Giro (one of them doubled with the Tour), the Dauphiné and the Dunkirk Four-Day, one in the Tour of Spain. He was a man of formidable energy. Once, having won the Dauphiné on the Saturday, he started at two the next morning in the 600km Bordeaux-Paris, winning that as well. And if the stories are to be believed, he spent the time in between not resting but playing poker. Yet even this did not endear him to the public. He was a great champion, but not in the style they most admired.

The French have an ambivalent attitude to the time trial. In calling it 'the race of truth' they acknowledge that it is the purest test of speed and judgement, but it doesn't excite them in the way that a showdown in the mountains does. And this lukewarm attitude to Anquetil's special talent very largely explained their warmer support for Poulidor, the man whom

Scarcely had Raymond Poulidor (left) seen the back of Anquetil, against whom he had fought a long and losing struggle, than he had to contend with the even more voracious Belgian, Eddy Merckx (right).

Anquetil invariably beat whenever they clashed in the Tour.

They shared a farming background, but little else. Anquetil was a fair-haired, pale-complexioned Norman, Poulidor a black-haired, deeply-tanned Limousin from La Creuse. Anquetil was the more sophisticated. Though reticent in a crowd, he was at ease with sponsors and managers and very soon became a successful businessman in his own right with cattle ranch, gravel quarry, property. At his peak, in 1958-65, he collected eleven million francs from one marginal source alone, the annual Pernod trophies. Poulidor, with his shy smile, may have been an even more private person, but he projected a reticent public charm which people took for natural modesty. He, too, was presumably well rewarded for his successes (Tour of Spain, three second and five third places in the Tour de France, several classics) and for his popularity, though he never displayed it. And while the differences in their approach to racing were more apparent than real, Anquetil was perceived as shrewd and calculating, and Poulidor as bold, straightforward – and unlucky, especially that. So Anquetil remained the distant Maître Jacques to his urban admirers. Poulidor was affectionately embraced as Pou-Pou (a nickname which in fact displeased him) by the rural followers who believed him to be the victim of northern guile.

There was more coolness than animosity between them. 'Contrary to what people think,' wrote Poulidor, 'I have never detested Anquetil.' And Anquetil confirmed, though in slightly loaded terms, that there was no personal dislike. 'Of course I would like to see Poulidor win the Tour de France in my absence,' he once told a reporter. 'I have beaten him so often that his victory could only add to my reputation.'

In 1956 Anquetil broke Coppi's one-hour record at the Vigorelli stadium in Milan and, after it had later been beaten by Roger Rivière, he returned there at the age of thirty-three hoping to regain it. To all appearances he did, setting a new mark of 47.493km. He described it as 'the last great joy' of his career. But it turned to ashes when he refused to take a drug test afterwards, and in turn the UCI refused to ratify the result. Independent and careless of public opinion to the end, he went on asserting that professionals should be allowed to take stimulants and, on being banned for his insolence from the 1967 French and world championships, he simply rode out on the sport.

After Anquetil came four one-time winners: the excellent twenty-two-year-old Félice Gimondi and the more forgettable Aimar, Pingeon and Janssen. And then in 1969, with the return to trade teams after the brief international experiment, came the Cannibal. There was never a more insatiable winner than Eddy Merckx: five Tours (with ninety-eight yellow jerseys and thirty-four stages), five Giros, one Vuelta, two Tours of Belgium and one of Switzerland; three world championships; thirty-two classics – 445 victories in all. Plus the world hour record of 49.431km set in Mexico in 1972. It's little wonder if he now treats LeMond as a talented cyclist but a bit of a dilettante.

Just over six foot tall, he was impressively built (like Freddy

Maertens he had to choose between a professional career in football or cycling). He had black hair, high cheekbones and, in public anyway, the grave, unsmiling features of an Aztec carving. Off duty he could be cheerful and sociable, and his manners were invariably correct, but since he worked so hard at cycling, and had such respect for his professional obligations, people rarely saw him when he was relaxed.

He appeared aloof even among his own riders, though they remained intensely loyal to him. Men like Josef Bruyère and Jos De Schoenmaecker preferred to stay with him even though they might have earned more promotion in other teams. This wasn't simply due to personal admiration, of course. Merckx had patronage to bestow. He was such a consistent winner that it was like working for a man with a private mint. He could also reward exceptional service with the gift of a stage win, and he didn't always confine his favours to his own team. One of his closest friends was the great track sprinter and six-day man, Patrick Sercu, and in 1974 he honoured that friendship by helping Sercu, who was riding for an opposing team, to win the points prize in the Tour.

Merckx was both Superman and war lord, with a personal bodyguard which became famous, when he was at Faema in 1968-69, as the Red Guard (in fact their jerseys were red above and white below, but it was their shoulders hunched over the handlebars that you saw from a distance). Like any other leader he relied on them to control the peloton on the flat and he needed their protection in the lower slopes of the mountains. But in the popular tradition of warlords he was a leader by example, and secured his position by being stronger than any of them. When he chose he would drop them as abruptly as he did his opponents and make all the running by himself.

In 1969, at twenty-four, he entered his first Tour. That season he had already won the Paris-Nice, Milan-San Remo, Tour of Flanders and Liège-Bastogne-Liège – and then been eliminated from the Giro, which he was leading, for failing a dope test. A great storm blew up over this since it seemed inconceivable that he should take stimulants when he knew that, being in the pink jersey, he would be tested every day. The Belgian press argued that he must have been a victim of a spiked drink, and the UCI were sufficiently unsure of their ground to reinstate him a few days before the Tour started in Roubaix near the Belgian border.

During the race Merckx voluntarily submitted himself for tests after every stage, and seemed determined to prove that he needed no artificial help. At the end of the first stage he put on the yellow jersey in his own capital, Brussels, and though he let it pass to one of his *équipiers*, Julien Stevens, for some days, he foreclosed on stage 6 by winning at the summit of the Ballon d'Alsace. Further victories, two in time trials and one in the Alps, had put him 8min into the lead, and in the final bout of climbing in the Pyrenees he had no need to do more than watch and wait.

J. B. Wadley, who wrote a short monograph on the race, remembered seeing a headline in the Belgian weekly, *Le Sportif* which read: 'The Prayer of all Belgium for her Super-Champion: EDDY – BE CAREFUL!' And carefully was how Merckx seemed to be doing it at the start of the four-peak stage 17 from Luchon to Mourenx. He began the Peyresorde climb under a close red escort, coming over the top with the leaders but making no aggressive move. The same on the Aspin. But on the Tourmalet he began setting the pace with his lieutenant, Martin Van den Bossche, to shed Roger Pingeon, the man lying second overall. And on the descent Merckx dropped like a stone, converting a 5sec lead into a minute.

He didn't know the last col, the Aubisque, and had no intention of climbing it alone. But after picking up his rations in the valley, and finding that there was still no-one in sight, he set off again. Such was his strength at that age that he crossed that summit with nearly a 7min lead, and although even he was flagging over the final 40kms, so were his pursuers. He preserved most of his gains as he took the stage at Mourenx, and went on to win the Tour – Belgium's first for thirty years – by almost 18min. On the way he also picked up all three jerseys, the points and the mountains as well as the yellow, which no-one had ever done before.

It was then that the French rider, Christian Raymond, gave him his nickname, the Cannibal. Had Merckx been simply a glutton for victory the sport might not have remembered him as fondly. But fortunately there was a lot more to him, including courage, gallantry and a highly developed sense of professional obligation. Merckx was not tediously invincible, either. In 1971, having determined to hold the yellow jersey from start to finish, he was morally beaten by the Spaniard, Luis Ocana, who at last paid up on his promising talent. Ocana outdistanced him in the Chartreuse, along with Thévenet, the Swede Gosta Petterson and Zoetemelk, who took the yellow jersey. And the following day in the Alps, Ocana attacked him once again, making off with Lucien Van Impe, the Portuguese Joaquim Agostinho, and Zoetemelk once again, but dropping all three on the col du Noyer to take 8min 41sec out of Merckx at Orcières-Merlette. It was the greatest affront the Belgian had received.

Merckx replied in kind and indignantly after the rest day, forcing Ocana to chase him and his companions for 250km. But although these tactics weren't to Ocana's liking, he stuck to the task and limited his losses to 2min. With 7min 32sec still to make up, Merckx left his next counter-attack to the Pyrenees where, on the col de Mente the rain and hail came down in a sudden violent storm which made the already dangerous descent even more treacherous. Water ran in rivers down the road as Merckx tried to shake off Ocana, who followed him closely until at one bend his brakes failed to respond and he crashed to the ground. Ocana was then struck by Zoetemelk, who couldn't see him in the mist, and in a semiconscious state was taken to the clinic at Saint-Gaudens. Merckx, although among the many who also fell, continued to the finish. Shocked by the accident to Ocana (who was to win the Grand Prix des Nations before the end of the season and the Tour two years later), he wanted to retire from the race. His team persuaded him to continue, but Merckx, to acknowledge the injustice of Ocana's misfortune, refused for the time being to take the yellow jersey which was his again.

If Merckx behaved sympathetically in that Tour, he did so at even greater cost to himself in 1975, when he held the yellow jersey from the sixth stage to the fourteenth, but with flagging resources. Trying to shake off Bernard Thévenet, who had been trailing him like a predator waiting for the kill, he attacked on the alpine stage from Nice to Pra-Loup and within 20km of the finish, appeared to have saved the race. Instead his strength suddenly drained away, and Thévenet came back at him to take the stage and the overall lead. Another day, another dolour: Thévenet dropped him on the Izoard. The race was over, but not Merckx's difficulties.

Next morning Merckx touched wheels with another rider and crashed heavily to the ground. He was sick and dazed but insisted on continuing, and did so again on the following day, even though by now he knew that he had broken a cheekbone. He had no sensation in his jaw, could take only liquid food and refused antibiotics in case they weakened him. But he not only declined the excuse, and the doctors' advice, to retire gracefully, he continued to ride competitively, twice regaining small segments of time. Only tokens, perhaps, but they allowed him to hold on to second place overall. And they gave Thévenet an honourable, not a hollow, victory like his own over Ocana. Merckx may have been the Cannibal, but he never spat out what he couldn't chew.

After the Cannibal, the Badger. No-one seems to know who first called Hinault *le Blaireau*, or exactly why. Presumably it had to do with the badger's apparently mild manner when left alone, but its ferocity when cornered. At any rate the name stuck and Hinault didn't disown it. After he lost the Tour to Fignon in 1984 he took out a full-page ad in *L'Equipe* to say: 'I shall be back next year. The badger has claws and intends to use them.' He had and he did, but not, as it happened, on Fignon who had tendon problems and didn't ride. He also looked as if he had been in a fight after he fell in the sprint at Saint-Etienne and finished with a broken nose, his face covered with blood. It was the start of the problems between himself and LeMond referred to earlier.

LeMond wasn't the only rider who found him perplexing to deal with, amiable one day, tight-lipped the next, frequently combative in manner and with a habit of turning questions back on the questioner. He was – still is – a handsome man, looking younger than his age and wearing clothes that might have just come out of the wrapper. While he may be a countryman, who used to list his hobbies as *bricolage* (which has a finer ring than DIY) and shooting, he is very much at home in management and media. And for all his ruthlessness in combat, he has more than a streak of sentimentality. When he retired in November 1986, after taking part in his last race, a

Popularising the Renault headband was not the greatest of Bernard Hinault's achievements, but it became the mark of his cool, detached style, as though proclaiming that no sweat would ever blind those wary eyes to what was going on.

neighbouring cyclo-cross event, he gave a party attended by Félix Lévitan, old champions like Roger Lapebie and Jacques Anquetil (though no transatlantic message, it was noted, from LeMond). 'All my friends, known and unknown, gathered in my native town in Brittany. We took our bicycles and rode along my favourite roads. I wanted it to be simple, but a celebration of friendship.' Afterwards there was a buffet and fireworks. It was a fitting end to a career which dominated cycle-racing for nearly a decade. But was this the real Hinault? The French reply is that Hinault is a Breton, not French at all, and they are very secret people (just as the English will say you can never tell with the Welsh).

Still there was nothing enigmatic about Hinault's gifts as a rider. He rode and won his first Tour at the age of twenty-three, having already that season carried off his first yellow jersey in the Tour of Spain. This was four days after Merckx gave up the sport, though their careers had already overlapped in the Paris-Nice where, asked what he thought of the great man, Hinault replied curtly, 'He has two legs like me.' Hinault, for that matter, was like Merckx in his appetite for victory, in his prowess in the mountains and against the clock and, with Cyrille Guimard as his manager, in controlling the peloton through his team. What he lacked was Merckx's deadly finishing sprint, which meant that although he won the Nations four times, and most of the other classics including the Paris-Roubaix, he was essentially a stage-race rider. Time, space and variety of competition gave him the best opportunity to wear down the opposition with strength. There not even Merckx surpassed him, and but for problems with his knee in 1983, when he was at the height of his powers, he would almost certainly have set a record of six Tour victories.

Since Hinault's retirement – he literally hung up his bike on a hook thoughtfully provided at his farewell party – the search for a new Superman has been unproductive. The most obvious candidate is LeMond. Three Tour wins, by definition, make him one of *les grands*. But apart from the fact that the French would be loath to elect an American to the part – a nice irony, that – it doesn't seem to appeal to LeMond either. He is a marvel, no doubt about that. He can overcome enormous difficulties, even if he has to make them for himself. But he is not an old-style boss of the peloton, more the personnel officer. He is friendly and buoyant, a good mixer with allies and rivals, but in the heat of competition is equally adept at playing riders off against each other and using their own strength against them. When he feels that it's time to attack, he does it with style and courage, but also with economy, and for the most part appears to ride with events instead of trying to dominate them. Four stage wins in three Tour victories is pretty self-effacing.

Laurent Fignon looked like filling the role at one time. His first Tour win in 1983 may have owed much to Hinault's absence and Pascal Simon's accident, but his repeat performance the following year was so overpowering that he relegated Hinault to more than 10min, LeMond to nearly 12 and Simon to 21. There was no glib answer to that. The slightly owlish young Parisian with his long blond hair and John Lennon glasses had, at twenty-three, become a major player. His approach to racing has changed very little over the years: he is strong and assertive, a naturally aggressive rider as he showed in his victories in the 1989 Giro and consecutively in the Milan-San Remo. And but for LeMond's final spurt – and maybe LeMond's tri-bar – in 1989, it's Fignon who would be the current triple Tour winner.

What changed after 1985 was Fignon's luck. He suffered a series of tribulations – injuries, tendon problems, sinusitis, even the indignity of a tape worm – which he bore with less than Job-like patience. He has one of those long, expressive faces which exaggerate emotion. And where previously the press and public had seen humour and cheerfulness they were now met, more often than not, with a surly down-turned mouth and a hostile suspicion.

The disappointment was on both sides. Fignon was still capable of winning the Tour, but not for much longer; he had already turned thirty. There was some consolation in the fact that Fabrice Philipot and Gilles Delion, the best-placed Frenchmen in the 1990 Tour, were both in their mid-twenties. But neither looked ready to run the family business as Hinault, or even Fignon, had done, and frankly the older boys, Charly Mottet and Jeff Bernard, may have proved nine-day wonders but they had been a bit of a disaster over twenty-three. For the French in the Tour it was Fignon or no-one.

Yet maybe this was missing the point, and the days of the Superman were numbered anyway. He belonged to a period which was different in several respects. In his time the route was longer, but the racing itself was confined to certain key stages: the time trials and the high mountain sections where a strong man could impose himself, take several minutes out of his opponents, bring them to their knees. Now even the heavy alpine stages were often less than 200km long: still decisive, but by seconds rather than minutes. And fewer men cracked on them. The flat and merely hilly stages, too, had been cut. The Tour no longer hit the doldrums as the peloton wound across the coastal plains. There was racing every day, making it harder to control the bolshier elements in the pack.

In Superman's day the peloton had been smaller and more

homogeneous, and everyone knew his place: he was either a leader, a lieutenant or a *domestique*. Now there were not only more riders but more, and smaller, teams, so increasing the number of leaders. And to complicate matters, some of those teams might have two leaders and perhaps one or two protected riders in addition. The favourites couldn't be sure until the final week where the main threat was coming from. There were ten or more riders from almost as many countries who couldn't be written off. Each, depending on form and fortune, had it in him to win the Tour. But none was a Superman.

CHAPTER 10

And still there were four

Thursday, 5 July. We will probably not see another Tour in which the links of each stage form an unbroken chain. There will always be gaps to be bridged by car, train or plane. One explanation for this is commercial. Towns prepared to pay the price of hosting a stage aren't always placed a convenient day's ride apart. And the start town nowadays insists upon a package which includes not only the prologue but a second day's racing on its own doorstep. But for that, the Tour might have reached Nantes on Sunday instead of Monday.

The other is logistical. The shortest distance between two points, a trunk road, say, isn't always available to the Tour; the authorities have other traffic to think of. Nor does a straight line produce the most interesting racing. In the Alps and Pyrenees the course is regularly doubled back on itself for the sake of taking in another climb. Finally the shortening of the race, both to keep inside UCI regulations and to sharpen up the contest, has imposed its own constraints. Even if you take short cuts, you can't trace the perimeter of France within a self-imposed limit of 3,400km.

So, after only five days' racing, came the Tour's longest transfer, from Normandy to the German frontier. The convoy travelled by autoroute to Paris, round the périphérique and eastward on the A4 via Reims – a distance of 650km. The riders, with their managers, flew from Deauville to Strasbourg where they were staying the night. Or all but one of them did. Eddy Planckaert, the Paris-Roubaix winner, had such dread of flying (he had already cried off from the world championships in Japan) that he preferred to make the journey cramped in a team car. And although Moreno Argentin made the flight his first visit was to a hospital near Strasbourg. There, following his fall on the way to victory at Nantes and then again on Wednesday, he was found to have internal bruising and torn muscles in his right thigh and was forced to retire from the race. De Wilde and Hermans also abandoned overnight.

As these things go, and they usually go wrong, the flight was without mishap. It was delayed by no more than ninety minutes. But contrary to what you might expect, unless they're in need of a short break to recover from injury, riders don't welcome rest days. They would rather keep up the daily rhythm and get on with the race. Transfers, being even more disruptive than stationary rest days, are even less popular. Still the pause was a convenient moment to take stock.

The Canadian Steve Bauer remained in command of the Tour and of the gang of four who escaped at the Futuroscope; he led Ronan Pensec and Frans Maassen by over half a minute, and Claudio Chiappucci by more than a minute. The new man, Gerrit Solleveld, had a presumably short lease on fifth place after his exploit on the stage to Rouen. And the best placed of the favourites, Raul Alcala of Mexico and Sean Kelly of Ireland, the two PDM men at sixth and seventh, were still more than 10min down. Panasonic's Steven Rooks, a notable climber on his day, was at 10min 9sec, Stephen Roche at 10min 31sec, another PDM prospect, Eric Breukink, at 10min 35sec, Greg LeMond at 10min 31sec, Miguel Indurain with Gianni Bugno at 12min 20sec, and Pedro Delgado at 12min 27sec.

What this meant, in effect, was that except for Bugno and Delgado, who were paying for their inattention on the approach to Mont-Saint-Michel, the favourites had lost and gained very little on each other. Their relative positions still reflected their results on stage 2, Sunday's team time trial. But equally they had made scarcely any impression on Bauer's lead. Take LeMond. On stage 1 Bauer had beaten him, and practically everyone else, by 10min 35sec. At the end of the day, with the team time trial over, Bauer remained 10min 33sec ahead. And now, four days later, he still had 10min 31sec in hand. It was like sitting and waiting for the grass to wither.

In other sections there had been a little more movement. Chiappucci still led the mountain competition, but he no longer had the freedom of movement he had enjoyed on the opening day and was being pressed by the Russian, Dimitri Konyshev, and the Frenchman, Thierry Claveyrolat. Soon he might have to decide between defending his mountain jersey or his overall placing. Kelly was still in the struggle for the points prize, but in addition to the handicap of his thirty-four years, he was burdened by garish cuts and scrapes on arm and thigh from two crashes, in both of which he had fallen on his right side. He already held the record with four green jerseys, and had hoped to win a fifth before he retired. But at present it was being worn down by the remarkably consistent East German, Olaf Ludwig, who had so far finished in the top four on every stage. The Belgian, Johan Museeuw, was also ahead of Kelly on points. Sprinters for the most part being indifferent climbers, the points contest often turned into an elimination race. In the end Kelly's chances might simply depend on whether Ludwig and Museeuw could get across the mountains within the time limit.

Stage 6, Sarrebourg – Vittel, 202.5km
Poitiers, where the Tour first hit the open road, was the city in which Joan of Arc's divine mission was first revealed to her in 1429. Rouen was where she was burnt to death by the English twelve years later. And three-quarters of the way through this flattish stage, which brought the race into the valleys of the Vosges, was the village of Domrémy-la-Pucelle where, as all the world knows, Joan was born in 1412. If that 'all' was meant to include the riders, it was something they had probably forgotten. There was another underlying theme of the Tour which concerned them far more closely. This was the weather, which remained cool, windy and showery, adding to the sum of daily crashes and the punctures which are a by-product of gritty wet roads.

Chiappucci was to puncture twice, and each time at the foot of the only two climbs of the day, little 4th-cat côtes which normally he would have sailed across as though they were hump-backed bridges. Both fell to Konyshev, with Claveyrolat in close attendance, and this trivial mischance cost Chiappucci the white jersey with the large red spots on which he had earlier set his heart. By the end of the afternoon it rested on the shoulders of Konyshev, the first Soviet rider ever to wear one of the leaders' jerseys on the Tour. It would not please Chiappucci, even if he had fresh ambitions now, but it might placate Konyshev's Italian sponsors, the door and window-frame makers, Alfa-Lum, who were rumoured to be having second thoughts about their support for this all-Russian team. Theirs was a curious arrangement anyway. The firm leased the team from the Soviet Ministry of Sport for around £150,000, but the riders – unlike 'Slava' Ekimov who had made his own deal with Panasonic – were the lowest-paid in the peloton.

With a 61km individual time trial to follow next day, the favourites weren't expected to waste any effort today on trying to recoup lost time. But after a slow first 100km, undisturbed by Konyshev's short forays, it was Bugno who suddenly accelerated just before the feed at Toul. The speed of the chase and the effects of a cross-wind produced a number of crashes, and shortly after Bugno had been retrieved, another high-powered attack came from Charly Mottet and his RMO team-mate, Michel Vermote, drawing in, among others, LeMond and Rooks. LeMond afterwards said he was riding at the front to keep out of trouble and had simply reacted to events. But while it lasted the pursuit was furious, splitting up the peloton, and it was not until km 173 that order was restored and the pedalling wounded were able to regain their places.

The last break was a more or less private affair organised 3km later by the sprinters. Jesper Skibby, Guy Nulens and Giovanni Fidanza set it up, and to their annoyance were joined by Ekimov, Museeuw and the Dutchman, Jelle Nijdam. The *bête noire* of sprinters because he doesn't play it their way, Nijdam is not a popular man at this sort of party. The son of Henk Nijdam, 1962 world professional pursuit champion, Jelle won the Dutch pursuit title in 1985, and although he has won sprints from a small group he is more inclined to take advantage of his speed over his old track distance of 5km. He has used it to win a number of stage race prologues, including that of the 1987 Tour de France. And he used it again today to foil the specialists. While Nulens was setting up Ekimov for the sprint, and the other three were manoeuvring for position with rash disregard for the approaching peloton, Nijdam took a flyer from 300 metres out and held them all off at the line. It was his fifth Tour victory, and Buckler's third in six stages. For the rest it was stalemate.

Stage 6 result: 1. Nijdam (Buckler) 5hr23'56"; 2. Skibby (TVM) s.t.; 3. Museeuw (Lotto) s.t.; 4. Fidanza (Château d'Ax) s.t.; 5. Ekimov (Panasonic) s.t.; 6. Nulens (Panasonic) at 3".

Overall placings: 1. Bauer (7-Eleven) 28hr45'1"; 2. Pensec (Z) at 34"; 3. Maassen (Buckler) at 37"; 4. Chiappucci (Carrera) at 1'5"; 5. Solleveld (Buckler) at 7'26"; 6. Alcala (PDM) at 10'2".

Stage 7, Vittel – Epinal, 61km (individual time trial)
The time trial from Vittel, the Cheltenham of French spas, to the old garrison town of Epinal, promised a good deal more than it delivered. In the equivalent stage from Dinard to Rennes in 1989 LeMond's win had earned him the yellow jersey, and the runners-up, Delgado and Fignon, were also the two men who ended up on the podium with him in Paris. A similar show of strength was expected from LeMond this time. The jersey might still be out of his reach, but at least he ought to win the trial and cut Bauer's lead by two or three minutes. Some of the papers made it sound as though this were a moral imperative.

It didn't happen. LeMond did neither outstandingly well nor hopelessly badly. He finished fifth. And that, from the point of view of the reporters, was even worse. It left the whole issue as clouded as before.

The weather added to the ambiguity, making it hard to compare like with like. The earlier riders certainly had the better of it, with dry roads on the half-dozen short climbs and descents and the snaking bends of a heavy course. And these conditions held good for three of the riders – setting off two and a half hours before the last man, Bauer – who were to finish in the top four. They were Miguel Indurain, putting up what looked a likely winning time of 1hr 18min 29sec, Bugno and Delgado. Those who started later ran into rain along the way and finished in a steady downpour.

LeMond was one of them. He made an encouraging start, and the word from the 20km time check was that he had gone through 12sec faster than Indurain – though this was followed by news that Eric Breukink had been 6sec faster still. At 41km LeMond, disturbed by the wet surface, was now 38sec down on Indurain. Breukink had lost ground too, though not so dramatically. At 51km LeMond's deficit had eased to 34sec, while Breukink's had steadied at 30sec. It would need an exceptional effort from LeMond over the last 10km to regain the time he had lost on Indurain. It didn't come. Breukink slipped out of contention on the run-in, but LeMond could manage only 1hr 19min 16sec, which left him in fourth place behind Delgado. And a score of riders had still to complete the course.

In fact only one of them, the broad-faced, high-cheekboned Alcala, would beat LeMond's time, but sensationally he would beat everyone else's too. The fastest man at each consecutive check and gaining all the while – 39sec . . . 1min 22sec . . . 1min 40sec – he took the descents nervelessly, cut corners to the quick, and although he prudently eased on the last slippery 3km descent to the line, knowing that he had already won, he improved on Indurain's result by 1min 24sec. If you went down the results you would not find a bigger gap until you reached the 1min 46sec opened up between the men at 189th and 190th.

This still left the gang of four, starting last, to defend their lead against the world and their relative positions against each other. Here Pensec, not the smoothest of riders, threw himself and his bike into a frenzied struggle which took him into seventh place, beating the more fancied Bauer (fourteenth) by 17sec. Chiappucci came a respectable fifteenth, 23sec down on Pensec. And even Maassen, twenty-second, produced a solid rearguard action which suggested that he would cling to his unexpected prominence at least until the mountains.

Since almost every rider finishes on a different time, races against the clock are an accountant's dream, a reporter's nightmare. But when finally the balance sheet had been drawn up it looked like this: Bauer still had the yellow jersey, but Pensec had closed to 17sec. Chiappucci and Maassen were third and fourth overall. And Alcala having moved up to fifth was now in a different category: no longer a fancied outsider but one of the favourites.

Perhaps he should have been accorded that status earlier. He had worked hard to improve his technique against the clock during the winter. Three weeks at 3,650 metres altitude in Otomi, Mexico, riding 200km in sections in the morning, lunching on nothing but dried fruit, and then riding a fast dozen kilometres in the afternoon was rather different from LeMond's idea of a winter break. But this is what had enabled him to cover today's course at an average speed of 47.870kph.

Since winning the Tour de Trump, Alcala seemed a much more assertive rider. He was more settled in Europe, having found a home with his wife and son in Switzerland among a small colony of Mexican expatriates. And he was happier at the multi-national PDM team now that Rooks and Theunisse had transferred to Panasonic. There was no friction between the three men who shared the leadership. He felt he would have the support of Breukink and Kelly, just as he would give them his if the situation changed. PDM, with all three, plus their East German, Uwe Ampler, in the first eleven overall, were in a strong position to keep their opponents guessing.

After his injuries Kelly, too, was a good deal better pleased with his seventeenth place than another Irishman, Roche, was with his result. Roche had started well, but in the chill of the finish he had run out of energy from lack of food – in a word he had got the knock – and lost 3min in the last 3km. Realistically he had lost any chance of winning the Tour, just as Charly Mottet had done. Three times a winner of that time trial classic, the Grand Prix des Nations, he had finished 3.5min slower than Alcala.

LeMond, who had lost time on four rivals and gained only 32sec on Bauer, believed that the trial had been falsified by the conditions, in which he had taken no risks in his anxiety to avoid falling. But he freely admitted they were the same for Alcala 'who produced a superb performance', and for Pensec 'who rode better than I ever saw him before'. If he had made a mistake, LeMond believed it was in overestimating the difficulty of the terrain, and holding too much in reserve. When he finished he didn't feel he had covered 61km.

That morning he had ridden over the course with Pensec, and now seemed to take a brotherly pride in his team-mate's achievement: 'I adore Ronan. He is so open and interested in everything.' But clearly a delicate situation was developing, even if LeMond was too tactful to admit it. How Roger Legeay, the team manager, spelt it out was that Z's objective was to win the Tour. For the moment the team had two leaders, LeMond and Pensec, and it would be left to the mountains to decide whether that was reduced to one.

Stage 7 result: 1. Alcala (PDM) 1hr17'5"; 2. Indurain (Banesto) at 1'24"; 3. Bugno (Château d'Ax) at 1'47"; 4. Delgado (Banesto) at 2'5"; 5. LeMond (Z) at 2'11"; 6. Bernard (Toshiba) at 2'26".

Overall placings: 1. Bauer (7-Eleven) 30hr4'49"; 2. Pensec (Z) at 17"; 3. Chiappucci (Carrera) at 1'1"; 4. Maassen (Buckler) at 1'16"; 5. Alcala (PDM) at 7'19"; 6. Solleveld (Buckler) at 7'23".

Stage 8, Epinal – Besançon, 181.5km
The atmosphere of the Tour began to change as it moved south through Lorraine and into Franche-Comté. Rain fell lightly at the start, but the air was distinctly warmer, and on the sides of the heavily-wooded valleys mist hung between the pines. Mist, perhaps, for heat. This was the last genuinely flat stage for eleven days, and since it was also fairly short there were several riders, for whom the mountains would be an anxious, arduous slog at the back of the field, who wanted to take advantage of it.

It's true that in the opening 14km there were two 4th-cat climbs, but so short as to pass unnoticed if they had been in the Alps, and doing nothing to check the rapid pace of the field. At the first Konyshev, the new King of the Mountains, succeeded in pulling rank, but the second was taken in its stride by a mixed quintet of strictly palm court quality more interested in the first bonus sprint at 24km. This went to the Frenchman, Pascal Lino of RMO, and shortly afterwards the break came to an end.

Even so the pace was maintained, leaving four riders who were off the back little option but to retire. One was Alvaro Pino, the second leader lost to the SEUR team, who must now have been doubting the wisdom of riding three major tours in one season. Another was the Colombian, Martin Farfan of Kelme, the smallest man in the race (5ft 2in) but at least with a growing reputation as a climber. Disappointingly he had not even reached the foot of the mountains.

At 33km the stage ran through the cobbled streets of Fontenoy-le-Château, and it seems almost too much of a coincidence that next to make an attack was Michel Vermote, a man from the *pavé* of Flanders and the only Belgian in the French RMO team. He made so much ground that at the feeding station in the streets of Lavencourt (94km) he had earned just over eleven minutes. It looked as though the stage was being run as a benefit for him. But due more to his own dwindling resources than to any acceleration by the field his lead first gradually, then dramatically, narrowed in the second part of the stage. At 155km he was caught and immediately dumped by the bunch, and in the final 26km lost a little more time – 11min 16sec – than he had gained in the previous 120. He came in last, which cost him eighty-five places on general classification – a lesson in the folly of the lone break from which, with any luck, neither he nor anyone else will learn a thing.

The way was now clear for the members of the sprinters' club to make the running. Fifteen of them broke clear in the streets of Besançon, and thirteen of them came together to the line where in an uphill finish Ludwig beat Museeuw, his

Olaf Ludwig wins at Besançon, strengthening his hold on the points competition. He was to become the first East German to take the green jersey, and since the two Germanys were on the point of reunion, he would also be the last.

151

closest rival in the green jersey competition, by half a length. He also added a historical footnote to the records. World team time trial gold medallist in 1981, Olympic road race champion in 1988, winner of the Peace Race twice and the Tour de l'Avenir once, Ludwig, in his first year as a professional had become not only the first East German but the first rider from eastern Europe to win a stage in the Tour.

He was unimpressed by that. To him the win meant that he had made up for his defeat by Museeuw at Mont-Saint-Michel, and effaced the memory of Vittel where Nijdam had outwitted his Panasonic team-mates, Ekimov and Nulens. In any case it was not a record he could take much further. Next time he rode the Tour it would not be as an East German but simply as a German.

Stage 8 result: 1. Ludwig (Panasonic) at 4hr26′53″; 2. Museeuw (Lotto) s.t.; 3. Kiefel (7-Eleven) s.t.; 4. Colotti (RMO) s.t.; 5. Kappes (Toshiba) s.t.; 6. Lavainne (Castorama) s.t.

Overall placings: 1. Bauer (7-Eleven) 34hr32′3″; 2. Pensec (Z) at 17″; 3. Chiappucci (Carrera) at 1′7″; 4. Maassen (Buckler) at 1′16″; 5. Alcala (PDM) at 7′19″; 6. Solleveld (Buckler) at 7′23″.

Stage 9, Besançon – Geneva, 196km
The last rain fell on the Tour as the riders signed on beside the grey river Doubs at Besançon. Soon the sun would be out, and future weather reports would talk only of heat, first welcome, then intense and finally oppressive. But not yet; this was a transitional stage. Moving on south towards the Swiss border, the riders wouldn't have noticed it but the roofs on the houses were getting longer; there were snow guards running across them and below the eaves the winter logs were stacked. And coming off the 1,325m crest of the col de la Faucille, even they, with their minds on more immediate problems, couldn't fail to see lac Léman and the white peaks of the Alps spread out ahead of them. They were looking into their future.

The present was trouble enough for some. This was what they call a stage of moderate difficulty. It was not, by the Tour's strict definition, mountainous; but except for the last

36km, as it crossed the border and made its way into Geneva, it certainly wasn't flat. After three low-category climbs in the first part of the stage, at 126km it reached the côte des Rousses, the first 2nd-cat of the race.

After climbing out of the valley of the Doubs the tempo of the peloton, reacting to numerous attacks, put several riders under pressure. Ludwig, the points leader, was beaten by Museeuw at the first of the intermediate sprints (this was the last day on which they would carry time bonuses) and was then dropped on the day's second climb, the côte d'Ornans. So too, more surprisingly, was Jean-François Bernard, and both had to chase to regain their places. Konyshev, in the red-and-white jersey, was also made to hustle for his mountain points, losing the first prime to Thierry Claveyrolat, his closest rival, but gaining the second and third.

After this spate of activity the escape by a score of ticket-of-leave men, which began to build up from 74km, came almost as a relief. But not to Bauer. Among them was the persistent Frans Maassen, taking the very last chance the Tour would offer to wipe out his 1min 6sec arrears on the Canadian and wear the yellow jersey, if for only one day. To the great satisfaction of the rest, 7-Eleven, on Bauer's behalf, were obliged to work furiously at the front until the escape was brought to an end at Morez (118kms), 'famous for its curious and audacious viaducts' and, of more interest to the riders, the feeding station just before the assault on the côte des Rousses.

Even then two riders escaped capture, the Italian, Massimo Ghirotto, and the Spaniard, Eduardo Chozas. This was no concern to 7-Eleven; they had got their man. But it was a blow to any sprinters who hoped to be in at the kill in Geneva. The 6km ascent of the côte des Rousses eased off into another uphill drag which took the course up a further 225 metres to the top of the col de la Faucille. This too was a 2nd-cat summit, but only when it was approached – as it had been in seven previous Tours – from the opposite direction, the south. Taken in reverse what the Faucille offered was a 900-metre serpentine drop in the space of 16km. If two riders had the nerve to swoop down its hair-raising curves they would reach Switzerland, which was at the bottom, long before their pursuers and build a sustainable lead for the last 20km into

Geneva.

For Ghirotto and Chozas it worked like a charm. At the summit of the côte des Rousses (where the peloton again shed Ludwig and Bernard) they had 20sec on the third man across, Chiappucci. At the Faucille they had 50sec. And after a reckless descent they reached the Swiss frontier with 1min 27sec lead on ten chasers (whose counter-attack would be thwarted) and 2min 20sec on the peloton. It was only just enough. Ghirotto took the sprint from Chozas 16sec ahead of the solitary Christophe Lavainne, a string of eight more riders who had tried to bridge the gap, and then the main part of the field at 37sec. For Ghirotto, a Paduan, it was his first stage-win since Guzet-Neige, 1988. That was the occasion when Robert Millar and a Frenchman, Philippe Bouvatier, with whom he was attacking, misread a policeman's signal and went off course 300 metres from the line allowing Ghirotto to slip by them. Ghirotto had got it right both times.

So nothing had changed except that Bernard – once reckoned a threat by Delgado – had slipped into the limbo of 110th overall. Konyshev was still in the mountain jersey, though having failed to score on the côte des Rousses was now only five points ahead of Claveyrolat. And Ludwig, despite losing almost quarter of an hour on the day, was still in the green.

Tomorrow the Alps. And then, as we had already said several times, the Tour will begin.

Stage 9 result: 1. Ghirotto (Carrera) 4hr47'7"; 2. Chozas (ONCE) s.t.; 3. Lavainne (Castorama) at 16"; 4. Holm (Histor) at 19"; 5. Louviot (Toshiba) s.t.; 6. Müller (TVM) s.t.

Overall placings: 1. Bauer (7-Eleven) 39hr18'47"; 2. Pensec (Z) at 17"; 3. Maassen (Buckler) at 1'6"; 4. Chiappucci (Carrera) at 1'7"; 5. Alcala (PDM) at 7'19"; 6. LeMond (Z) at 10'9".

CHAPTER 11

Proof positive

Cycle racing has earned a bad name for not simply turning a blind eye to drug-use, but giving it a confidential wink. On the other hand it deserves some credit for trying harder than many sports to discourage the practice through dope tests, sanctions and, in the case of some more enlightened managers, by active dissuasion. But clearly it hasn't tried hard enough or been sufficiently effective. The penalty for being caught out is a *suspended* three-month ban, a small fine which normally comes out of team funds anyway, and demotion to the bottom of the day's result sheet. In other words a warning to be more careful next time. Disqualification – and then for no more than six months – comes only if the rider fails another test within two years.

The UCI can't be taken seriously as opponents of doping until they bring in immediate bans for the first offence and life bans for repeated offenders; make it obligatory to hold dope tests in all events, not just the big one; and punish the team for the misdeeds of its riders. The last would probably be the most effective move of all. Some of the riders take drugs independently, though rarely without the knowledge of their teams. More often it is the managers and soigneurs themselves (with a number of shining exceptions) who create the climate of tolerance towards doping, supplying the drugs and encouraging their use. They do it to improve their results by cheating, and they would stop if they were held responsible for their riders' conduct as, for instance, football clubs are for the violence of their players on the pitch. The threat of suspension from World Cup races or major tours (easily accomplished by simply deducting FICP points) would do wonders to concentrate the minds of managements and sponsors.

In the end the sport will have to get rid of drugs, not just because they can be fatally dangerous, or because they are an unacceptable means of cheating, or even because their use is

illegal. It's because they are simply old-fashioned and inap-
propriate. However sophisticated the products become, the
drug culture of sport belongs to a more superstitious age. It is
repellent to a lot of the current generation of riders – the
LeMonds, the Bauers and the Delions – who are far more self-
aware and would like to leave the sport with their winnings,
their reputations and their health intact. And it frightens off
the big corporations whose money the sport would like to
attract.

The summer of 1990 brought good news and bad from this
particular front. And in the Gert-Jan Theunisse affair the two
were mixed. In 1988 Theunisse, a strong, hirsute Dutchman,
then with PDM, was penalised when a test revealed traces of
testosterone in his urine sample. He was penalised 10min,
which effectively meant that he finished the race in tenth
place rather than fifth. Still, he was allowed to finish it. His
career continued, and next year he was King of the Mountains
in the Tour and finished fourth.

In 1990, and now with Panasonic, he was riding the Giro
when word came through that he had again tested positive for
testosterone after finishing third in the Flèche Wallonne in
mid-April. That was twice in two years, and so the six months
ban should have applied. But because of a technical error – it
was said that the French Federation hadn't informed the
Dutch of the earlier offence, though everyone knew of it of
course – Theunisse was given another suspended sentence
and again was free to ride on.

The good news was that instead of taking their usual there-
but-for-the-grace-of-God attitude, the other managers and
riders (except those of Panasonic) delayed the start of stage 6
with a protest against Theunisse's continuing presence in the
race. And when that produced no results, twenty-one teams
demanded a meeting with a UCI representative. It took place at
Brescia on 28 May – with Guimard (Castorama), Legeay (Z)
and Stanger (Château d'Ax) forming a delegation from the
managers, and Hein Verbruggen, the UCI vice-president, leading the official group – and immediately got bogged down in
technicalities. Verbruggen agreed that Theunisse had been
positive twice, and that this had been notified by the president
of the jury on the Tour de France. But since the matter hadn't

gone through the proper channels, the Belgian Federation (within whose jurisdiction the matter fell) had only the second offence on their books. He could promise no more than that the UCI would discuss the subject again in August during the world championships in Japan.

Afterwards, however, Verbruggen did say: 'In the Tour of Belgium last year Sean Yates, positive with anabolic steroids, was given the benefit of the doubt. And Delgado in the Tour of 88 received the support of a minister. Why not Theunisse?' One reason why not was that the others were quite different cases. Yates had been found positive in one test, but negative in all the others. And since traces of the drug did not disappear overnight, it was accepted that a mistake had been made, probably in the labelling of samples. As for Delgado, he had taken a drug, but one which the UCI had neglected to ban. Legally he was in the clear. It looked as though the UCI were using these cases to confuse the Theunisse issue and avoid taking action.

By now, though, the French, stung by the suggestion that they had behaved incorrectly, had challenged the UCI's reading of their rules. And the absurdity of the situation had to be faced. On 13 June at the request of the UCI, and after France had confirmed the truth of what everyone already knew, the Belgian Federation revised their sanctions on Theunisse who was riding in the Subida A Arrate in northern Spain: he was disqualified from the race, suspended for six months, and fined 5,000 Swiss francs. Theunisse still protested that he was innocent, and that his body produced the testosterone naturally; but that was up to him to prove.

There were two more disquieting items that summer. The first was the publication of *A Rough Ride* by Paul Kimmage. He had started 1989 as a fourth-year professional cyclist and had ridden the first twelve stages of the Tour; and he had ended it in a new career as Irish Sports Journalist of the Year. There was no denying the book's unique insight or its painful honesty, and it depicted a world in which hormone doping was widespread and – in minor races if no longer in the big tours and championships where regular testing had more or less driven them out – amphetamines were taken with cheerful casualness.

The other item was a report in *L'Equipe* in late May listing the number of riders who had died of heart attacks during their careers or shortly after retiring from racing. There were many familiar names in the sport, among them the Briton Tom Simpson, the Spaniard Vincente Lopez-Carill, the Belgians Marc De Meyer and Ludo Van der Linden. But the greatest concentration was in the Netherlands, where sixteen riders had died young in the past twenty years, and twelve of these in the past four. It was difficult to prove a direct link between this rising mortality rate and the use of drugs (and in one or two individual cases it could be ruled out), but the anecdotal evidence was strong. A number of riders had been so shocked that they wanted to give up the sport, and the Dutch Federation had set aside a fund to investigate the cause of these deaths.

In particular there was concern about the growing use of EPO, a natural hormone injected straight into the veins. It had been developed in hospitals for use in dialysis and had never been openly sold. But supplies had slipped through to cyclists and those doctors and soigneurs who treated them. The advantage of EPO to the rider was that it increased the number of red corpuscles and so muscle-tone, improving performance by 10-12 per cent. Its effect was similar to blood-doping by transfusion, now banned from sport. And it was undetectable. Its disadvantage was that it eventually killed him. It increased the density of the blood, which became deposited on the artery linings, obstructed them and caused an embolism.

Because of its excessive demands on strength and stamina, long distance cycle-racing, and in particular a marathon like the Tour, has long attracted quacks with magic potions which promised to make the rider as strong as a horse. Systematic drug use in a more modern sense goes back at least to the 'twenties. Amphetamine was available from the early 'thirties. And Dr Pierre Dumas, who was the Tour doctor in the 'sixties, once described the immediate post-war situation as 'medicine from the heart of Africa . . . healers laying on hands or giving out irradiating balms, feet plunged into unbelievable mixtures which could give rise to eczema, "magnetised diets" and everything else you can imagine'. But this was less damaging than what followed as drugs became more powerful and more specific in their action – relaxing muscles, increasing the flow of blood and helping with breathing. Riders experimented with these without medical supervision, or on advice of the wrong sort from soigneurs who were about as well qualified to look after young sportsmen as the cut-man in the corner at a prize fight.

Cycling first woke up to the fact that it had a serious drug problem in 1960 when a Danish cyclist died in the Olympic road race in Rome. It was announced that he had suffered sunstroke, but more credence was given to specific allegations that his death could be traced to nicotinyl tartrate, a mild vasodilator drug which had been issued to increase the blood supply to the leg muscles. A special Olympic committee was set up to investigate drugs and cycling (in ignorance of the fact that there were other sports which used them). And in 1965 a law was passed in France making it a criminal offence to consume, prescribe or offer certain listed drugs which might artificially improve an athlete's performance. The penalty was up to a year's imprisonment and a fine of roughly £400. In Belgium a similar law empowered the police to search cyclists and their helpers during races.

In France this law was not enforced, mainly it seemed because professional cyclists regarded it as an intrusion on their personal liberty, and on the whole public opinion was behind them. Random testing was introduced into the Tour in 1966, briefly and ignominiously. Two doctors accompanied by a gendarme appeared at the door of Poulidor's bedroom in Bordeaux and requested a urine sample for analysis. They had clearly decided to test a national hero rather than some minor figure in the race in order to avoid any charge of timidity. Under protest Poulidor agreed to provide it. But the news that he had been subjected to this indignity spread through the race. Next morning the whole peloton rode out of town, dismounted and walked. The implication was clear: any more testing, no more Tour. The samples taken from Poulidor's bedroom were never mentioned again.

There was a price to pay for this insubordination. The Tour organisers, which in effect meant Félix Lévitan, decided that there had to be a showdown with the trade teams, who were behaving as if they ran the race and putting it into conflict with the law. The demonstration provided an additional pre-text for reverting to national teams in 1967. And during that Tour the riders were confronted with an even more shocking consequence of drug taking: the death of Tom Simpson on Mont Ventoux. Although heat and stress contributed to his collapse there was never any real doubt that amphetamine was the fatal ingredient. As Dr Dumas, who had striven to save Simpson with mouth-to-mouth resuscitation, told the press with deliberate understatement a few hours later: 'I consider it abnormal that a young and physically well-prepared athlete should die in the course of a competition.'

The old guard still wouldn't have it. At the end of the world championship road race at the Nurburgring the previous season, the winner, Rudi Altig of West Germany, and the next five riders placed, all famous figures – Anquetil, Poulidor, Motta, Stablinski and Zilioli – had unanimously refused to take a drug test. Yet Altig kept his title and the others were only briefly suspended. Now Anquetil, writing in *France Dimanche*, went so far as to blame Simpson's death on the new anti-doping measures. He wrote that to climb Mont Ventoux in such temperatures, 'it was absolutely necessary to take something simply to breathe. Some solucamphre, for example. But with this idiotic prohibition of all injections, it is possible that Tommy that day used a product less proven, less understood and perhaps more dangerous than solucamphre.' And Anquetil was to have another brush with the authorities later in the season after his unratified hour record. 'Young people setting out in amateur sports should never take stimu-lants,' he said afterwards. 'But when you ride 200 days of the year, it's practically impossible not to do it.'

That summed up the attitude of most of the riders of his generation. As swotting students and long-distance truck drivers took benzedrine to keep them awake, and practically everyone took a coffee-break when he was flagging, so cyclists were entitled to some form of artificial aid to help them through the extreme rigours of their trade. Drugs were no more than medication, and generally prescribed by private phys-icians. But even that didn't save some of the leaders from addiction or worse. And for *domestiques* all that was available was the loaded advice of older riders and the witch-doctrines of the soigneurs.

In the 1968 Tour, the second and last for national teams, Lévitan took some account of these attitudes. Not by dropping dope controls – which instead were stepped up to cover six to eight men a day – but by decreasing the riders' work-load and therefore their excuse for taking drugs. There were no desperately long stages, no great set-pieces like Mont Ventoux, and no mountains at all until stage 12. Instead there was a series of shorter runs with intermediate prizes intended to encourage the sprinters and the opportunists rather than the hard men. The race, which started appropriately from the spa town of Vittel, was sub-titled the Tour of Health, and despite its good intentions was deadly dull. For one reason or another the Italian trade teams withheld their top riders, which included the young Belgian world champion, Eddy Merckx. The field of 110 was the smallest for fourteen years. And one comparative nonentity followed another in the yellow jersey.

Finding little to enthuse over, the press yearned for the good old days, drugs or no drugs, and were highly critical of the present regime in their columns. Lévitan stoutly defended it. He went on television to say that for this modern style of Tour younger reporters were needed. The regular, admittedly rather elderly, press corps were observing it 'with worn eyes'. More out of boredom, perhaps, than heartfelt indignation, the journalists went on strike on the way to Bayonne – the very stage chosen by the cyclists for their action two years before – refusing to attend the start and driving 72km up the road to wait for the race in a car park. When it arrived they held up banners bearing witticisms like 'Field glasses for Félix' and 'Riders – Worn Eyes are Watching You.' They honked their car-horns at Lévitan, who smiled silkily as he passed. Poulidor gave a clenched-fist salute. Dr Dumas remarked, '*Ah, la Sorbonne des vélos.*' And that was that. In the absence of more stirring events the press had manufactured something to write about.

That Tour didn't win the campaign against drugs, but it did change the rules of engagement. Two men tested positive, the youngest rider in the race, and the oldest, Jean Stablinski, a past world champion and the captain of the French team. Both were disqualified, but even in Stablinski's case there was no public protest by the other riders. Nor was there ever again. There were times when the testing was lax, when positive results were not proceeded with, when apparently well-found rumours of a scandal were followed by silence. But the principle of testing was accepted, and those who wanted to continue to use drugs set about trying to beat the system by other means: cheating the controls, going easy on the stuff except in events when they knew they wouldn't be tested, or experimenting with those substances which, according to the current folklore, defied analysis.

In the most popular type of fraud, the rider gave the urine sample of a clean-living friend in place of his own. If the official in charge of the dope control was complaisant, or more often embarrassed, about the whole business, and left the room to allow the rider some privacy, then this could be done by pouring from a bottle into the flask provided. If not, the rider would provide the sample from a *topette*, a rubber bulb and tube which he concealed in his shorts. In 1976 the supervising doctor discovered two Peugeot riders doing this after the Etoile des Espoirs. Worse, when he made them give genuine samples, one of them drove ahead from Dax to Paris, intercepted him at the gare Austerlitz on his way to the laboratories, and with an accomplice put him under so much pressure that he destroyed the flasks. It was only after a week-long fight with his conscience that the doctor told the authorities and the riders were punished.

If the *topette* had failed so ignominiously in a minor race, it's hard to believe that two years later a rider would risk using it in the Tour de France. And not just any rider, but the man in the yellow jersey. Michel Pollentier, who was the Belgian national champion at the time, took the lead in the race by winning at l'Alpe-d'Huez which, on both counts, obliged him to visit the dope control. Two hours later news reached our unusually solemn press room in the church of Our Lady of the Snows that he hadn't done so and the doctor was looking for him. This was followed with surprising speed by a communiqué which turned the suspense story into something closer to black comedy. For attempting to defraud the control, Pollentier had been banished from the Tour, fined 5,000 Swiss francs (then about £1,200) and suspended from racing for two months. This would cost him all his lucrative post-Tour contracts.

The story was that he had concealed a rubber-bulb of urine in his arm-pit with a tube winding round his body to his shorts. And this had been uncovered as soon as the doctor, more conscientious than some, had insisted on applying the letter of the UCI rule – that the rider being tested should be naked from his knees to just above the waist.

On the rest day which followed, Pollentier, a polite, sympathetic and highly embarrassed man of twenty-seven, with a pale, thin face below thinning fair hair, stood on the balcony of his alpine hotel and explained himself with candour. He had used the apparatus, he said, after taking a branded preparation 'for the breathing'. It was permitted in Italian racing, but since he wasn't certain whether or not it was on the UCI list of proscribed drugs, he had decided to try and trick the control.

He made no bones about that, but if he had grievances they were that at least 50 per cent of the riders were using products – 'I'm not saying they are drugs' – that previous controls in the Tour had been more lenient, and that one rider, whom he named, had deliberately dropped back to third place on a stage because only the first two were automatically tested. 'They were looking for me,' he added illogically, 'because they want me out of the race.' Yet while nobody courted trouble more ardently than Pollentier, the whole testing system had so many random elements that 'Why me?' seemed almost a logical question to ask.

Compared with the knockabout of the Pollentier case, the Pedro Delgado affair in 1988, also involving the yellow jersey, trod a much finer moral line. Delgado, a quiet, reticent man from Segovia, well liked in the peloton (unusually for a Spaniard, he had spent two seasons riding for a Dutch team, PDM) had emerged from the Pyrenees with a 4min lead and the prospect of an uneventful ride to victory in Paris on the final week. Then in Bordeaux his problems began. The television channel, Antenne 2, began asking about rumours that Delgado had failed a dope test.

This was the first that most people had heard of them, but the following morning the Tour organisation confirmed that they were true. However Delgado had asked for a second test on the sample, as he was entitled to do. It would be two days before the results of this analysis were known, and meanwhile Delgado remained the Tour leader.

This was unprecedented. The positive result of the first test ought never to have been made public. It should have remained confidential until the result of the second test came through. Then, only if it confirmed the original result, would it have to be published, along with any penalties imposed by the jury. If it was negative, that was the end of the matter and nothing needed to be said.

Instead Delgado had to suffer two days of speculation and suspense. The events of the race were forgotten as everyone waited for the announcement which was to come at Clermont-Ferrand. But that, too, was botched – this was not the Tour's finest hour – because at the critical moment the president of the jury could not be found. It was late in the evening before the communique was issued. And that was as unsatisfactory as everything else had been. The second analysis confirmed the first. Delgado had taken probenecid (a drug which helps the kidneys clear uric acid from the system and so staves off fatigue). But here was the catch. Probenecid was on the banned list of the International Olympic Committee, which the laboratory had taken as its guide, but it was not due to be added to the UCI list until a week or so after the Tour was over. Delgado, then, was both positive and innocent at the same time. And had it not been for the original leak of information, the world need never have known. But it did know, and while Spain prepared a victory celebration, the favourite image employed in the French papers was of a laundered yellow jersey.

CHAPTER 12

The lost leader

It's true that a course is only as hard as the riders choose to make it. If they put their minds to it, they can turn a short, flat stage into an agony of effort and apprehension. Equally they can climb a range of mountains at a snail's pace so that, by common consent, nobody is put to any inconvenience. What they can do little to control is a stage which finishes on a summit. At the foot of the final climb there is no point in keeping anything in reserve and it's every man for himself.

The conventional wisdom was that the 1990 route was 'easier' than most recent years. For one thing it went clockwise for the first time since 1985, which meant that the Alps came before the Pyrenees, depriving them of their dramatic role as the setting for the grand climax. A role which many believe is their natural right. The Alps are generally sunny, with the occasional *son-et-lumière* of an electric storm for effect. The Pyrenees are often clouded with mist. The Alps attract bigger crowds of summer visitors. And although the highest point of the Tour would in fact be reached in the Pyrenees – the 2,114-metre Tourmalet – most riders would tell you that the climbs in the Alps were more difficult – steeper, less regular and with more wrenching hairpin bends. They also tended to be hotter and, unlike the wooded lower flanks of the Pyrenees, more exposed.

For another thing there were only three alpine stages, against five in 1989. Or to be more precise there were two in the Alps and one in the Vercors, the mountainous national park to the west of Grenoble. But each of these had an uphill finish – at Saint-Gervais on the skirts of Mont Blanc, at l'Alpe-d'Huez and, in the case of the mountain time trial, on Côte 2000 at Villard-de-Lans. Even if they didn't bring down the curtain on the drama – which seemed highly unlikely considering how tangled the plot had become – at least they ought to reveal to us at last exactly who the main characters were.

Stage 10, Geneva – Saint-Gervais, Mont-Blanc, 118.5km

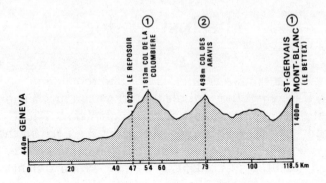

Tuesday 10 July, and for the first time since Nantes, exactly a week before, the sun shone at the start. Opposite the Quai Wilson the fountain on lac Léman rose in a thick column with not enough breeze to widen it into its usual plume. Out over the water the black kites swooped for food as though they thought they were seagulls. It was all very pleasant and restrained, though it beats me why the Tour bothers to come here, except perhaps to show its face to the Union Cycliste Internationale, which is based in Geneva. In French-speaking Switzerland they are not exactly hostile to the race, but neutral to a degree – like those people who make a point of saying that they never read the sports pages. And since the city hadn't allowed the Tour to put up any of its untidy cardboard arrows, finding the way into the start area was even trickier than usual.

There were no route arrows out of town either. So, in the absence of crowds on the pavement, you might not have guessed that the Tour was about to pass through but for a fair-haired young mother with two blond boys and a placard. Even they were unlikely to have been Swiss since their message read, 'Go for it, Greg.' Still none of this greatly mattered since after what was called the 'fictitious start' on the quai, the race would be appropriately neutralised and under escort for the first 10km. The Tourists wouldn't begin to ride their bikes in anger until they reached Annemasse and were safely inside the Haute-Savoie.

Even then they seemed reluctant to fall out before they had to, which was at 39km, when they reached the foot of the 1,613-metre col de la Colombière. This was one of the modern classics, scaled ten times since 1960, a 16km climb through the alpine postcard village of le Reposoir, averaging a little over 1-in-14 for most of its length, which meant it was a good deal steeper along some stretches and at the bends. At the top it disappeared into the cleft between two rocky peaks hung with cloud.

As the field arrived in close formation, the first to attack it was Omar Hernandez. Thierry Claveyrolat gratefully took his wheel but, once the Colombian weakened, he hit the front and stayed there, shaking off several other riders who tried to join him. When the Spaniard, Federico Bahamontes, was in his prime as a climber in the 'fifties he was called the Eagle of Toledo. Claveyrolat is known, a little less grandly, perhaps even ironically, as the Eagle of Vizille, after the village near Grenoble in which he lives. But although his main role in the RMO team was to help Charly Mottet win the race – a job with diminishing prospects it now appeared – this was not in conflict with his own ambitions to win the mountain jersey. He had been wearing it the year before when, after fracturing his wrist in a fall, he was forced to abandon in the Pyrenees. He had suffered other disappointments. In the late summer of 1989 he had led the attack throughout the world championship road race at Chambéry, only for Fignon to counter-attack in the final lap and, certainly not by intention, present the title to LeMond. And this June, having apparently won the Dauphiné Libéré in the mountains, he had lost it to Robert Millar in the time trial on the final day. But near-misses didn't seem to discourage him.

At the head of the Colombière he was alone with 35sec advance on Roberto Conti and 1min 23sec on Patrick Robeet, whom he had shed 2 or 3km back down the road. Another 11sec further back were Chiappucci, Millar and Martinez Torres. And at 2min 10sec were all the favourites with the exception of the yellow jersey himself, Bauer. But we'll come back to that, and stay with Claveyrolat.

While he had picked up 30 points on the Colombière, Konyshev had scored none, so Claveyrolat was already King of the Mountains 'on the road'. Now he went on to consolidate his position. As the leaders to his rear regrouped and slackened their pace, he proceeded to take the shorter and less severe col des Aravis at 79km, crossing the summit 2min 40sec before Conti who was still battling along alone, and 3min exactly ahead of the leading peloton. Christian Rumeau, the deputy racing manager of RMO, drove up beside him on the descent to give him this news and for the first time Claveyrolat thought seriously of winning the stage. But he had been disappointed before: 'The public were encouraging me strongly, and in that situation a lot of things cross your mind. You question yourself, you grit your teeth, you get a little worried. You can't be sure of anything.'

The long descent held obstacles which he could negotiate more easily alone – in particular wet, unlighted tunnels through the cliffs, one of them a mystery trip into total blackness since there was a sharp bend in the middle. By now there were those – though not necessarily the leaders – who were straining to close the gap; instead it was gradually widening as Claveyrolat showed no sign of failing strength. At the foot of the final climb, he still had 2min on the stubborn Conti, and 2min 25sec on a posse of fourteen pursuers, including Konyshev who must have been expecting Claveyrolat to crack and was hoping to pick up some of the pieces. And the main field – in quality if not quantity – were at 3min 40sec.

For a *massif* quite so massive, Mont Blanc is peculiarly inconspicuous for much of the time. We were driving towards it long before we realised that the greyer patches in the cloud above us were parts of its ice-covered surface showing through. On that scale Saint-Gervais was simply a base-camp, but the final 8km climb towards the ski station of Le Bettex was, in the matter of gradient at least, tougher than the Colombière. Claveyrolat faltered only once, 4km from the top, but quickly recovered to take his first stage ever in the race by nearly 2min, RMO's first that year, and also France's first if you set aside Marie's prologue. And since he had won maximum points on the cols, the mountain jersey, which he held by 62 points, also looked to be his for keeps.

The domes of discovery and crystal palaces of the Futuroscope, a scientific theme park near Poitiers where the 1990 Tour began.

(Below) Laurent Fignon in the carpenter's dungaree strip of Castorama, a DIY chain. Twice a Tour winner in the early 'eighties, Fignon lasted less than five days of this race.

The gang of four whose stage 1 escape turned into a twenty-one day wonder. (Above l-r) Frans Maassen, Dutch winner of that stage but the only member of the quartet not to wear the yellow jersey. Steve Bauer, the Canadian who doggedly led the Tour to the foot of the Alps. (Below l-r) The Breton, Ronan Pensec, who took over from him at Saint-Gervais. And Claudio Chiappucci, the Italian who held off Greg LeMond up to the eve of the finish in Paris.

Thierry Claveyrolat, 'the Eagle of Vizille'. Although the title may have been bestowed tongue-in-cheek, Claveyrolat went on to earn it with his adventurous defence of the mountain jersey. His was the only star performance by a Frenchman.

L'Alpe-d'Huez: the original summit finish in the Tour (1952), and the
Netherlands' favourite mountain playground. Gianni Bugno of Italy was
the first to the top in 1990, but yet another Dutchman, Eric Breukink, was
individually timed the fastest man on the climb.

For over two hours the main street has been closed to private traffic. Only the publicity caravan has passed through, filling the air with noise and the pavements with litter. Now, at last, the Tour. Here and gone in 30 seconds. But still the only world event you can glimpse from your own doorstep.

My enemy's enemy is my friend. On stage 13 from Villard-de-Lans to Saint-Etienne, Eric Breukink (Above right) and Greg LeMond, noticing that the new race leader, Claudio Chiappucci, is not going well, make common cause to cut his lead. On the slope to Luz Ardiden, LeMond attacks again, but this time his temporary allies are Miguel Indurain (Below centre) and Marino Lejaretta.

The last act of defiance. In the Pyrenees everyone waited for Pedro Delgado to attack – or everyone but Chiappucci (here on the Tourmalet), who decided to get his blow in first. He lost the stage but won a pyrrhic victory, saving his yellow jersey by just 5 seconds.

On the sport's most exclusive criterium circuit, the Champs-Elysées, Greg LeMond, at last in the yellow jersey, is borne home by a guard of honour from his Z team. The race isn't his until he is inside the last of the 3,400km.
(Below) Later on the podium he signals his delight at becoming only the sixth man to win the Tour de France three times.

Then third across the line, awarded the same time as the second man, Uwe Ampler of PDM and East Germany, was RMO's leader, Mottet. Claveyrolat was delighted for the team, especially since their success had come practically on the doorstep of RMO's headquarters in Grenoble; for Charly, since it proved that 'they had been wrong to bury him'; and for himself – 'I would have been happy to win any stage, however small, but this was one of the big ones.'

Still, Claveyrolat's exploit, appealing as it might be, was only the supporting feature. The main film was rolling a couple of kilometres behind him. Here Bauer, dropped on the way up the Colombière, regained 36sec and his place on the way down, and from there on the favourites remained grouped. Le Bettex would provide all the action they needed. Pensec only learned of Bauer's difficulties from his team-mate, Jérôme Simon (the gathering of intelligence in the field is often hit-or-miss). But he decided to do nothing foolhardy, like chasing after Claveyrolat on the Aravis, but simply to stay with the best in the peloton.

This was Z's general strategy, too. They would keep the tempo going to discourage attacks until Le Bettex, and then make their own bid. And although only the next few days would tell whether they had made a mistake in letting Ampler escape, broadly their policy worked. If there was safety in numbers, they had achieved it. Seven of their nine riders were with the top echelon as it arrived at the bottom of the climb.

They used their strength to maintain the pressure, Millar, Simon and Atle Kvalsvoll setting a pace which burnt off Bauer 4km from the line. What they couldn't control was the brusque acceleration of Delgado shortly afterwards. As we watched these moves on the television sets in the press room, we saw first Marino Lejaretta follow his wheel, then Pensec do the same. The voices of the commentators rose excitedly, scenting a third French victory to outshine even Claveyrolat's and Mottet's. And a Dutch journalist, finding this triumphalism slightly nauseating, trumpeted the opening bars of the *Marseillaise* as Pensec surged uphill. There were guffaws from other Dutch and Belgians, and a little embarrassed laughter from the French.

In fact Pensec couldn't hold the Spaniards' wheels, and a

kilometre from the line they dropped him. But it was no great matter. He was carried along by the next group led by LeMond and containing Indurain, Bugno, Chiappucci and the PDM troika of Alcala, Kelly and Breukink. Delgado and Lejaretta had finished at 2min 10sec. LeMond and company were only 19sec behind. And Bauer was to finish alongside Maassen at 4min 7sec. The old gang of four still led the race, but now the order read Pensec, Chiappucci, Bauer, Massen. Pensec had taken the yellow jersey by 50sec, and it was on his twenty-seventh birthday. 'To tell you the truth I have surprised myself,' Pensec told reporters who, if they're French, can usually do a pretty fair impersonation of the likeable, un-guarded Breton. 'I am very calm, and to tell you the truth, I am astounded with myself because that isn't truly my usual tem-perament.' But even if the truth he told wasn't the whole truth, and underneath he was highly excited, he still refused to bring out the words that everyone demanded. 'Listen, I'm not going to say to the whole of France, it's me, Ronan Pensec, the Jack the lad, who is going to win.'

Things would be clearer by Friday. But as LeMond told it, everything had gone to plan so far. He had not been feeling at his best, but he had come up to Pensec at the approach to Le Bettex and said: 'Stay with Alcala and don't concern yourself with Bauer, he's cooked.' And except for his short effort to match Delgado, that is what Pensec had done.

For his own part LeMond felt that Z were in a tactically perfect situation. 'I have no need to make a move, just to follow Delgado, Bugno or Alcala if they make an attack. And so much the better if I can help Ronan win the Tour. I am paid by Z. What is necessary is that a Z should be in yellow on the Champs-Elysées.'

Bauer, meanwhile, reacted in his usual decent way. He might have reproached Hampsten and Lauritzen for their ab-sence when he needed them on the climbs. But all he said was that he'd had a bad day, that he had done his best, and that he had 'without doubt lost all chance of winning the Tour.'

Stage 10 result: 1. Claveyrolat (RMO) 3hr24'31"; 2. Ampler (PDM) at 1'54"; 3. Mottet (RMO) s.t.; 4. Montaya (Ryalao-Postobon) 2'10"; 5. Lejaretta (ONCE) s.t.; 6. Boyer (Z) s.t.

Overall placings: 1. Pensec (Z) 42hr46'4"; 2. Chiappucci
(Carrera) at 50"; 3. Bauer (7-Eleven) at 1'20"; 4. Maassen
(Buckler) at 2'27"; 5. Alcala (PDM) at 7'2"; 6. Ampler (PDM)
at 9'22".

Stage 11, Saint-Gervais – l'Alpe-d'Huez, 182.5km

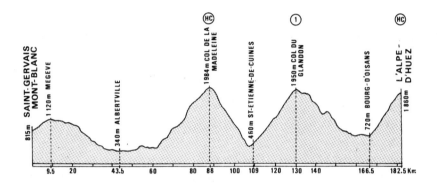

L'Alpe-d'Huez is to the Tour nowadays what the Galibier used
to be in those days when it was said of someone who had tried
and died in any attempt that 'he had met his Galibier'. It is not
that the Galibier has become any shorter (though its surface
has improved a bit since 1911), or that it has been neglected.
But l'Alpe-d'Huez has taken over from it as the climb on
which riders' fortunes are made and lost.

It was introduced in 1952 when the Tour first experimented
with summit finishes (two more followed that year), and it got
off to the most auspicious start when it was conquered by the
Campionissimo, the champion of champions himself, Fausto
Coppi. Later Coppi said, 'It is in winning at l'Alpe-d'Huez that
a rider knows he has become the champion of the world. You
always keep the memory of l'Alpe-d'Huez.' In spite of that
testimonial the mountain was dropped from the schedule until 1976, since when it has been included in all but the 1980
and 1985 Tours, and in 1979, to make up for its omission the
following year, it was climbed twice on consecutive days.

At 1,860 metres, it is not among the Tour's highest spots, nor
at 13.8km is it one of the longest climbs. And since it rises at a
steady 1-in-11 for almost its entire length, some riders reckon

that its regularity compensates for its steepness: it is not that hard if you take it comfortably. But that's a luxury few riders with ambition can afford, and coming at the end of a series of high-category cols, the climb deals out *coups-de-foudre* and *coups-de-grâce* impartially among the leaders. Curiously, since Coppi no rider who finished first there has gone on to win the Tour. But this is where Fignon has three times taken the yellow jersey, and only once, in 1989, failed to keep it.

Two other peculiarities make the climb unique: first, the twenty-one numbered hairpin bends (each displaying a telephone number to call in case of breakdown) which gradually jack up the road from the pleasant little tourist village of Bourg d'Oisans to the all-year ski resort. If you stop below in the valley of the Romanche you can see the whole of the ascent traced out in a zig-zag pattern of bold scratches on the face of the mountain.

The second is the overwhelming presence of the Dutch on its slopes. The attraction of opposites draws them from the Low Countries to the Alps each summer in any case. But all winter in the Netherlands coach companies offer two or three nights at l'Alpe-d'Huez as a special feature of their alpine tours. And those Dutch families who don't come by coach, park their campers and pitch their tents along the narrow ledges beside the road like sea-birds nesting on St Kilda.

Winter resorts look better when their raw edges and concrete footings are hidden in several metres of snow. And l'Alpe-d'Huez, described by its publicists as the Juan-les-Pins of the Alps, also has its share of brutally ugly buildings and straddling pylons. But it is older established than most, and more lived in. Its first ski run, called the Piste des Idiots, was built in the 1930s, and there are still remnants of the 'old' town.

But the Dutch haven't adopted the l'Alpe-d'Huez simply because it is sunny and agreeable, or even because the modern, funnel-shaped church, Notre Dame des Neiges, has a Dutch priest, Father Reuten (until a few years ago, it was used as a press room, and was probably the only church in France where, for one day of the year at least, there were ashtrays in the nave and a bar in the vestry, or where an organist was once asked to leave because he was disturbing the writers' concentration). No, what draws the Dutch to l'Alpe-d'Huez is the remarkable run of success their riders have had there.

A Dutchman had never been King of the Mountains until 1988 when Steven Rooks took the title, to be succeeded a year later by his friend and countryman, Gert-Jan Theunisse. But the Netherlands has consistently produced riders capable of making one great performance in the climbs, and this has been their favourite stage. Out of thirteen winners here since Coppi, seven have been Dutch: Joop Zoetemelk, Hennie Kuiper (twice), Peter Winnen (twice), Rooks and Theunisse. They have invariably played to a packed house of supporters from home, and because their enthusiasm heightens the sense of theatre, the Tour is happy to keep coming back.

This morning Rooks received a telegram from Theunisse, who was following the race from home and still contesting his disqualification for taking testosterone. It read: 'You, the donkey, you can win.'

The white pyramid of Mont Blanc was clear to see, and in its shadow the air was quite sharp as, shortly after ten o'clock, the peloton made its way upward towards the chalets of Megève before plunging down through the gorges de l'Arly, strung out by the new-found urgency of the RMO team at the front. Claveyrolat had a mountain jersey to defend, and Mottet a point to prove about the upturn in his personal fortunes. Everyone assumed that Banesto would launch a frontal attack today; they had little choice if Delgado was to recoup his losses over the first ten days. And although Z and PDM might watch and wait until l'Alpe-d'Huez before making a move, anyone who wasn't in at the kill there could forget about contesting the Tour this year. And that, of course, included anyone who trailed off on the two preceding cols, the Madeleine and the Glandon.

The Madeleine was the first *hors-catégorie* or super climb of the Tour (beyond category because once you have attributed 1st-cat status to the Colombière and Glandon, there's no further you can go in numbers). It began with a series of hairpins to gain height and then rose steadily, hugging the side of the mountain and getting some shade from a scrubby woodland of beech, ash and rowan. A shallow descent, which had to be paid for later, and on up to more exposed roads. Finally, passing the trees, it came out on a ledge which crept up the contours on the right-hand side of a high valley. In just over 25kms it lifted from 380 to 1,984 metres, and you could hardly deny that like l'Alpe-d'Huez itself, and the Tourmalet, Luz-Ardiden and the Aubisque in the Pyrenees, it belonged in a special category.

The first man Banesto threw into the battle was Juan Martinez-Oliver who attacked just after Albertville and 17km before the Madeleine. But it was to take a bigger sprat than that to catch any mackerel. The peloton refused to be drawn, and after the first 5km of the ascent he was nearly 3min ahead. Halfway up it was another matter; natural selection had begun to take over. Martinez-Oliver's lead was down to 1min 50sec, and only the fittest were surviving on the peloton. Bernard was on the point of abandoning. And in the rear Ludwig and the other sprinters were forming themselves into chatty little social clubs whose sole aim was to beat the time limit. Their time would come when they were back on the flat.

Martinez-Oliver was gathered up 7km from the summit, where the unflagging Claveyrolat took another 40 points – 7sec ahead of Indurain and 10sec ahead of a much reduced peloton of thirty-three riders which included all the old favourites apart from Bauer and Roche. So far stalemate. But on the descent Banesto threw in a far more serious contender, Indurain, who plunged down to reach the valley of the Maurienne with 35sec on Claveyrolat and a minute on the yellow jersey group. And the whole purpose of this move was to ensure that Delgado would find a reliable ally waiting for him when the favourites made their final moves before l'Alpe-d'Huez.

Next, after little more time than it took to pick up fresh rations at St Etiennes-de-Cuines, came the Glandon. Shorter than the Madeleine by 4km and allotted only a first category, the Glandon, in the opinion of the past Tour winner, Bernard Thévenet, was the hardest col in this section of the Alps. This was because its steepest section came in the last few kilo-metres when the riders were close to exhaustion. It took its toll on Indurain, who was caught then dropped by Claveyrolat, who went on to put his mountain lead virtually beyond chal-lenge at the summit. But Indurain had done what was required of him.

On the descent and in the 10km of straight valley road along the Romanche, where often in the past the head of the race has regrouped, the ONCE rider, Eduardo Chozas, caught Indurain and set off in pursuit of Claveyrolat. And the reason for Indurain's unusually measured progress downhill became apparent when moments later Delgado attacked. Although Alcala fatally hesitated, Delgado was unable to shake off LeMond and Bugno. The three joined up with Indurain, who then, to take the pressure off Delgado, led the pursuit of Chozas and Claveyrolat who in their turn were caught. At 20km from the finish these six had 1min 40sec on the Pensec group, and although it was being towed along by PDM – Kelly and Ampler in particular – the gap had widened further by the foot of l'Alpe-d'Huez.

There the remainder of the action unfolded, though the tall, courtly figure of Indurain played no further part in it. Having done all he could for Delgado, he settled for taking the climb at his own relaxed pace to finish in fortieth place. Chozas was the next to drop out, then at Bend 19, Claveyrolat. The three original favourites were left to fight it out between themselves, or so it seemed. Delgado led the trio, as he had to in order to strengthen his advantage over Pensec. Bugno sat in, and so did LeMond who, for Pensec's sake, could not and would not do anything to help the Spaniard.

Behind them Millar was sacrificing himself for Pensec just as Indurain had done for Delgado, though in his different style, staying close to his man, leading him up through the bends and finally towing six other riders – among them Breukink, Parra and Hampsten – as he closed the gap on the leaders. Claveyrolat, meanwhile, having been left for dead, was working his way through the field and staging a recovery as remarkable as any of his mountain conquests over these two days.

Three kilometres from the finish Delgado cracked, to be left floundering as Bugno and LeMond abandoned him, and then to be caught and dropped by Breukink, Parra and Claveyrolat. As the front-runners came round the final bend and into the finishing straight LeMond opened up his sprint and only just saved himself from hitting the right hand barriers (he had damaged a finger when he hit a pot-hole and crashed at the feeding station, and found it hard to grip the brake-lever). He recovered and surged forward again, and still seemed likely to take the stage until Bugno outsprinted him in the final metres. He was the first Italian winner at l'Alpe-d'Huez since Coppi. Breukink took third place and Claveyrolat fourth, which, since this was also a mountain prime, brought his climber's points to 228, compared with the 96 of Chiappucci in second place.

So, as the rest of the field straggled in for the next hour and three-quarters, who were the losers? Delgado certainly. He had managed to save himself from collapse, and helped by the timely arrival of his team-mate Aberlado Rondon, came through to finish eighth. But he had lost 40sec on LeMond, and for all the sacrifice that had gone into the day's campaign, had gained only 8sec on Pensec, who came in two places behind him, keeping the yellow jersey. Chiappucci had lost 38sec on Pensec, though he was still in second place overall. Marino Lejaretta, who had been threatening one of his famous late runs, was 3.5min down, Alcala 5min 41sec, Ampler 7min 58sec and Mottet 10min dead. And both Bauer at 21min 45sec and Frans Maassen at almost half an hour had finally declined from the eminence they had earned as members of the gang of four.

The riders now ranked behind its two remaining members were LeMond, Breukink and Bugno. Breukink had certainly provided the Dutch supporters – as vociferous as usual on the climb, though not quite as numerous – with a winner on the day. As an innovation the ascent of l'Alpe-d'Huez had been officially timed from base to finishing line, and since his was the fastest (43min 19sec, beating Parra by 4sec) he received a gold watch and bracelet worth, or at any rate valued at, £2,000. But of more importance, he had taken over as undisputed leader of PDM. After Martin Earley's retirement that morning, it had looked as though the team would be left with four chiefs and four indians, which could only cause trouble. As it was Kelly, their senior pro, had found himself fetching water from the team-car for the others towards the end of the stage. But LeMond had already noticed Alcala's decline in form since Epinal. And Alcala had admitted as much to Breukink that morning. Now Breukink was left as PDM's only credible candidate for the yellow jersey.

Bugno modestly declined to be compared with Coppi but, having risked humiliation by taking on a race for which he hadn't prepared so soon after winning the Giro, he had now abundantly justified his presence. He had done everything that Château d'Ax could reasonably have expected of him. But you never knew, with his confidence raised he might now come round to thinking of the double.

And LeMond, he was surely a winner – or was he? He had raised himself above all his supposed peers on a stage which Z had finally controlled more successfully than either Banesto or PDM. But he was still 9min 4sec down on the one man whom, in all conscience, he couldn't attack. If he was to win then Pensec would have to bring about his own defeat. And of all of them Pensec was the *victor ludorum*, having actually increased his overall lead in probably the hardest stage of the Tour.

You could sense a certain uneasiness about it. Everyone liked Pensec, he was so transparently honest; there was no guile in him. Everyone shared his own pleasure at having taken the yellow jersey and defended it by pure graft. But there was also something slightly snobbish in the way the news- papers depicted this affable rider with his shock of untidy black hair, his enthusiasm for Dire Straits and the Blues Brothers and, at twenty-seven, a conspicuous lack of substan- tial wins in his past record. Was he really, they seemed to be asking, champion material? It was one thing for Pensec to hold the jersey, another for him to wear it into Paris. But that evening in l'Alpe-d'Huez it looked remarkably as if he might. As Millar, his bodyguard over the mountains, put it: 'Today, in his head, he must be the winner of the Tour. Beyond that, I hope for him.'

By way of a footnote to Stage 11, Eric Vanderaerden, the Belgian sprinter with the Dutch Buckler team, was disqual- ified from the race that day. This year there were *commis- saires*, or referees, not only in cars and on motorbikes but flying in helicopters over the race. One of them looked down to see Vanderaerden holding onto the door of a team car on the Glandon as he tried to regain his place in the group which had dropped him. He was the spy-in-the-sky's first victim.

Stage 11 result: 1. Bugno (Château d'Ax) 5hr37'51"; 2. LeMond (Z) s.t.; 3. Breukink (PDM) at 1"; 4. Claveyrolat (PDM) at 4"; 5. Parra (Kelme) at 6"; 6. Rondon (Banesto) at 40".

Overall placings: 1. Pensec (Z) 48hr24'43"; 2. Chiappucci (Carrera) at 1'28"; 3. LeMond (Z) at 9'4"; 4. Breukink (PDM) at 9'28"; 5. Bugno (Château d'Ax) at 10'39"; 6. Delgado (Banesto) at 11'5".

Stage 12, Fontaine – Villard-de-Lans, 33.5km (individual time trial)

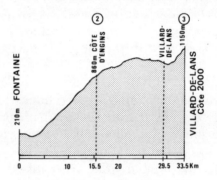

The temperature had dropped from the high eighties to the mid-seventies, and the rounder heights of the Vercors national park seemed comfortably fresh and leafy after the rocky expanse of the Alps. The region has sombre memories as the assembly centre for the Resistance, and the scene of a costly and unequal battle which they fought here against three German divisions in June 1944. But today the region, which boasts of being, according to its season, either all green or all white, is a favourite place among the French for walking and caving, for winter sports and children's summer camps.

Grenoble is as close to the Vercors as it is to the Alps, and although the time trial course started at Fontaine on the outskirts of the city, within a few kilometres it had begun its approach to the côte d'Engins, which had a 2nd-cat rating. From there it rose another 160 metres before dipping down to Villard-de-Lans, and finally climbed for just over 2km to the telecabin station on the 3rd-cat côte 2000. And since the earlier starters left at intervals of two minutes, and the last twenty – the favourites – at intervals of three, the stage took best part of seven hours to complete. A spectator who sat down at a café table with his mid-morning glass of white wine to watch the first riders pass by would have been in no state to recognise Pensec, the man who brought the procession to an end.

Thierry Marie, winner of the prologue, led in the early afternoon by returning 58min 18sec (which was to give him twelfth place), but it was only in the last hour and a half that the results began to take on any real significance. The first to set a potentially winning time of 57min 35sec was Indurain who by easing off on l'Alpe-d'Huez had kept something in reserve for today. Bauer, next man in, was over the hour; and two likely candidates, Lejaretta and Parra, were 11sec and 15sec slower than Indurain. But already there was word from the course that while Delgado was 46sec faster than Indurain at the check-point on the summit of the côte d'Engins, Breukink was faster by over a minute. And when the times began to come in for LeMond, who had started after them, they showed that although he was closing on Breukink and Delgado it probably wasn't quickly enough to beat them.

So it proved. Breukink, none the worse for his fast ascent on l'Alpe-d'Huez the day before, won in 56min 52sec. Delgado was only half a minute behind him, despite trouble with a rear wheel which was out of true and forced him to change his bike in the final kilometre. Indurain was squeezed down into third place ahead of Lejaretta. And LeMond, the time trial specialist, could manage no better than fifth place, as at Epinal. He had lost almost a minute to Breukink and 26sec to Delgado, whom he still regarded as the strongest man in the race.

And while the would-be leaders were counting their gains and losses an even greater upset was being signalled from the course where the *de facto* leaders were completing the trial. At the top of the côte d'Engins, with only 15.5km covered, Chiappucci had all but recovered the 1min 28sec by which he was trailing Pensec overall. He came up the final slope and through the finish in eighth place with 57min 57sec. And once 4min 29sec had passed and there was still no sign of Pensec coming up the hill, Chiappucci was led up onto the platform to claim his yellow jersey. He was still there when Pensec finally arrived in a state of near-collapse. He had yielded 3min 50sec to Breukink but, of more immediate consequence, 2min 45sec to Chiappucci.

He couldn't explain why suddenly his energy had drained away. He had ridden over the course with LeMond that morning, and had felt perfectly happy with himself. In fact he had even told Legeay, his manager, that if he felt the same in the afternoon he would make the watch explode. Instead he could find no rhythm, and over the last couple of kilometres had almost come to a stop. He was desperately disappointed, though he took the defeat with his usual good grace. That night he went into a bedroom of his own instead of sharing, as he usually did, with Jérôme Simon, and he slept for eleven hours.

It was now the rest day, and by the afternoon, he was prepared to explain it all as a *jour sans*, which could happen to anyone. He talked of going on the attack, though when someone asked him whether Chiappucci would win the Tour, he said he couldn't tell. He had seen him ride only once before, in the Paris-Nice: 'On the other hand I know very well who has lost the Tour.'

Nobody knew much about Chiappucci (*'prononcez Kiapouchi'*, advised *L'Equipe*). He was twenty-seven and lived in Varese; his widowed mother had a dress shop; he was a former cyclo-cross international and the most loyal of Carrerans; he was brave and industrious, a stakhanovite of the bicycle, Italy's Lejaretta. But even the Italian public, dazzled by Bugno and Argentin, and having already been forced to come to terms with the success of the unconsidered Marco Giovannetti in the Vuelta and the Giro, found it hard to see Chiappucci as more than the water-carrier he had been until recently.

Clearly we should have taken more notice of him when a few days before he said that he was saving himself for Villard-de-Lans. Two stages of sensible, defensive riding in the Alps had cost him only 21sec on Pensec, and now 33.5km of concentrated effort had recouped that and more. Here he was, the first Italian to wear the yellow jersey (which he dedicated to his fiancée, Rita) since Francesco Moser in 1975. And he would not be prepared to surrender it lightly.

On the face of it this had been a bad day for Z. Pensec was gone, and nobody really expected him to make a come-back. And LeMond, who had not been imposing, would now have to think of Breukink as well as Delgado as a serious rival. But at least the air was cleared and he could make his own race, without inhibition, in the future.

Stage 12 result: 1. Breukink (PDM) 56'52"; 2. Delgado (Banesto) at 30"; 3. Indurain (Banesto) at 43"; 4. Lejaretta (ONCE) at 54"; 5. LeMond (Z) at 56"; 6. Parra (Kelme) at 58".

Overall placings: 1. Chiappucci (Carrera) at 49hr24'8"; 2. Pensec (Z) at 1'17"; 3. Breukink (PDM) at 6'55"; 4. LeMond (Z) at 7'27"; 5. Delgado (Banesto) 9'2"; 6. Alcala (PDM) at 10'44".

CHAPTER 13

Tri-bar warfare

When Maurice Garin won the first Tour de France in 1903 he did so on a La Française bicycle with a fixed rear wheel. This meant that he had to keep pedalling as he went downhill. He could, I suppose, have put his feet on the handlebars (there were no toestraps to undo) and let the pedals twirl around below him. But on the rutted horse-and-carriageways of his time that would have been asking for it. In any case his bike would have been out of control. There was only the most rudimentary hand-brake which pushed a pad vertically down on the front tyre, and it was only by slowing the fixed wheel with his pedals that Garin could be sure of coming to a halt. The bike didn't have any other accessories, either; it was just a skeleton on wheels. But those wheels had fat pneumatic Dunlop tyres, there was a big leather saddle, and the frame was of steel. All told the bike weighed 13 kilos, nearly 29lb, about twice the weight of the machines in present use.

Garin, by contrast, was only 5ft 3in, weighed 9st 12lb and sat astride like a jockey. Yet he pedalled this bike, fixed wheel and all, at over 25km an hour for 2,428km. 'To me he was a little devil,' said Desgrange, the founder. 'He was the toughest of them all. Very powerful, a human dynamo, full of incredible resistance and endurance. He was a brute of a fellow, very provocative and high-handed.' And that was what counted to Desgrange, the man not the machine.

It mattered to the manufacturers who sponsored the riders, of course, whether the Tour was won on a La Française, a Peugeot, an Alcyon, a La Sportive or an Automoto, and whether it was equipped with Dunlop, Wolber or Hutchinson tyres. The *vélo du Tour* became a best-seller in the months that followed the race. But Desgrange had it right. A bike was the only vehicle whose engine could think, change its mind, show courage and feel pain and triumph. That is what interested him and excited the public. The bike itself was just the means to an end and, considering how much innovation there had been just before the turn of the century, the early years of the Tour stimulated surprisingly little.

Instead there were regular technical refinements. The free-wheel came first. It was introduced into the 1907 Tour by Emile Georget who demonstrated its advantages in the first true mountain stage in the Alps. On the col de Porte there was a tremendous duel between François Faber and himself which was unresolved until Faber, pedalling away furiously at his fixed wheel on the descent, was still unable to hold Georget who raced away to win at Grenoble. In all Georget took six stages that year, and would have come better than third overall if he hadn't been penalised for borrowing a bike after a puncture in the Pyrenees. But he had already made a sufficiently strong case for the free-wheel (as well as for a brake which squeezed laterally on the rim instead of bearing down on the tyre). Over the next few years almost everyone adopted it, and eventually it was made compulsory as a safety measure. In cornering at speed with a fixed wheel there had always been a danger that the inner pedal would touch the ground and bring the rider down.

The Tour was far slower in tackling the problem of gearing, where Desgrange stood stubbornly in the way of progress. The *derailleur* mechanism, a system for moving the chain along a series of different-sized cogs on the back axle while still keeping the bicycle in motion, had been used by cycle-tourists since 1905. It made its first appearance in the Tour of 1911 on the bike of a *touriste-routier*, one of the group of amateur enthusiasts who were then allowed to ride the Tour alongside the professionals. He didn't complete the course. The *derailleur* was written off as unreliable, leaving too much to chance. And although the mechanism had been much improved by the mid-'twenties, it was 1937 before Desgrange, coming to the end of his career, allowed the pros the benefit of it.

They had the use of gears, but it was tedious business changing them. The typical racing bike in the early 'thirties had a single chainwheel and four sprockets on the rear wheel, two on either side, to give the rider a choice of ratios. But to make the change he had to dismount, loosen the back wheel, move the chain across and reset the wheel. And if he wanted one of the sprockets on the other side he had to take the wheel out completely and turn it around. It was a nice choice whether to sacrifice time and make that effort or to plug on in the wrong gear; and it helped a lot to know what kind of country lay ahead.

The fact is that apart from his lack of interest in technical matters, Desgrange was at odds with the manufacturers who, he felt, were getting too much publicity from the Tour and putting too little into it. This led to his decision in 1930 to provide the pros in the national teams with identical and anonymous yellow bikes. He stuck to this policy for the rest of the decade, imperiously keeping out brand-named machines until 1939. It worked, even if it did inhibit experiment. But over the *derailleur* Desgrange was forced to relent. It did the reputation of the Tour no good when some unknown *touriste-routier*, smoothly changing gear in flight, left the pros tinkering with their chains and sprockets at the roadside while he rode off to claim a stage victory which his prowess didn't merit. It was also embarrassing that rival events, where the *derailleur* was permitted, were putting up faster times. As a matter of principle the Tour had to be the pace-setter. In secrecy Desgrange made his choice from the various *derailleurs* on the market, and ordered it to be supplied with no maker's name stamped on it. But something as complex as a gear system is harder to disguise than a bicycle frame, and everyone who knew about such things immediately identified it as l'Elu. The great man's ideal of the anonymous machine was badly dented, and the manufacturers could complain that he was giving free publicity to a rival.

Desgrange had some reason to be suspicious of innovation. For most of the inter-war years racing cyclists still rode on wooden rims, which were generally serviceable, though they might be distorted by prolonged exposure to heat and rain. In the late 'twenties, however, duralumin rims were introduced. Desgrange, not to be rushed into things, waited until 1935 before equipping the Tour bikes with them, and then the result was all that a sceptic might have wished. As soon as the race hit the alpine descents, one after another the tyres rolled off and riders began to demand the return of their old wooden rims. The cause of the problem was that continual braking had heated the rims and melted the adhesive which kept the tyres in place. And although it was easily solved by changing the cement not the rims, Desgrange's Luddite instincts seemed to be justified.

One innovation he did introduce in 1923, much against his will, was the neutral service car which followed behind the race to replace equipment for riders who got into mechanical trouble. And by 1937 he was providing each team with its own service car. Until then the rider had been responsible for his own repairs, and was obliged to return to Paris as he had left it, with the same bicycle frame and even the same wheel hubs. As a result the men raced as if they were mobile mechanics, with a bag of tools cemented to the frame. It would typically contain a spoke key and spare spokes, a pair of wing nuts, a pair of brake blocks, an eight-hole or a shifting spanner, replacement pedal straps, and rolls of Chatterton compound (an English product intended for insulating electric wires) which

Breaking for a fag in the 1927 Tour. Notice the goggles as protection against the dust, and the spare tyres slung across the shoulders. Service cars had been introduced four years earlier, but riders still took their own precautions against punctures. 185

they used at one period for attaching the tyres. They also carried an obligatory spare tyre under the saddle and another two spares across their shoulders. Plus, of course, a pump. And even with the new arrangements, riders continued to equip themselves to deal with punctures since, like policemen, service cars were never there when you wanted them.

All the same, the benefit of independent service was felt immediately. While riders were, and still are, handicapped by punctures and mechanical breakdowns, none in future lost the Tour through having to repair a broken frame or fork. The immediate influence of the *derailleur* was less apparent, but only because there were only to be three more Tours before the second world war broke out.

After the war, with the number of sprockets available increasing from three to four then five, and with a second chain-wheel added to double the options, the *derailleur* was seen to put a couple of kilometres an hour on the average speed of the race. It was not the only accelerator. Lighter materials were now used in making the frames and accessories, and tyres became a circular puff of air. But it was the *derailleur* which made the essential difference to post-war racing.

The early tours were like massed start time trials; within half a dozen kilometres the riders became separated and were strung out along the road from strongest to weakest. Later they were more like running marathons, the favourites forcing their way ahead, trying to keep each other in sight, while the rest remained in loose and gradually disintegrating groups. The *derailleur*, by allowing more flowing, continuous movement, encouraged a different style of racing to develop. The peloton became the mobile base of operations.

A leader no longer led from the front throughout the race. He stayed with his *équipiers* in the peloton until he judged that the time or place was opportune for an attack. Or else an opponent did so first, in which case he broke away in pursuit or, with the help of his team, forced up the speed of the peloton to narrow the gap. On a long flat stage he might start and finish in the peloton and never leave it all day, gaining nothing but also giving nothing away. Even on a mountain stage the peloton might remain intact for most of its distance with the leaders saving their energy for the last cols or the climb to the finish. There was safety in numbers; other members of the team were always close by to lend support in case of emergency.

It did not mean that solo breakaways and duels in the peaks were a thing of the past. But there was more negative riding in the intervals between the great set-piece showdowns in the Alps and Pyrenees and in the time trials. Tactical racing had arrived, and more than anything else, the *derailleur* had made it possible.

For a period in the 'sixties and 'seventies the technology of racing cycles stood fairly still except in the application of lighter materials – titanium and carbon fibre for frames; nylon and various alloys for accessories. Leisure cycling, with mini-bikes, stowaways, choppers and mountain bikes, was perceived as the growth area and distracted the manufacturers' attention. But in the last decade there has been another inventive surge. It has given racing the strapless pedal binding to supplant the toestrap and toeclip; the 'black box' handlebar computer to measure time, distance, speed, gradient, altitude, pedal rhythm and heartbeat; and those narrow, mean-looking shockproof sunglasses, popularised by Greg LeMond, without which no rider with any sense of style nowadays feels properly dressed.

Once lightness had reached an almost irreducible minimum – and heretics had begun to question whether further reduction would serve any purpose anyway – what began to preoccupy designers was the question of aerodynamics, particularly in the time trial. The result was the low-profile bike plunging down to the smaller front wheel. The rider crouched forward, rodeo-fashion, keeping a grip on bull-horn handlebars which bent outward and upward instead of forward and down. And to that was added the *lenticulaire*, the carbon disc wheel which prevented the wind catching in the rigging of the spokes.

The other problem which attracted just as much attention was how to deal with that bulky, vertical object which was the bike's most important accessory, but also the hardest to streamline: the rider. First he was put into new kit. Lycra and other synthetic fibres in place of cotton and silk for every day;

smooth, seamless and wrinkle-free skinsuits for time trials. Hard shell safety helmets and, again for racing against the clock, the coal-scuttle helmet coming to a point between the shoulder-blades. Some ergonomists believe this headgear so important that in future they visualise individual fitting and testing in wind-tunnels.

Then fresh attention was given to the rider's posture in relation both to the mechanical functions of the body in driving the bike forward and to wind resistance. And the answer that Scott, the American manufacturer, first came up with was the delta-shaped tri-bar. Yet again its use was restricted to the time trial, but that had become such a crucial sector of the Tour that it was well worth separate study. And because the other riders were convinced that for Greg LeMond the tri-bar produced a measurable improvement in performance, they adopted it with more alacrity than any previous innovation in their field.

At its simplest, the tri-bar is a loop of tubing attached to the centre of the handlebars and sloping upward and forward. When it is gripped, with the forearms resting on two padded supports just behind, it brings the body forward with the arms tucked in. This is the position adopted by the downhill skier. The theory is that the airstream flows around the rider's body instead of building up resistance between his outspread arms, and the theory appears to be borne out. Whether or not the same could be said for the tri-bar which LeMond went on to use in 1990 – a single joy-stick model, the LeMond Extreme – is open to doubt. Second in the prologue and a couple of fifth places later on proved nothing either way.

There was some ill-feeling in France over LeMond's pioneering use of tri-bars in 1989, even though it was authorised. The ruling had come late and caught other teams out; they hadn't the same equipment available and they hadn't any real experience of using it. And although, a year later, everyone who wanted them had tri-bars, there was further resentment when Castorama's plea to use a saddle with a rear support in the prologue at the Futuroscope was rejected. Thierry Marie had ridden with one in his 1986 prologue victory – it had passed unnoticed until afterwards – and both he and Fignon wanted to use it. In other races, too, the *commissaires* had sometimes given clip-on tri-bars and back supports their blessing, and sometimes frowned upon them, an inconsistency which the UCI dealt with at their meeting in Japan in August 1990. They ruled that both were permissible, and relaxed Article 49, which defined the racing bicycle, to a point where the only limits on design related to minimum sizes, but with two provisos. No fairings could be fitted, or anything that acted as a fairing, and any equipment used had to be commercially available. In other words no team could monopolise a new development.

The future trend seems to be towards *monocoque* design with the frame and rear forks moulded in one piece; wheels without spokes and eventually without pneumatic tyres; hydraulic brakes. Desgrange wouldn't have approved at all, but Garin probably would.

CHAPTER 14

Alone against everyone

Greg LeMond spent the rest day which followed the Villard-de-Lans time trial with his family at Grenoble, cycling 30kms or so back to his team hotel at Autrans – his one stint of training – shortly after five in the evening. The previous year the rest day had been restlessly consumed by end-to-end interviews, and he had been determined not to make that mistake again. But now on his return he talked to the press and reviewed his situation. In short, he had more confidence in himself or Delgado winning the Tour than he had in Breukink, whom he felt was relying on him to do the attacking. But he also added that Chiappucci was more dangerous than anyone had thought.

In eight days' time at lac de Vassivière-en-Limousin the Tour would reach the third and last individual time trial, a stage which had become the great tie-breaker in recent years. If on the eve of the entry in Paris there was still unsettled business, that is where the final accounts would be paid. But really it shouldn't come to that. Over the next week there was a 1st-cat finish at the Causse Noir in the Aveyron; a *hors-catégorie* finish at Luz-Ardiden; a second stage in the Pyrenees which came back to earth at Pau but included the Aubisque; and a run through the Dordogne and Haute-Vienne to Limoges which, though not mountainous, covered scarcely a metre of level ground. What more opportunity could the leaders need to attack Chiappucci and each other?

The reporters asked LeMond what tactics he would use. 'Even if I had a tactical plan I would not reveal it,' he said, which couldn't have surprised them. 'What I hope for, simply, is that the racing will be hard.'

Stage 13,Villard-de-Lans – Saint-Etienne, 149km
Saturday, 14 July. Bastille Day, and an Italian in the yellow jersey. So, as you might suppose, when the race moved north-

west towards the Ardèche and the Loire with large crowds enjoying a continuous *buffet campagnard* at the wayside, the fireworks started early. Not that the French riders themselves did much more than light the blue touch paper and retire.

In fact it was an Australian, Phil Anderson, who caused the first panic, leading the descent from Villard-de-Lans and down through the narrow gorge of the Bourne at such a wild pace that the police motorcyclists had to pull over and let him pass. They could only hope that the road ahead was clear. When Mottet chased after him the peloton, for old time's sake, refused to let him go, and that skirmish petered out at 33km. But thanks to Anderson's initiative they had shortened their working day by covering 51.25km in the first hour.

Immediately there was another break by five men which lasted until 40km. Then came an attack by Tolhoek and Vermote who held the stage for 16km. And this was followed in turn by a thirteen-man escape composed mainly of sprinters but supported by Bauer, who must have hoped that lightning would strike twice.

So far the favourites had stood aloof, like lions watching their cubs at play and knowing that one cuff from their paw would restore order. But at 90km was the 4th-cat côte d'Ardoix, and shortly before it Pensec and Claveyrolat led a counter-attack which, after chasing and retrieving, put thirty riders into the lead.

Still LeMond, Breukink and Delgado made no move, but LeMond couldn't but notice that Chiappucci – anxious that Pensec should not steal time on him – was getting little or no support from his Carrera men who were at the tail of the field. Instead of being given the comfortable ride he was entitled to expect, he was having to lead the pursuit himself and looked surprisingly vulnerable. This gave LeMond ideas.

Chiappucci's efforts brought the main peloton up to the breakaway at Annonay, 27kms from the summit of the day's last climb, the 2nd-cat col de la-Croix-de-Chaubouret, from which it was only 18km downhill to the finish at Saint-Etienne. Just at the juncture of the two groups, another attack was launched by ten riders, and this time LeMond, his team-mate, Eric Boyer, Breukink, Hampsten and Indurain were among them. This, unlike the earlier by-play, was serious stuff.

At the foot of the col Delgado, Bugno and Lejaretta set up a counter-attack which left Chiappucci stranded in the main field. But although the loyal Indurain dropped back from the front group to help his leader, LeMond led his party over the summit 30sec ahead of Delgado's and more than 4min ahead of the Chiappucci peloton. And with LeMond and Breukink making common cause, these gaps were maintained to the finish.

There Eduardo Chozas, who had come along for that very purpose (and had ridden, he admitted, 'a little like a tourist', not putting in any effort) won the sprint from Breukink, Hampsten and LeMond (not to forget Conti, another opportunist). It was his fourth Tour stage win, but his first ever in a sprint finish, and he was looking forward excitedly to seeing the photographs. What interested the others was the half-minute they had gained on Delgado and Bugno. And it didn't end there. An intermediate group including Alcala, Roche and Parra came in at 3min 9sec. Chiappucci and company were at 4min 53sec. And the unlucky Pensec, whose mid-stage raid had rebounded on him and had provided LeMond with the springboard from which to attack, did not arrive until 7min 47sec had passed.

The ironical result was that Chiappucci had actually increased his overall lead. Instead of being 1min 17sec ahead of Pensec, he now had 2min 2sec on the new runner-up, Breukink, and 2min 34sec on the number three, LeMond. But there wasn't much doubt which was the more comfortable situation. If the race went on like this he'd see the last of his yellow jersey before he saw the Pyrenees.

Stage 13 result: 1. Chozas (ONCE) 3hr20′12″; 2. Breukink (PDM) s.t.; 3. Hampsten (7-Eleven) s.t.; 4. Conti (Ariostea) s.t.; 5. LeMond (Z) s.t.; 6. Lejaretta (ONCE) at 30″.

Overall placings: 1. Chiappucci (Carrera) 52hr49′13″; 2. Breukink (PDM) at 2′2″; 3. LeMond (Z) at 2′34″; 4. Pensec (Z) at 4′11″; 5. Delgado (Banesto) at 4′39″; 6. Bugno (Château d'Ax) at 6′25″.

Stage 14: Le Puy-en-Velay – Millau (Causse Noir), 205km

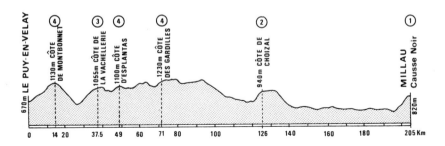

Causse, we eventually discovered after many blank looks from people who supposedly spoke the language – the French, for instance – is the regional dialect word for a mountain split by a river or a gorge. It is not a term you have a lot of need for in most parts of the country, but it certainly had its place on today's route through a selection of the geological freaks and splendours of the Auvergne and the Midi-Pyrénées.

Le Puy-en-Velay, an hour by road from Saint-Etienne, is called 'the strangest city in France', being dominated within its limits by two grotesque spires of rocks, one capped by a 16-metre statue of Notre Dame made of bronze from 213 cannons captured at Sebastapol, the other by a Byzantine-style chapel. It was an apt introduction to a stage which ran through granite and volcanic mountains and along the gorges du Tarn to finish at the heart of the Grands Causses, and in particular on the Causse Noir, a twisting 1-in-16 climb less than 8km long but hard enough to be rated 1st cat. With five other lesser climbs along the way, including the 2nd-cat côte de Choizal at 126km, and the sinuous gorges in which an escape could be out of sight in less than 100 metres, this was inviting terrain for guerilla warfare. Not that you would have guessed it from the calm of the tented village where the hard local Cantal cheese was being offered, and Steve Bauer sat at a table auto-graphing posters of himself in the yellow jersey. Those nine days in which he led the Tour already seemed an age away.

The peloton began to fracture from 8km, the start of the first hill, Claveyrolat following on the wheel of his team-mate Jean-Claude Colotti as though he still felt insecure in his mountain jersey. They were brought back but Colotti went again, taking three men with him, and provoking a counter-attack by thirteen, including Millar and Kvalsvoll; clearly it was Z's policy to make the stage as difficult as possible both to unsettle Chiappucci and forestall an orderly arrival at the foot of the Causse Noir where Delgado could choose his opportunity to climb away.

Again the group were caught; again Colotti attacked; and again Millar joined a posse of seventeen chasers who caught him at 91km. But this time the peloton didn't resist. The air was heavy and humid – 'Why doesn't someone turn the heat off?' Roche asked – and the favourites decided that, for the time being, they could leave it to natural wastage to solve their problem. The lead of the breakaway reached 5min before it began to decline, and at the summit of Choizal was down to 2min 45sec. On the descent leading to the dark shelter of the gorges du Tarn, Jean-Claude Bagot, following the example of his RMO team-mate Colotti, decided that he would have a better chance if he escaped alone. But he was only partially successful, for five of his confederates had rejoined him before the banner announcing 20km to the finish.

Now, too, the peloton, led by Delgado's Banesto team and Bugno's Château d'Ax, were in full cry. By the time they reached the foot of the Causse Noir they had recaptured all but the six leading escapers, and these had only a few minutes' liberty left. At 4km from the top what had been a bunch of riders was now stretched out in an unravelling string, with a dozen men, nearly all of them past or present favourites, detaching themselves from the front. Indurain was at the head of this group, Chiappucci at the rear being aided and encouraged by his team-mate, Gianelli. At 3km Lejaretta abruptly left them, with Indurain and Bugno following at a gradually increasing distance, and LeMond, Breukink and Delgado locked together in their private feud a little further back.

So ended in that order – except that Alcala nipped ahead to take fourth place from LeMond – a hot, fractious stage of what the Tour would describe as 'moderate difficulty'. There were no momentous changes. LeMond had lost 9sec on Bugno, but he had held Delgado and Breukink and gained, as they had, 13sec on Chiappucci. The Italian's overall lead on Breukink was now down to 1min 49sec, and he admitted that he would need a good deal more insurance than that to protect him when it came to the time trial at the lac de Vassivière.

Marino Lejaretta, although he hadn't moved up from seventh overall, was now only 5min 15sec behind LeMond. The Pyrenees, practically his home mountains, were ranged on the horizon. And at thirty-three, a veteran of ten Vueltas, six Giros and seven Tours de France, he had just won his first Tour stage. If he showed no emotion when he crossed the line, it was only because he was convinced that someone, he didn't know who, had crossed it ahead of him. But even after the pleasant shock of finding that he had, after all, achieved one of his remaining ambitions, he didn't go on to contemplate the yellow jersey. He had finished the Giro in seventh place a month before, and said he would be content to do the same here. Instead his hopes were for the team.

With Chozas's victory on Saturday, it had been a splendid weekend for ONCE, and they were now second to Z in the team competition. They had won this prize in the Vuelta and Giro, and since few teams contemplate riding the three great tours in one season, to come top in them all would be quite a performance. And although Lejaretta didn't say so, it would also be in a good cause. The letters ONCE are the initials of the national organisation for the blind in Spain, the most surprising sponsors in the sport.

ONCE, in fact, is a highly prosperous concern, its wealth based on a state-granted monopoly in the sale of lottery tickets. And under the astute direction of Miguel Duran Compos, who is himself blind, this has been increased by investment in real estate, industry and communications to the point where in 1989 it had a turnover of £1,500 million. In that year ONCE came into cycle racing sponsorship for the normal commercial reasons and, with a budget of around £2.5 million, its team is one of the most prosperous in the field. Otherwise it is indistinguishable from the others. It employs a soigneur, Miguel Angel Rubio, who is blind, but even that is not unique. Coppi chose a blind soigneur to look after him too.

Stage 14 result: 1. Lejaretta (ONCE) 5hr12′3″; 2. Indurain (Banesto) at 24″; 3. Bugno (Château d'Ax) at 25″; 4. Alcala (PDM) at 33″; 5. LeMond (Z) at 34″; 6. Breukink (PDM) s.t.

Overall placings: 1. Chiappucci (Carrera) 58hr2′3″; 2. Breukink (PDM) at 1′49″; 3. LeMond (Z) at 2′21″; 4. Delgado (Banesto) at 4′26″; 5. Pensec (Z) at 4′55″; 6. Bugno (Château d'Ax) at 6′3″.

Stage 15, Millau – Revel, 170km
Although it was hilly enough to conjure up one 2nd-cat and three other lesser climbs, today's countryside was rounder and more domesticated, and the racing a good deal less craggy than we had become used to. It was a stage of incidentals. The Kilometre 92 buffet was in fact at km 96 in a side-street at Brassac, a change of address which was quickly forgiven since it served a fine cassoulet, the regional dish of white haricot beans, goose and sausage. Robert Millar was forced by stomach trouble to quit the race. And Charly Mottet was urged by some other inner force to remind us that he was still part in it. On the eve of the first stage in the Pyrenees, the leaders simply rode defensively, stirring themselves only when Chozas threatened to join their exclusive club.

There was a quiet start, but after Johan Museeuw, still nagging away at Olaf Ludwig's hefty lead in the points contest, had beaten him in the sprint at 29km, the first attack was launched by Adrie Van der Poel. It was not a clean-cut affair. Eleven riders gained half a minute, and when the peloton approached them at 50km, three surrendered while eight held out and were joined by reinforcements, notably Roche and Mottet in the first wave, and by Chozas and Claveyrolat in the second. At the summit of the col de Sie at 69km they numbered nineteen and had 3min on the field, which seemed prepared to ignore them. At 80kms their lead was over 5min.

By now Millar had abandoned the race. He had felt perfectly well at breakfast, but almost as soon as the stage got under way he began suffering from diarrhoea. This is a common enough complaint among long-distance cyclists, and had it started earlier he could have taken something to relieve it. Now it was too late, and he had no choice but to retire. It was a sorry end to a Tour in which, although he had ridden for his team rather than himself, he was probably stronger than at any time since he had won the mountain jersey in 1984. It was also a blow to LeMond, who had been counting on his help in the Pyrenees next day.

The leaders in the peloton, meanwhile, had woken up to the dangers of the breakaway. At Brassac (the cassoulet having long since been disposed of) the group had a lead of 8min, and although this didn't affect the prospects of most of its members, it was enough to put Chozas into fourth place overall between LeMond and Delgado. And Chozas wasn't the kind of person you gave a lift to.

From this point Z, Banesto and PDM worked together at the front of the bunch to shorten the gap and limit the damage. Expecting such a reaction, and knowing that, anyway, he stood little chance of winning the stage if he stayed in the company of so many sprinters, Mottet slipped away from them with 30kms to go. Living up to his reputation as a time trialist for the first time in the race he finished over 2min in front of his nearest pursuers, and nearly 5min ahead of the peloton. And since this split in two on the run-in, Chiappucci was presented with the bonus of a 3sec gain over his chief rivals.

Mottet, who had been disparaged for achieving less in the race than his public demanded, is an honest man. All the same this victory may have made it easier for him to say what had been in his mind for several days: that he wasn't cut out to win the Tour de France. In future he would concentrate on the classics, and although he remained the leader of RMO on the Tour, from now on he was prepared to work as an *équipier de luxe*, protecting the position of Claveyrolat.

Stage 15 result: 1. Mottet (RMO) 4hr13'56"; 2. Calcaterra (Château d'Ax) at 2'2"; 3. Ekimov (Panasonic) s.t.; 4. Van Hooydonck (Buckler) s.t.; 5. Claveyrolat (RMO) s.t.; 6. Cassani (Château d'Ax) s.t.

Overall placings: 1. Chiappucci (Carrera) 62hr20'47"; 2. Breukink (PDM) at 1'52"; 3. LeMond (Z) at 2'24"; 4. Delgado (Banesto) at 4'29"; 5. Pensec (Z) at 4'58"; 6. Bugno (Château d'Ax) at 6'6".

Stage 16, Blagnac – Luz Ardiden, 215km

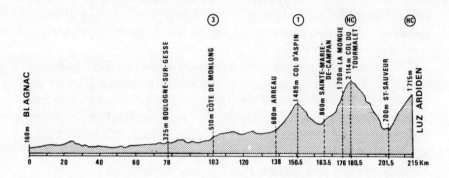

This was the day marked down in everyone's diary for the eclipse of Chiappucci, though it was a matter of individual opinion whether this would be accomplished by LeMond, Delgado or Breukink, a combination of any two of them, or perhaps all three. It ended with LeMond staring up at the clock on the finishing line, wide-eyed and open-mouthed, just as he had been on the Champs-Elysées the previous year as he waited for his rival's time to come up. But this time there were no North American whoops of triumph; instead, the baffled incredulity of a hunter who has seen his quarry jump out of the trap.

All the dramas and difficulties of this stage came towards the end. Starting from Blagnac, the airport of Toulouse and the birthplace of Concorde, it gently rose 520 metres over the first 138km, passing under an overcast sky across fields of maize and sunflowers and along avenues of plane trees. But in the next 77km it would climb some 3,000 metres. Not in one go, of course (even the Tourmalet, 2,114 metres above sea level, is only 1,109 metres high from its base) but in a series of peaks and troughs. First the Aspin, then the Tourmalet and finally Luz-Ardiden. With all this in store for them the riders saw no point in wasting effort on the approach and took three hours to cover the first 82km: in their terms a crawl.

This gave us ample time to do justice to a 10.00am buffet offered by the mayor of Boulogne-sur-Gesse in his indoor market. A simple matter of country ham and melon and mutton stew to be rinsed down with a red Domaine de Cahuzac, the kind of breakfast most of us keep for Sundays. And by the time we had digested it, the riders were approaching the first small côte – taken by the insatiable Claveyrolat – and Bugno's Château d'Ax was winding up the pressure at the front.

It was from this point that Chiappucci endeared himself not only to a global television audience but to the tiny, critical world of the Tour's camp followers. They had never been able to take him seriously, regarding him as the lucky beneficiary of a deplorable loss of concentration by the favourites on the opening day. They compared him with Roger Walkowiak, the obscure twenty-five-year-old leader of an unfashionable regional team, Nord-Est-Centre, who benefited from a similar lapse in 1956. That year thirty-one riders took 18min out of the peloton on stage 6 and Walkowiak, who inherited the yellow jersey, kept it to the end. The crowds, far from honouring him, turned on the French national team for allowing him to win and made a hero of the *lanterne rouge*, a joker named Chaussabel. Now it was said that if Chiappucci should win he would do so *à la Walkowiak* – which was cruelly unfair to both men.

Chiappucci had always worked for what he got, and his pride was without vanity. But he had cheek. Once he had been Stephen Roche's *domestique*; now he was race-leader and Roche was trailing thirty-five minutes. Would he like to come and work for him next season, Chiappucci asked as they rolled along in the peloton. And today his refusal to be overawed by those with bigger reputations took another turn. Most men in his position would simply have dogged the riders who were waiting to depose him, let them make the running and try to match them turn by turn. Instead Chiappucci got in his counter-attack first.

It was he, not Delgado, who made the first move on the 12km Aspin, a sweeping, open climb, unlike the close hair-pins of the alpine cols, though you had only to lift your eyes to the fringe of spectators on the skyline to appreciate how severe it was. With Chiappucci went six other riders: Jorg Muller and Johan Bruyneel and the Colombian, William Palacio, all in a freelance capacity; Bagot, Sunday's lone escaper, but now apparently as a forerunner for Claveyrolat; Miguel Martinez-Torres keeping alive ONCE's interest in the team competition;

and Jérôme Simon, representing LeMond. And as they moved away Breukink was seen to be in trouble, first summoning his team car, then exchanging bikes with a team-mate, Jos Van Aert, and still seeming as unhappy with the deal, as if he'd bought the machine from some shady character in a street market.

Half way up the Aspin the leading group were joined by another Colombian, Omar Hernandez, and the Russian, Konyshev. Later Claveyrolat got across to them. And after Chiappucci had led them over the col, 34sec ahead of the peloton, the Italian, Roberto Conti, joined them on the descent. Here Muller made a short-lived bid for freedom and in the helter-skelter Chiappucci almost came to grief on a bend. But having survived this panic he found when he reached the valley that he was 2min ahead of LeMond on the road and so 4min 25sec ahead overall. If he could maintain that, it might be enough to hold LeMond in the time trial.

So the race moved on to its next battle-ground, the 13km Tourmalet, a sombre climb among quarry-like cliffs, beneath concrete avalanche shelters and through the architecturally brutal resort of La Mongie – 10km of it 1-in-12, the last 700 metres steeper than 1-in-10. Not a place to conjure with your profits until you were safely over the summit.

Here not only the front group but the peloton broke into fragments. Martinez-Torres attacked alone, knowing that if he reached the final climb he would have the support of thousands of Spaniards who had crossed the frontier in anticipation of a victory by one of their own. Palacio followed him across the col at 1min 24sec. Then at 1min 42sec came Conti and Chiappucci who had formed an Italian alliance – blood ties being stronger at this moment than commercial strings – with Bruyneel and Simon still playing the gooseberry. And at 2min 4sec was Claveyrolat whom, surprisingly, they had dropped.

Back down the slope LeMond, who had been tagging Delgado, waiting vainly for his first aggressive move, decided to take matters into his own hands. He attacked with such purpose that Indurain had to help Delgado to regain his side, a service which Alcala was unable to perform for his troubled leader, Breukink. Indurain led this little party over the summit at 2min 50sec, with Breukink another 40sec in arrears. And then LeMond resumed command, stringing them out in a reckless descent to close on Chiappucci. This they did in Saint-Sauveur, at the foot of Luz-Ardiden, leaving everything to be decided on the climb.

Chiappucci might have been caught, but he would not give way. He insisted on taking the head of the group as it mounted the hill. But he was tiring. Twice he was dropped, and twice he came back, each time resuming his place at the front. When a spectator handed him up a bottle of water he offered it behind him to LeMond and Indurain as though they were guests at his table. They declined it. But courtesies came to an abrupt end 6kms from the finish. Fabio Parra jumped away on the right-hand side of the road. LeMond went with him, followed by Lejaretta and Indurain, and Chiappucci could only look across at them. He was able to continue at his own steady pace, but any further acceleration was beyond him.

LeMond was now in control. Parra was dropped immediately, Lejaretta in the next few kilometres and Martinez-Torres – still plugging away ahead – was caught and discarded 2.5km from the summit. Only Indurain remained, and having ridden in LeMond's slipstream all the way, had no difficulty out-sprinting him by 6sec to win in the Pyrenees as he had done the year before. The Spanish fans had hoped for Delgado, instead it was his deputy, but at least their journey hadn't been wasted.

LeMond really didn't care. He had made his attack and, economical as it was, it had devastated his main rivals. Instead of trailing Breukink by 32sec he now led him by 3min 49sec. His gain of 1min 32sec on Delgado was less dramatic, but on a stage made to be exploited by the Spaniard's special talents it surely ended his challenge. Provided that LeMond looked after himself, he had little need to extend his advantage over either of them.

As the seconds ticked off on the clock at the finish line, the one question was whether or not LeMond had the yellow jersey already. Singly and in ones or twos the next eleven finishers came into view, and then the small, stocky figure of Chiappucci making a last tired sprint for the line. He had dropped 2min 19sec on LeMond, but he had saved his jersey

Singing and dancing Indurain. The young Basque may have failed to win the Tour of Spain, in which he was Banesto's main candidate, but he was to prove more at ease in the Alps and Pyrenees than his leader, Delgado.

by 5sec. We may have seen the best, but we hadn't seen the last of him.

Stage 16 result: 1. Indurain (Banesto) 7hr4'38"; 2. LeMond (Z) at 6"; 3. Lejaretta (ONCE) at 15"; 4. Martinez Torres (ONCE) at 59"; 5. Parra (Kelme) at 1'18"; 6. Corti (Ariostea) at 1'24".

Overall placings: 1. Chiappucci (Carrera) 69hr27'50"; 2. LeMond (Z) at 5"; 3. Delgado (Banesto) at 3'42"; 4. Breukink (PDM) at 3'49"; 5. Lejaretta (ONCE) at 5'29"; 6. Bugno (Château d'Ax) at 7'48".

Stage 17, Lourdes – Pau, 150km

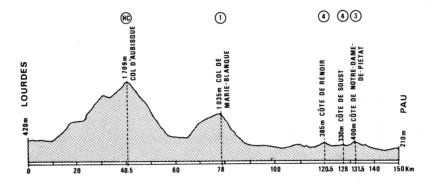

Today's stage didn't possess the previous day's clear potential for drama. It had the *hors catégorie* col d'Aubisque at 41km, and the 1st-cat col de Marie-Blanque at 78km, but that was its farewell to the Pyrenees, and apart from a ripple of small hills towards the end, the second half was pretty flat. It could still cause trouble, but this wasn't the kind of terrain that any of the dwindling band of favourites would choose to exploit. A hit-and-run raid in the mountains was a mug's game if you then had to ride two hours over the plains to avoid capture.

Of course riders with nothing to lose and only one day's notoriety to gain would see it differently, and from shortly after the start nineteen of them, soon to be augmented by another four, detached themselves from the front of the field. They included a few former yellow jerseys, Bauer, Da Silva (1989) and Pascal Simon (1983), a recent mountain leader, Konyshev, and several other riders who have figured in attacks over the past few days: Colotti, Ekimov, Bruyneel for instance. But there was nobody there who would make the leaders' blood race at this point of the Tour. Provided that they didn't go too far, they could stay away for the day if they wished. As a reward for good behaviour even Z gave their captain, Gilbert Duclos-Lassalle, and Atle Kvalsvoll leave to go with them, indeed encouraged them since they would balance the the two ONCE riders, Stephen Hodge and Melchor Mauri, and stop them stealing a march in the team race.

At the foot of the Aubisque they had over a minute in hand on the peloton, and at the summit the Colombian, Oscar de Jésus Vargas, now away on his own, had nearly 7min. Nothing to worry the leaders there. Or even when, at the base of the Marie-Blanque, Delgado's one French lieutenant, Dominique Arnaud, who had succeeded Vargas as the front-runner, was 10min 20sec clear.

The stage was unrolling just as LeMond might have wished, the release of the more restless spirits allowing their bosses to take things quietly. Delgado seemed reconciled to losing the Tour, though he was still keen to finish in the first three for a fourth year in succession. Breukink appeared to be relying on the time trial to put him on the podium in Paris. And Chiappucci, whose mother had lit a candle for him that morning in the grotto at Lourdes, could only wait on some unforeseeable incident to upset the even tenor of the racing.

Such a crisis came a kilometre from the top of Marie-Blanque when LeMond wobbled to the side of the road with a flat rear tyre. Nothing very terrible in that. Punctures are commonplace. A quick wheel-change by the team-car, a short, collective chase and everything would be as it had been. But this time, after their previous exemplary team-work, Z had bungled. LeMond was completely on his own.

As they filed past him up the climb other riders whom he had left behind saw him standing helplessly beside the road-side, holding up his rear wheel and looking back for service with genuine panic on his face. Duclos-Lassalle and Kvalsvoll were at least 5min ahead of him. Eric Boyer and Jérôme Simon, tired after their efforts the day before, were a kilometre or so back down the climb and making slow progress. Pensec, Cornillet and Lemarchand were even further to the rear. So there was nobody whose bike he could commandeer and, worse, there was no sign of his team-car.

The reason for this was that a group which was led by Fabrice Philipot, and included Kelly and Claveyrolat, was less than one minute behind the more select group – with Chiappucci, Delgado and Indurain – from which LeMond had just parted company. A team-car may not drive in gaps of under a minute, otherwise it would help to close them and so interfere with the racing. Therefore the Z-car, despite its name, could not reach LeMond any faster than Philipot and company could pedal. Although the delay could not have amounted to more than 1min 20sec, it must have seemed to LeMond that his painfully compiled advantage was draining away.

Boyer and Simon arrived as the car did (they had put on speed after hearing from spectators, who had heard it on the radio, that LeMond had punctured), but still they could not get the chase under way. LeMond's new wheel was touching the frame, and in a couple of hundred metres he had to stop again, this time changing his bike altogether. But once the summit had been reached, 1min 27sec after Chiappucci had crossed it, the pursuit was hectic. If LeMond had feared for his victory, he showed no fear on the descent (he is, of course, a skier). 'I have never seen a rider come down so fast,' said a race official who had watched the American in action from the pillion seat of a motorbike. 'I have never seen anyone take so many risks.' And even Boyer, straining with Simon to keep up with his leader, said wryly, 'We didn't touch the brakes very often.'

Ahead were reinforcements. Legeay, the Z manager, sent a message over his CB radio to his deputy, Serge Boucherie, who was in the car covering the breakaway group, telling him to stop Duclos-Lassalle and Kvalsvoll in their tracks. And at whatever cost to themselves in the lost opportunity to win a stage, the two riders dismounted with no reproach at Lurbe-Saint-Christau, where the course had levelled out, to wait for their leader. So, protected by four of his men, though certainly not sparing himself in the effort, LeMond regained the main field at 98km after an operation which had taken half-an-hour and 21km of hot and anxious pursuit.

Unaware of all this the escapers, now reduced by wear and tear to thirteen men, completed the day's business. Bruyneel attacked at one of the little hills outside Pau, and was joined by Konyshev who, though a climber by reputation, beat him in the sprint by a single second. It was the first Russian stage win in the history of the Tour, but even so it was clouded by the hot air of a lively moral debate over Carrera's behaviour during the LeMond crisis.

There is a tradition in professional cycle racing that the leaders don't take advantage of a rival who's involved in a crash. It is occasionally breached – as Fignon felt it had been by LeMond at Mont-Saint-Michel, even though it turned out that nobody had crashed, least of all himself – but it is generally respected. The proper reaction in the case of a puncture or mechanical breakdown is far more debatable. Many riders feel that this is one of the natural hazards of the game, and have no special sympathy for the victim. Especially if it happens in the middle of a stage and costs him no more than a spell of sweaty discomfort. Anyway, they argue, you can't slow down the race and wait for him when an attack is already on.

What happened today was that Chiappucci's team certainly increased the pressure when they knew that LeMond was in trouble, with Perini, Gianelli, Maechler and Da Silva (who had dropped back from the front group) forcing the pace downhill and along the flat. 'One doesn't do things like that,' said LeMond angrily. 'I will not forget it. It's a stupid attitude. One day or another it will be paid for.'

Da Silva wasn't penitent: 'We have raced,' he said. 'This is the Tour, and in the Tour you don't give anyone a present.' And Chiappucci echoed this: 'No-one gave me a present in the Saint-Etienne stage when I wasn't well. It was bizarre how everyone happened to race that day.' Indeed he was convinced that the Z team had learned of his unspecified indisposition from other Italian sources in the peloton, which was why first Pensec, then LeMond had attacked him so vigorously. 'And today,' he went on, 'I didn't find anyone to help me, unless it was Banesto [whose help appeared to have been minimal] . . . In the Tour I am alone against everyone.'

Stage 17 result: 1. Konishev (Alfa-Lum) 4hr8′25″; 2. Bruyneel (Lotto) at 1″; 3. Bauer (7-Eleven) at 11″; 4. Colotti (RMO) at 32″; 5. Cassani (Ariostea) s.t.; 6. Montoya (Ryalcao-Postobon) s.t.

Overall placings: 1. Chiappucci (Carrera) 73hr41′46″; 2. LeMond (Z) at 5″; 3. Delgado (Banesto) at 3′42″; 4. Breukink (PDM) at 3′49″; 5. Lejaretta (ONCE) at 5′29″; 6. Bugno (Château d'Ax) at 7′48″.

CHAPTER 15

Making the wheels go round

It was a common complaint by the early 'eighties that the Tour was too commercialised. Its saturation in advertising messages was criticised by the socialist government, and some newspapers suggested that perhaps the race should be State-run. But clearly Félix Lévitan, co-director with Jacques Goddet and the man whose job was to oil the wheels, was of the opinion that it wasn't commercialised enough. Before he unveiled the outline of the 1982 Tour at his annual autumn press conference, he delivered a thirty-four-minute lecture on the finances of the race and a homily on the need for commercial exploitation.

He said, and then said slowly a second time: 'Unless it were taken over by the State, the 1982 Tour could not take place without being financed in the same way as its predecessors. And even if the State did take it over, it could not take place if it did not have the same sporting image as in the past.'

He reminded his audience that the organisers (then *L'Equipe* and *le Parisien-Libéré*, now the Société du Tour de France, a subsidiary of the Aumary Group which owns the two papers) also ran the Paris-Roubaix, the Bordeaux-Paris, the Grand Prix des Nations and the Tour de l'Avenir (now the Tour of the EC). These made a loss, and so the only way to pay for them was out of the two million pound revenue which came in from the stage towns and sponsors of the Tour de France.

The Tour, Lévitan pointed out, cost tax-payers 'not one centime' – which would no longer be the case if the State took over. How was the Tour's publicity caravan more scandalous, he asked, than the commercial practices 'of football, tennis, rugby or motor racing – especially motor racing with its illegal advertising for tobacco and alcoholic products.' As for the publicity logos worn by the riders, they were the only recompense for sponsors who spent £400,000-£700,000 a year on their trade teams: 'And this is without considering that these sponsors assure the well-being of professional cycling, which would otherwise disappear.' He admitted that some people would like to return to national teams, 'but the conditions for such a formula no longer exist. We are a long way from the financial climate that existed in the 1930s.'

Warming to his subject Lévitan said that the French cycle industry depended on the Tour for international publicity, which in effect was guaranteeing employment for 6,000 factory workers, 7,000 assembly workers and 60,000 people in the retail trade. The Tour's stage-town sponsors also drew prosperity from their association with the race. A mayor had written, in the bygone style of testimonial ads: 'The Tour has served, beyond our expectations, to promote our town as one of dynamic ability, which is much appreciated in attracting new business and employment to the area.'

Lévitan then went on to reveal how the income was spent: nearly £300,000 to government departments for police control and tele-communications; over £400,000 for salaries and fees for permanent and casual members of the Tour staff; over £200,000 for their living expenses on the race; almost £85,000 for petrol; some £30,000 for race officials' expenses; £7,500 for information and press assistance; nearly £40,000 for air and rail travel during the transfer between stages.

'It is not the aim of the Tour de France organisation to make excessive profits,' Lévitan concluded, 'but simply to pay its way.' He was loudly applauded for his performance, and for the moment criticism in the press was stilled.

Ten years on the same complaints could be made, and the same rebuttals offered by the Tour. But now in 1990 the figures were very different. The Tour had receipts of ten to eleven million pounds which came from three main sources: sponsorship £6.5-7 million; television rights, £2-2.5 million; and stage town fees, £1.5. The outgoings had also risen, of course – to nine to ten million. Prizes alone had been boosted from £250,000 in 1982 to one million. Indeed they had gone up by a third in the past year, and the winner's £200,000 put the Tour on roughly the same footing as the big snob event of the season, the French tennis championships at Roland Garros – another sports production which did not shrink from making a pretty sou out of its commercial contacts. And then there were the fixed and running costs of administration – no small item of which was the hire of 11,000 policemen to guard every access road along the route. These came to nine to ten million pounds, so leaving a surplus of a million. The Société du Tour de France, or STF, was not making a mint, but it was doing a good deal better than breaking even, and a certain gloss of prosperity reflected this.

The STF, whose total income came to around thirteen million pounds, had admittedly taken on additional commitments. Its list of promotions now read: four World Cup events (Paris-Roubaix, Paris-Tours, Liège-Bastogne-Liège, and the special time trial finale), the Critérium National, Grand Prix des Nations, the EC Tour and a new track meeting at the Bercy stadium in Paris, replacing the old and unloved Paris Six-Day. But these, too, it seemed well equipped to cope with.

By far the biggest contributors to the 1990 Tour, making up two-thirds of its income, were the sponsors. The STF had reduced their number but increased their quality. In 1988 it had seemed a good wheeze to invite as many as possible to take a share in the action, and the figure had risen to fifty-two. Many of them sponsored special jerseys and prizes for a variety of internal contests: the *maillot de la Performance* (though nobody could quite remember what that was awarded for), the leader of the intermediate sprints classification, the leading team on points as well as on time. Things were getting out of hand. At the end of the stage thirteen different riders had to go up to the podium to receive awards and kisses, and the only people to benefit were the florists who made up the bouquets. The *cérémonie protocolaire* dragged on and on. The public got bored and confused. Riders were kept from their television interviews. Most ominous of all, the major sponsors were aggrieved that their publicity was being diluted.

By 1990 the STF had slimmed down the system. There were four big spenders – 'The Great Partners of the Tour' – who each contributed between one and £1.8 million to the Tour coffers. They were Crédit Lyonnais, Fiat, Coca-Cola and Panasonic. Crédit Lyonnais sponsored the yellow jersey and was also the bank of the Tour – the only one in France allowed to open on Bastille Day. Fiat provided the official vehicles. Coca-

Cola – whose ousting of Perrier as the drink of the Tour had brought an end to French civilisation as we knew it – donated the stage-prizes and provided both the riders' *bidons* and the rations that they picked up along the route; also 2,500 mini-cans of Coca, Fanta and Sprite for the thirsty scribblers in the press room. (In passing, another effect of this switch of sponsor should perhaps be recorded before it's too late. In the old days the riders, having drunk their fill of Perrier at the end of the stage, would pour the sugarless mineral water over their heads and swollen feet. This wasn't something you would care to do with Coca-Cola). And Panasonic, the only one of the four which also had a team in the race, sponsored the green points jersey.

In addition there were smaller, though still considerable sponsors like the Japanese firm, Ricoh, who paid to have their name on the riders' numbers, and between them contributed some £500,000. And there were others, 'technical partners', who provided goods and services: Hewlett Packard printing the communiques, for instance, and Aspro providing the medical services. If it moves, was the principle, slap a logo on it.

Of the two million pounds or so from television – just under a quarter of the STF income – roughly half came from the French station Antenne-2, though probably a million more had to be spent on technical costs. ABC, the US network, were thought to have paid £600,000 for their rights. NHK of Japan also had their own commentators on the race. And Eurovision took up the rest of the market.

Stage-towns, whatever their size, paid a flat £50,000 for the privilege of welcoming the Tour, though to exploit the year's most popular event in the municipal calendar, they would probably multiply that figure several times over in publicity, receptions and various supporting events. But there is still no shortage of applicants for inclusion, even if some of the dots on the map are hard to join up. In 1991, for instance, the Tour ends its big mountain stage at Val-Louron, and the deal between the STF and the general council of the Hautes-Pyrénées is that the Tour will finish a stage in the *département* ten times in the next ten years. Although it contains such regularly climbed cols as the Aspin, the Tourmalet and Luz-Ardiden, and has the Aubisque on its borders, that may not always be convenient. To get around the problem the Tour may have to finish two stages there another year.

The Tour has always been a commercial enterprise, and although you hear complaints about its excesses, its vulgarity doesn't appear to give widespread offence. After all, if you can't stand the noise and flashing lights, you simply keep out of the funfair. And the most raucous element of the whole carnival, the publicity caravan, is the one which would be most sorely missed. On a flat stage the race takes only a minute or so to pass any given point, and it's the caravan which whiles away the previous hours for the six million people who crowd the route.

Except that many of the major sponsors also take part in it, the caravan is not the financial mainstay it was when Desgrange introduced it in the 'thirties. Nor is it as flourishing and inventive, and the hucksters who try to sell things are having a thin time. Spectators expect to be given them, and are. Z, for instance, showered out 1,600,000 plastic carrier bags along the way, not so much adding to the litter as providing a solution for it (the Tour is having a clean-up campaign). Coca-Cola gave away 400,000 mini-cans and cardboard caps, Mars 150,000 icecream bars, Crédit Lyonnais 500,000 lapel pins, PDM 100,000 packets of chewing gum.

The only huckster who did well was Pépé with his Mini-vélo, a toy racing bike drawn along by a string, and the one product specially produced for the Tour. He had over 7,000 sales. The newspaper vans, however, reported business down by 20 per cent. It used to be regarded by visiting American reporters as a stroke of genius that French journals should solve their waste paper problem by packaging the week's issue with half a dozen back numbers. But now there are fewer takers – even with a Fignon tee-shirt thrown in. The fact that Fignon abandoned early was held to blame. That and the fact that the Alps came before the Pyrenees – always a bad omen apparently.

It will be different next year but, even if it's worse, the caravan will have to keep rolling. Without it the Tour would be like the Rose Bowl without the marching bands and majorettes.

CHAPTER 16

Fifth man first

The argument over Chiappucci's attack on LeMond when he punctured ran childishly on, threatening to sour the last four days of the Tour. LeMond went on insisting that the Italian's behaviour had been unsporting, Chiappucci replying that he had only done as he had been done by. But at least the words were exchanged through intermediaries in the press; they were not delivered face to face. Although the two riders pointedly ignored each other, the heat went out of the quarrel. One evening in an English-language television interview LeMond referred to Chiappucci as Cappuccino, and instead of pretending that it was a slip of the tongue, just gave a private smile. The nickname was patronising, and unfair: there was a lot more than froth to his opponent. But it wasn't belligerent, and whatever annoyance he may have felt at Pau, LeMond had no cause to make an enemy of this man whom he had helped to promote in the first place.

In three days' time, unless we were all mistaken, the matter would be settled in his favour at the lac de Vassivière. The more obscure question was, out of Chiappucci, Breukink and Delgado, which two would be with him on the podium in Paris.

Stage 18: Pau – Bordeaux, 202km
Most of the riders looked on the stage which took the Tour north from the Pyrenees through the pine forests of the Landes and the vineyards of the Gironde – rugby and pelota country all the way – as the start of the holidays. No more mountains. Little risk of being dropped and getting eliminated. Two stages of no great difficulty. A time trial which you could take as it came. A trip by TGV to the outskirts of Paris. Then the final swoop onto the Champs-Elysées. Only the leaders had anything to worry about.

Even the official 'film' of the stage entered into the spirit of it: 'Nothing to report until the sprint at km 32.5: Colotti (6pts), Ludwig (4pts), Redant (2pts). The speed is feeble and the humour joyful until km 139 where Anderson suddenly attacks.' There always has to be someone to spoil a good thing.

Phil Anderson, a great exponent of the long-range attack in his days, was in fact alone for only 10kms, after which six escapers caught him, and in turn were caught by the peloton in another 24kms. Then the joyful humour returned, but the speed picked up and the next break when it came, 20km from home, was a more serious affair.

Bordeaux, with a flat run-in across the coastal plain, has always been celebrated for sprint finishes: more particularly when the stage ended on the old municipal velodrome of Bordeaux-Lescure, but even recently after transferring to the exhibition centre out at the lake. But although there were sprinters among the 19 who broke away, they were unflattered to find themselves in the company of LeMond, Chiappucci, Breukink, Bugno and Alcala. Of the great, only Delgado and his henchman, Indurain, were missing. The true specialist sprinters hadn't had much of a look-in at the finishes in this Tour, and again they weren't going to have it their way.

At 10kms to go three men – Breukink, Bugno and his Château d'Ax team-man, Roberto Gusmeroli – split from the rest of the group, who put up no great resistance to the closing peloton and were caught at 5km. The trio, however, stayed clear, and though Gusmeroli's role was to lead his master out in the sprint, Bugno outran him as he comfortably beat Breukink to the line. He was the first rider to win two stages, and the contrast between them – the summit at Alpe-d'Huez and the flat at Bordeaux – together with a third place in the Epinal time trial and another on the Causse-Noir, defined his remarkable versatility. He may have been in two minds about riding the Tour so soon after winning the Giro, but he had done more than fulfil his contract.

Breukink said he had been less concerned about winning the stage than regaining 18sec on Delgado after the collapse of his effort at Luz-Ardiden. It was just enough to allow him to leapfrog the Spaniard into third place overall. And depending on the result of the time trial, it might still be sufficient to put him into second place in Paris.

Stage 18 result: 1. Bugno (Château d'Ax) 5hr41'33"; 2. Breukink (PDM) at 1"; 3. Gusmeroli (Château d'Ax) at 3"; 4. Fidanza (Château d'Ax) at 19"; 5. Baffi (Ariostea) s.t.; 6. Museeuw (Lotto) s.t.

Overall placings: 1. Chiappucci (Carrera) 79hr23'38"; 2. LeMond (Z) at 5"; 3. Breukink (PDM) at 3'31"; 4. Delgado (Banesto) at 3'42"; 5. Lejaretta (ONCE) at 5'29"; 6. Bugno (Château d'Ax) at 7'29".

Stage 19, Castillon-la-Bataille – Limoges, 182.5km
Chiappucci was sure that LeMond would attack him on this stage, and he had good reason for his fears. If LeMond chose his moment, a short, sudden attack towards the end might easily wipe out his 5sec lead. It would not need a heavy commitment. And if LeMond did pull it off he would win the advantage of starting last in the next day's time trial, 3min behind Chiappucci. It was always more encouraging to be the pursuer than the pursued: to have your rival as the quarry not the hunter. LeMond would also get the yellow jersey one day sooner, of course, though that was probably not the main consideration. Having waited three weeks for it, he could contain himself another day.

Needless to say, the impeccable logic of this forecast was ignored. The tactical opportunities of a heavily corrugated run through the Dordogne and the Haute-Vienne were allowed to slip by. Neither LeMond nor any of the leaders made an aggressive move all day. So at last there was a stage dedicated to the sprinters? Well, yes and no. It was won by a sprinter, but not in a sprint.

The stage was more than half over before, at 110km, the Spaniard, Jésus Rosado, detached and was joined by fourteen other riders, including Gusmeroli, Bontempi, Van Der Poel, Pensec and Rominger. The peloton showed no interest. Rosado dropped back, but the other fourteen continued and were reinforced at 145km by Hernandez, Ruiz-Cabestany, Nijdam, Bauer and Ekimov. Still no reaction. And at 153km another quintet, in which Rosado reappeared, jumped across what was now a gap of nearly 4min. Even so these five were too late to catch what proved to be the decisive move when, at

150km, Guido Bontempi, the *équipier* of Chiappucci, attacked alone.

This wasn't like Bontempi. In the great days of 1986, when he won five stages in the Giro and three in the Tour de France – crowned by leading the cavalry charge on the Champs-Elysées – he could have counted on imposing himself on a mixed bunch of sprinters and *rouleurs* like this. But now he was thirty-one and his finish was less explosive. He felt he stood a better chance if his only opponent was his own tiring muscles. It was a remarkable effort of will. At 10km to go he had only 1min 40sec on his eight most determined pursuers and seemed sure to get caught. Yet at the line his lead on the runners-up, Lauritzen of Norway and the Belgian, Roes, had been cut by only 12sec. It was the first race since he was an amateur that he had won in a solo attack, and it brought him over 6min of individual attention from the media before the peloton with all the leaders together reached Limoges.

Although most of the caravan and all the riders were un-aware of it, the Tour had been forced to side-step another sheepfarmers' demonstration during the stage. In a narrow lane somewhere in the Haute-Vienne in the last third of the route we found our way blocked by farm carts, and when we stopped hand-printed leaflets were put through the windows. 'Shepherds of Limousin, must we disappear?' they asked. And below was the now-familiar argument against privileged cheap imports of lamb from New Zealand, eastern Europe and the U.K. Gradually we were filtered down a dirt track from which, after a farcical wrong turn into a farmyard, we hit a road running parallel with the course. So we reached Limoges well ahead of the race, which had been so neatly diverted before the barricade that nobody noticed the difference.

On an otherwise unremarkable day we felt diverted by the incident too. The delay was short and there was no brow-beating or aggravation. But perhaps we were lucky that when one of the farmers came along to question us it was Samuel Abt of the *International Herald Tribune* who had his window open.

'What nationality are you?' he was asked in French.

'American,' said Sam.

'You've come a long way.'

'No, just from Paris.'

After which surreal exchange, the shepherd thought better of interrogating the rest of us.

Stage 19 result: 1. Bontempi (Carrera) 5hr16'4"; 2. Lauritzen (7-Eleven) at 1'28"; 3. Roes (Lotto) s.t.; 4. Gusmeroli (Château d'Ax) at 1'32"; 5. Nijdam (Buckler) at 2'6"; 6. Van der Poel (Weinmann) s.t.

Overall placings: 1. Chiappucci (Carrera) 84hr45'46"; 2. LeMond (Z) at 5"; 3. Breukink (PDM) at 3'31"; 4. Delgado (Banesto) at 3'42"; 5. Lejaretta (ONCE) at 5'29"; 6. Bugno (Château d'Ax) at 7'29".

Stage 20, Lac-de-Vassivière, 45.5km (individual time trial)

It was beyond all reasonable doubt that LeMond would beat Chiappucci today by more, a good deal more, than 5sec. Equally that Breukink and Delgado would be unable to make up their deficit of 3.5min plus. So LeMond would take the yellow jersey and the Paris stage would just be ceremonial. But you could never be absolutely certain. It's at times like these that the mad dog syndrome is invoked . . . Only a cloud-burst/broken fork/runaway dog on the road could stop LeMond winning. But this is only another way of touching wood.

LeMond had good days and bad days, but not *jours sans*. Once he had hit form his powers of recuperation between stages were perhaps his greatest asset. He might be, as Robert Millar had put it in a rare sentimental moment, 'the boy next door, the kind you'd like your daughter to marry'. But though he had nice manners and liked to be liked, in competition he was as self-centred as a McEnroe or Carl Lewis or almost any American athlete.

There were only two counts against him. He couldn't sleep: he would go to bed at eleven and be wide awake by four; though Roger Legeay, his manager, regarded that as a good sign. It was also widely known that he had a deep wound, 4cm long, in what the French call 'the saddle' (professional cyclists, like U.S. Presidents, are expected to reveal their most intimate physical infirmities to the public). This had opened up on the Epinal time trial, and had responded very little to treatment. But since he had borne it stoically for a fortnight, it seemed unlikely to make a crucial difference in his ride against Chiappucci today.

L'Equipe made a comparison of the riders' results against the clock this season. In the Giro Chiappucci had lost to LeMond once and beaten him twice for a net advantage of 1min 3sec. In the Tour LeMond had been faster than Chiappucci in all three trials so far with a gain of 1min 9sec. If they had thrown in the result of the Paris-Nice prologue (there was no contest in the col d'Eze time trial, since LeMond failed to qualify for it), the balance would have swung to Chiappucci by 7sec. But all this was about as relevant to the issue as collecting train numbers is to locomotive engineering.

What it really underlined was LeMond's gradual improvement through the season. Perhaps Chiappucci, too, had changed. He was convinced he had: 'The yellow jersey has helped me to find new strength. I am no longer the same man.' But it was hard to believe there was all that room for improvement in a man who had started the season as though he had been let out of a trap, and had won his first race in Sicily in mid-February.

If there was anything to learn from the past it might be better to go back to 1985, the only other year that the lac de Vassivière circuit had been used for a time trial. It was also the last occasion that LeMond had ridden as number two to Bernard Hinault (next year the roles were reversed – in principle, anyway). His subservience to Hinault had been frustrating since LeMond was convinced he could have won if he had been free to ride his own race. But the lac de Vassivière, coming as now on the eve of the arrival in Paris, had given him the chance to declare himself. If by only 5sec he beat Hinault, the most powerful time trialist of his day, to become the first American to win a stage in the Tour de France.

Even if it hadn't held good memories, the area around the lake, some 60km east of Limoges, would have been a hard place not to respond to. The lake was man-made as a feeder reservoir for a nearby underground hydro-electric plant, but with its apparently random shape, its inlets and islands you would never have known this. The waters are used for dinghy sailing and sail-boarding, and the deeply-furrowed valleys around, with their forests and banks of broom and small granite villages, form another of those holiday retreats which only the French get to hear of.

The clockwise course has its technical attractions too. Though it ends where it begins, at the beach and harbour of Auphelle, it is far longer than the perimeter of the lake. It spreads into the countryside, threading in and out of these valleys, becoming a test not only of the rider's strength but of his ability to find at the same time both his right gear and his rhythm. In short it is the kind of course on which the English wouldn't think of holding a time trial in the first place. Or not one of any importance.

LeMond used it to do what was needed and no more. He had asked not to be given any time checks; he found them distracting and he preferred to set his own schedule. It's hard to believe that his orders wouldn't have been disobeyed if Chiappucci had begun to gain on him, but in the event he wasn't required to go any faster. He was effectively the race leader after only 5km. At 10.2km he had 11sec lead on the Italian; at 22km he had 31sec; at 33.4km, 1min 17sec; and at the finish, 2min 21sec. The last of the gang of four had been rounded up, and LeMond was finally in the yellow jersey. But he was only fifth on the stage, just as he had been at Epinal and Villard-de-Lans. 'I wasn't forcing myself at the end,' he said. 'I was thinking of the general classification not the individual victory.'

Chiappucci was forcing himself, but the strength was no longer in his legs and he struggled to find a measured tempo. Yet though he buckled, he didn't crack. Just as he had saved his yellow jersey by 5sec at Luz-Ardiden, so he managed now to reserve second place overall, 13sec ahead of Breukink, a position nobody could begrudge him.

Breukink, meanwhile, was fighting a fierce battle with his PDM team-mate, Alcala, for the stage. And when the Mexican, having been 6sec down on Breukink at 10.2km, was one second up on him at 22km, it looked as though he might be making the kind of charge that had brought him victory at Epinal. But Breukink was 6sec up again at 33.4km, and over the last quarter of the circuit eased ahead to win his second stage of the Tour by 28sec. He had failed in his ambition to finish next to LeMond, but at least he had ensured that he, not Delgado (eighth at 2min 21sec), would stand beside him in Paris. Provided, of course, that the mad dogs were kept chained.

Stage 20 result: 1. Breukink (PDM), 1hr2'40"; 2. Alcala (PDM) at 28"; 3. Lejaretta (ONCE) at 38"; 4. Indurain (Banesto) at 40"; 5. LeMond (Z) at 57"; 6. Ruiz-Cabestany (ONCE) at 1'28".

Overall placings: 1. LeMond (Z), 85hr49'28"; 2. Chiappucci (Carrera) at 2'16"; 3. Breukink (PDM) at 2'29"; 4. Delgado (Banesto) at 5'1"; 5. Lejaretta (ONCE) at 5'5"; 6. Chozas (ONCE) at 9'14".

Stage 21, Bretigny-sur-Orge – Paris, 182.5km
By custom nobody attacks the race-leader on the final day. Or to put it another way, nobody attacks him unless the final stage is a time trial. The Dutchman, Jan Janssen, certainly attacked the Belgian, Herman Van Springel, on the time trial into Paris in 1968, coming from behind to win the Tour by the smallest margin ever, 38sec. And LeMond did the same to Fignon in 1989, reducing the margin to 8sec.

Or to put it yet another way, nobody has attacked the leader since 1947 when the Breton, Jean Robic, turned the tables on the overnight leader, Pierre Brambilla of Italy, during the final stage from Caen. Perhaps personal hostility had built up between them in the mountains – both were climbers – or Robic resented Brambilla's assumption that the race was as good as won. At any rate as the peloton climbed out of Rouen, Robic noticed that Brambilla was badly placed and attacked with Edouard Fachleitner and others. Brambilla was too exhausted to follow and Robic won a Tour which he had never led.

So to put it more exactly, in most years the yellow jersey is treated as inviolate on the final day. But it isn't something you should put your shirt on. And particularly not that one.

The Z team, from LeMond downward, were well aware of this. They were highly nervous from the start in case someone or something should rob them of their victory. It would be cynical to say this was just a matter of money, and naive to suggest that money played no part. LeMond would take none of his £200,000 prize for winning the Tour; that would be distributed among the others, swelling their total prize money over the month to £248,480 (this compared with £115,830 for Chiappucci's Carrera team, and £2,207 for the least-successful, SEUR, though there were only four riders left to share that). In addition Roger Zannier, the Monsieur Z of his sponsors, had promised his champion a personal bonus of $300,000 if he won the Tour, and LeMond said that he would also share this with his team.

But LeMond hadn't just bought popularity with his team. He had repaid their loyalty with his own. He had played absolutely fair with Pensec. He may have known that Pensec wouldn't stay the course, but for as long as he was in the yellow jersey, LeMond supported and encouraged him, and the two went out together to ride over the time trial courses. Naturally gregarious, LeMond found no trouble getting on with the others. He might detach himself to talk to his father, Bob, who was always in the background. And at Villard-de-Lans he had left the hotel to spend the rest day with his whole family. But when he was with the team he was affable and open. And while he was exacting as a leader, he did not, as he showed on the day that he punctured on the Marie-Blanque, expect them to take any risks that he wouldn't take himself.

Finally he did the business; he was a winner. And if you cannot win the Tour yourself, the next best thing is to ride into Paris with the winner, knowing that you have earned the right to share the glory. Having passed an uneventful journey so far – a puncture by Delgado and a successful return with four of his team-mates providing the only diversion – the Z team massed around LeMond at the front of the peloton as it swung on to the Champs-Elysées. They would probably have carried him home on a litter if the rules had allowed it.

Since mid-morning this pretty raddled grand avenue sloping up from the Place de la Concorde to the Arc de Triomphe has been busy with strollers, as it would be any Sunday morning. There are barriers along the pavement, and temporary stands in front of the Elysées Palace with the giant screen relaying the race obliquely facing them. Every 50 metres or so loudspeakers broadcast a commentary on the race. And just beyond the Drug Store at the Rond-Point the PDM supporters' band with black umbrellas and black balloons is playing European Community oompah music. But while the scene is animated, it lacks the focus of a football crowd. Along the barriers the serious spectators are standing no more than two or three deep, and there's little call for the cardboard periscopes which vendors are trying to push. Paris, as they say, is not France. Nor is it exactly a hotbed of enthusiasm for the Tour de France.

From 1904 to 1967 the Tour finished in greater privacy at the Parc des Princes, a dingy stadium with a pink cement cycle track where the waiting crowd were entertained by a programme of sprints and motor-paced races until the first of the marathon riders appeared through the tunnel from the street. Appropriately Raymond Poulidor, cycling's matinée idol of the 'sixties and 'seventies, took the last curtain call there (as stage winner, of course, for he never won the Tour). But it was to a half-empty house. Already much of the seating had been ripped out to make way for building the new international rugby and football ground.

The finish was then moved for seven years to another of cycling's ancient monuments, the Cipale velodrome at Vincennes. But that, too, wasn't a grand enough setting for an event which was beginning to feel a sense of its own international importance. And in 1975, after a great deal of political lobbying, France's most famous street was closed for the day and turned into a criterium circuit. The Tour has finished there ever since, and in terms of global publicity, the city struck a good bargain.

The citizens, too, were attracted to the spectacle in vast numbers in the early days, not least because they saw a succession of French winners. In the first eleven years nine victories were shared between the two Bernards, Thévenet and Hinault, and Laurent Fignon; and after Hinault's third victory the sign above the motor showroom on the Champs-Elyseés read HINAULT, RENAULT, BRAVAULT. The dark days of Eddy Merckx were over. But they were to return in the altered shape of an American, an Irishman and a Spaniard.

This year was particularly discouraging for the French.

Claveyrolat had performed impeccably in the mountains. And there was some consolation in the fact that LeMond was riding for a French team. But for the first time since 1925, and only the second time ever, there was not a French rider in the top ten. In fact the situation was worse than in 1925, for the best placed Frenchman, Fabrice Philipot, was only fourteenth.

It was too easy to put all the blame for falling support on xenophobia. Fignon, after all, had looked a certain winner the year before, and still the crowds had been thin. Instead the Tour had decided that, even though it produced the Tour's most exciting climax, the time trial finish had been a mistake. It wasn't spectacular enough. What the public preferred was to see the whole field racing together and then sprinting in a bunch for the line. This time there would be eight full circuits of the Champs-Elysées instead of the usual six – 50kms of racing lasting 1hr 20min. But still there was ample standing room. Still the visitors outnumbered the natives. Maybe the Parisians had seen it all before. Or if they wanted to see it all again they knew they could see it better on television.

What they saw were ritual attacks for the television cameras, the riders' equivalent of the fans' Hello Mum cards; a do-or-die effort by Stephen Hodge to gain 15sec, the margin needed by ONCE to snatch the team prize from Z; a swirling finishing sprint which went by a length to Johan Museeuw, adding a second stage to his first at Mont-St-Michel; and LeMond trying to push through a crowd which wouldn't give way. Standing behind him was a large expressionless man in a Coca-Cola cap and blazer whose role on the Tour was just that – to stand at the back of the winner and get photographed. LeMond no longer looked elated, but hollow-eyed and tense, as though lack of sleep had really caught up with him and the last stage had been as nervously demanding as the climb to Luz-Ardiden.

The night before, when he had given a press conference in the village school near Auphelle on the lac de Vassivière, he said that getting to the end of the Giro had been harder for him than winning the Tour. He was still sensitive to the criticism he had received in March (after which he had stopped reading the papers), in particular the silly, but particularly French, suggestion that he had brought his troubles on himself by a diet of hamburgers, chips and Coca-Cola. 'Those same journalists forget the hours I spent in training, the suffering I endured when I was regularly dropped at the start of the season, the tears that came when I was riding in the [motorcycle] slipstream of Otto, my trainer . . . I hated cycling because I suffered, and thought that no-one understood. I got the impression that I could win all the races, give away my salary, and there would still be people who would criticise me. Then again, do you believe that I could return to the top level as I have done if I had led a dissolute life outside the normal practices of my profession?'

No Tour is easily won, and this showed in LeMond's eyes. But the contrast between his experiences in the Giro and the Tour wasn't simply a matter of his personal condition. The Tour turned out to be the kind of race in which the strongest man (as LeMond had now become) could impose himself without needing to reach the precarious limits of his strength. As, for instance, Stephen Roche had to do in his counter-attack on Delgado at La Plagne in 1987.

The escape by the gang of four had confused the pattern of the race, creating a sub-plot which threatened to take centre stage. But LeMond was convinced it had been helpful: 'The presence of Pensec forced Breukink and Delgado to work. Besides we were right to play the Ronan card because he had better credentials than Bauer and Chiappucci. Our opponents feared him more. For my part I felt I had shed the weight of the race and I profited from that relief. No, on the whole I think it was a good move.'

Pensec it was, too, who cleared the way for LeMond with his attack on the unexpectedly stubborn Chiappucci during the Saint-Etienne stage. As for LeMond's major opponents, they fell away as a result of their own frailties rather than through any excessive pressure put upon them. He had needed only two frontal attacks, one in the Alps and another in the Pyrenees, to establish his position. And although he might have liked to take the yellow jersey earlier, he could afford, in all logic, to leave the outcome to the final time trial.

LeMond was reminded that he was the first Tour winner since Lucien Aimar in 1966 not to take a stage. And he in turn reminded his questioner that he had beaten Hinault in 1986 and Fignon in 1989 when he and they had been far stronger than any of their rivals. This had been a different race. The standard of the peloton had been far higher, with a dozen men (though he only mentioned six: Delgado, Alcala, Bugno, Breukink, Chiappucci and, by implication, himself) capable of winning the Tour. But none of them was able to dominate both the time trials and the cols, and he had simply adapted to the situation, concentrating on his overall position not on stage wins.

Now it was all over. The American had joined Philippe Thys of Belgium and Louison Bobet of France on three Tour wins; only Jacques Anquetil, Merckx and Hinault were ahead of him with five. And although this had not been his most dramatic Tour, it had certainly been spent in the best company. In 1986, he said, only Bauer and Hampsten had

Whatever their rivalries on the road, whatever bitter things may have been said at the time, Chiappucci, LeMond and Breukink become comrades in arms on the final podium in Paris.

been happy to see him win; the other members of the team would have preferred it to be Hinault. In 1989, out of sorts with ADR, he had won for his family. 'This year I have won for a team of which my family is part.'

Chiappucci was soon on his way to Italy where from midnight until two in the morning he was due to answer telephone messages from readers of the *Gazzetta dello Sport* and then travel on to a celebration party at Uboldo, the village where he was born. Breukink was returning to the criteriums of the Netherlands, knowing that when he came back it would be as the only Dutchman thought capable of winning the Tour. And LeMond and his team were bound for an all-night party aboard a *bateau-mouche* on the Seine. As someone was sure to point out to Pensec, it was called *le Bretagne*.

Stage 21 result: 1. Museeuw (Lotto), 4hr53′52″; 2. Baffi (Ariostea) s.t.; 3. Ludwig (Panasonic) s.t.; 4. Aboudjaparov (Alfa-Lum) s.t.; 5. Phinney (7-Eleven) s.t.; 6. Kelly (PDM) s.t.

Final overall result: 1. LeMond (Z) 90hr43′20″; 2. Chiappucci (Carrera) at 2′16″; 3. Breukink (PDM) at 2′29″; 4. Delgado (Banesto) at 5′1″; 5. Lejaretta (ONCE) at 5′5″; 6. Chozas (ONCE) at 9′14″; 7. Bugno (Château d'Ax) at 9′39″; 8. Alcala (PDM) at 11′14″; 9. Criquielion (Lotto) at 12′4″; 10. Indurain (Banesto) at 12′47″; 11. Hampsten (7-Eleven) at 12′54″; 12. Ruiz-Cabestany (ONCE) at 13′39″; 13. Parra (Kelme) at 14′35″; 14. Philipot (Castorama) at 15′49″; 15. Delion (Helvetia) at 16′57″; 16. Palacio (Ryalcao-Postobon) 19′43″; 17. Bruyneel (Lotto) at 20′24″; 18. Conti (Ariostea) at 20′43″; 19. Boyer (Z) at 22′9″; 20. Pensec (Z) at 22′54″; 21. Claveyrolat (RMO) at 23′33″ . . . 25. Konishev (Alfa-Lum) at 31′21″; 27. Bauer (7-Eleven) at 35′5″; 30. Kelly (PDM) at 38′42″; 33. Rooks (Panasonic) at 42′9″; 44. Roche (Histor) at 1hr0′7″; 49. Mottet (RMO) at 1h6′57″; 64. Maassen (Buckler) at 1hr22′14″; 156 and last, Massi (Ariostea) at 3hr16′26″.

Final Placings:
Points winners: 1. Ludwig (Panasonic) 256pts; 2. Museeuw (Lotto) 221; 3. Breukink (PDM) 118; 4. Colotti (RMO) 117; 5. Kelly (PDM) 116; 6. LeMond (Z) 108.

Mountains: 1. Claveyrolat (RMO) 321pts; 2. Chiappucci (Carrera) 179; 3. Conti (Ariostea) 160; 4. Indurain (Banesto) 153; 5. LeMond (Z) 135; 6. Bruyneel (Lotto) 124.

Teams: 1. Z 272hr21'23"; 2. ONCE at 14"; 3. Banesto at 23'42"; 4. PDM at 33'3"; 5. RMO at 56'29"; 6. Ryalcao-Postobon at 1hr9'34".

CHAPTER 17

Tour d'horizon

The Tour might be over, but the wheels continued to turn. A few days after the finish, Roger Legeay announced that LeMond would be making an attempt on the world hour record, which currently stood at 51.151km and in the name of Francesco Moser, who had set it in Mexico in January 1984. Provided that LeMond was in condition at the time, he might go for it in August 1992, following the Tour. Z were considering suitable tracks at altitude, and although Mexico and La Paz (3,660 metres and so a bit lofty for an hour's flat-out effort) hadn't been ruled out, Colorado Springs (1,900 metres and less humid than Mexico in August) seemed the current preference.

LeMond seemed to find the more immediate prospects less enticing, and his season ended fairly quietly. He came second in the Championship of Zurich to Charly Mottet who felt he had now proved beyond reasonable doubt that he would be right to concentrate in future on one-day races. Mottet then broke his wrist and was unable to lead the French team at the world championships in Japan. He didn't miss much. The road race title went to one Belgian sprinter, Rudy Dhaenens, from another, Dirk de Wolf, while the favourites – is that an echo we hear? – failed to react soon enough to an earlier breakaway. 'It was a tactical race, and we got it wrong,' said LeMond, who finished fourth behind the ubiquitous Bugno. Later LeMond started in the Irish Nissan Classic, but he retired towards the end of the first stage complaining of stomach trouble and fatigue and leaving behind an aggrieved promoter. So his European season came full circle.

A week after the Tour Bugno won the Wincanton classic at Brighton, boosting his lead in the World Cup series, which he eventually won by 34 points from the new world champion, Dhaenens. Bugno also finished at the head of the FICP table. Having lost his fear of heights, he was now on top of the world.

In front of his own Breton crowd of 35,000, Pensec, another man who had bounded back, took the Critérium de Chateaulin, 'which was as important to me as wearing the yellow jersey'. He was shortly to announce his departure from Z to join SEUR as a replacement for Marco Giovannetti. The unexpected Tour of Spain winner had been invited home to sign up with Bugno's Château d'Ax.

ONCE merged with Alfa-Lum, having been joined by Malcolm Elliott, whose Teka team had folded under him. Café de Colombia pulled out of racing altogether after having failed to qualify for the 1990 Tour; their most celebrated rider, Herrera, moved on to Postobon. And 7-Eleven, for five years the flagship of US cycle racing, also quit. There were rumours for a time that they would simply make economies, but in October the car radio manufacturers, Motorola, announced that they had taken over the operation – riders, manager, staff and all. And in 1981 the team would be riding the full European programme with no American distractions.

Roche had unfruitful negotiations with his old team, Carrera, and with Toshiba, and when he finally left Histor it was to take up a two-year contract with Tonton Tapis (Belgium's biggest carpet warehouse), a sponsor who was new to the game. It was Roche's sixth team in ten years.

Kelly, who finished third in the World Cup despite missing the early classics through injury, decided, at thirty-four, to remain with PDM for a further year (with the option of a second). And to scotch earlier stories that he had ridden his last Tour de France, he insisted that it was again on his schedule. The third Irishman left on the circuit, Martin Earley, stayed with him, signing a two-year contract.

Fignon missed the world championships but was back on the road soon afterwards for competitive training. The promise that he would be more assertive when he returned the following season, however, was implicit in Castorama's signing of two experienced mountaineers, Frédéric Vichot and Jean-Claude Bagot, to support him in the major races.

Interestingly, though, Castorama lost Fabrice Philipot and Gérard Rue who both went to join Gilles Delion at Paul Koechli's Helvetia-La Suisse. This meant that the best of the new generation of French riders were gathered together on foreign though friendly soil. It was surprising, but it was no bad thing. Koechli was the man who asserted that with proper attention to diet, training and recuperation, it was possible not only to ride the Tour de France, but to win it, without resorting to drugs. 'One day the immense majority of riders, the immense majority of the public, will confirm that.'

The curtain was now coming down on the fifth act of the season. Some of the players were off to see their managers about contracts which had still to be hammered out. A few were going on to make guest appearances in the winter cabaret of six-day racing. But most would be resting through November and early December before pulling on their woollen caps and arm warmers to start winter training. It was time to allow a sneak preview of the next big attraction. On the morning of Tuesday, 23 October a few of the principal actors and most of the reviewers turned up at the Congrès d'Issy-les-Moulineaux in the Paris suburbs for the unveiling by Jean-Marie Leblanc of the route for the 1991 Tour de France. And afterwards, although they made polite noises, most of them didn't know quite what to say. There were so few surprises.

As was well-known already, the start was to be in Lyons. It had paid the Tour £150,000 for the usual package of prologue, short morning stage beginning and ending in the city, and afternoon team time trial. Nothing as bizarre as the Futuroscope about the settings, although the third part did end at somewhere called Eurexpo. But the situation of Lyons posed some problems with the route. Unless the race took an eccentric cross-country course, there was only one way to go. Being already on the doorstep of the Alps, it couldn't go south or east since this would have meant sending the riders up the mountains in the opening days. It had to travel north and take the long way round anti-clockwise to the Pyrenees. That much was practically pre-ordained. The rest was a matter of race logistics and commercial deals.

While it was about it, the Tour wanted to spend some time in Brittany, which had recently been neglected (the 1990 stage from Nantes to Mont-Saint-Michel had really only brushed its fringes). But dalliance has to be paid for. After eleven flat and almost continuous stages, north to the Belgian border at Valenciennes (but carefully avoiding the *pavé*), west through

ROUTE OF 1991 TOUR

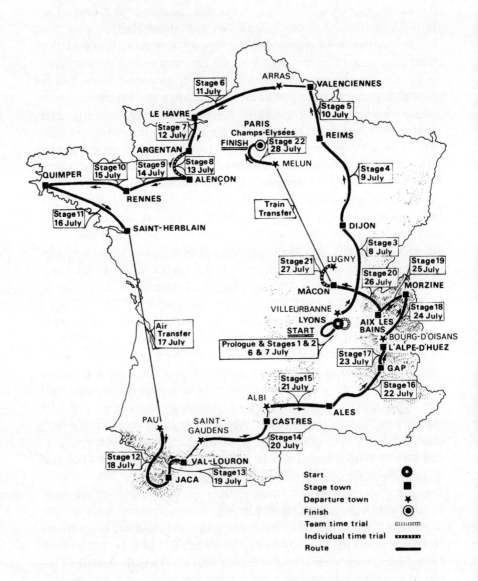

ARRAS

VALENCIENNES

Stage 6
11 July

LE HAVRE

Stage 5
10 July

Stage 7
12 July

PARIS
Champs-Elysées
FINISH   Stage 22
28 July

REIMS

ARGENTAN

Stage 9
14 July

Stage 8
13 July

Stage 10
15 July

MELUN

Stage 4
9 July

QUIMPER

ALENÇON

RENNES

Train
Transfer

DIJON

Stage 11
16 July

SAINT-HERBLAIN

Stage 3
8 July

Stage 21
27 July

LUGNY

Stage 19
25 July

Stage 20
26 July

MORZINE

MÂCON

VILLEURBANNE
LYONS
START

AIX LES
BAINS

Stage 18
24 July

Air
Transfer
17 July

Prologue & Stages 1 & 2
6 & 7 July

BOURG-D'OISANS

L'ALPE-D'HUEZ

Stage 17
23 July

GAP

Stage 15
21 July

ALBI

Stage 16
22 July

ALES

PAU

SAINT-
GAUDENS

CASTRES

Stage 14
20 July

Stage 12
18 July

VAL-LOURON

Stage 13
19 July

JACA

Start		◉
Stage town		■
Departure town		★
Finish		◉
Team time trial		⊓⊓⊓⊓⊓
Individual time trial		⊓⊓⊓⊓⊓
Route		▬▬▬

Normandy and on to three Breton stages, the Tour would still have got no further than Nantes. It needed by now to reach the mountains. The answer was simple. Fly the riders from Nantes to Pau, 'the belvedere of the Pyrenees', leaving the rest of the entourage to cover the intervening 500kms by road. This would, in fact, be the only day without racing; there was to be no official rest day, but Fignon spoke for most of the riders when he said, 'That won't bother me; quite the contrary.'

From Pau the race would cross the Pyrenees to Jaca, its first Spanish stage town since 1974 (when it was Seo de Urgel). It would spend a second day in these frontier mountains, then move steadily eastward for three days in the Alps. Finally there would be two days among the vineyards, with a time trial from Lugny to Mâcon to tie up any loose ends. TGV from Macon to Melun. Entry of the gladiators onto the Champs-Elysées. Very neat. Apart from the two long transfers, the stages dovetailed nicely with only a couple of short gaps. Lots of *fruits-de-mer*, you could hear the journalists thinking, plenty of Burgundy. But what about the racing?

Well, look at the details. At 3,940km the race covered 540km more than 1990, though the organisers had tried to keep a balance between long (230km) and short (170km) stages. The longest, the 289km from Dijon to Reims, was still a little shorter than the 301km trek from Avranches to Rouen in 1990. There wasn't much to take issue with there. The un-broken sequence of flat stages making up the first half of the Tour was a bit uninviting, but they carried the same time-bonus at the finish and in the intermediate sprints, and if 1990 was anything to go by, they wouldn't be uneventful. Anyway what was flat? There is not much level ground in Brittany, and even Normandy can pitch and roll. As for the individual time trials, they added up to 134km compared with 153km in 1990, which was neither here nor there.

But the mountains, that was the thing. For the second year running they seemed to have been played down. There would be one great heroic showpiece, stage 13, the second in the Pyrenees, running, if that's the word, 231km from Jaca to Val Louron. That was like a row of dragon's teeth with, in turn, the cols du Portalet, d'Aubisque, du Soulor, du Tourmalet and d'Aspin and, after they had done their worst, a 7km climb to the finish. The appearance of the Joux-Plane, the steepest climb of all with 10km of 1-in-10, on a 249km stage from Bourg-d'Oisans to Morzine, was also going to bring on some heavy breathing. But there would be only two summit finishes (against five in 1990), the stage which ended at the top of l'Alpe-d'Huez had only a 128km preamble and, unusually, there would be no mountain time trial.

The route went down well with most of the favourites. Fignon preferred the Pyrenees before the Alps since he had never finished a clockwise Tour. Roche said that on the whole it was pretty good. And LeMond described it as ideal. He didn't regret the absence of a mountain time trial, because it had never helped him gain time on his opponents. He would only miss the rest day since he liked to be joined by his wife and children in the final week. Except for small reservations there were no complaints except from José-Miguel Echavarri, the *directeur-sportif* of Banesto, who was concerned for the prospects of Pedro Delgado and Miguel Indurain. 'Basically, the route is not favourable to climbers. I would even say that the Tour is a little Italianised [the Giro is generally considered a gentler option as far as mountains go] perhaps on account of the influence that Italian cycling is beginning to exercise. The course is appreciably softened, which I regret a little, for the legend of the Tour was not created by making it easy.'

The one novel feature was that the Tour was to start a week later than usual on Saturday 6 July, the day that French schools broke up for their summer holidays. Beyond that there were no surprises, and even *L'Equipe* seemed a little disappointed, making the best of it by summing it up in a copy-writer's phrase, 'A Tour for today.'

This was apt enough. Leblanc is not a man with grandiose ideas as Desgrange was, and as were even Jacques Goddet, with his idea of a brave new *mondiale*, or Félix Lévitan, with his admiration for American enterprise. The Tour is no longer a one-man or two-man band; it is more an orchestra. In the 1990 Tour manual there was a pull-out spread of thirty-four studio portraits of its members, from Jean-Pierre Carenso, Directeur Général, to Fabrice Gaspard, Technicien Radio. All the same size, even if the seven in the top row − which included Carenso, Leblanc (Directeur des Compétitions) and

Hinault (Conseiller Technique) – were in slightly closer close-up. As in the new logo, a sketchy figure of a rider in the yellow jersey and the two words, LE TOUR (as if asking what other tour is there?), you could see the hand of the corporate image-maker at work.

Teamwork, however, matches the personal style of Leblanc, a relaxed, approachable and responsive man who spends more time asking questions than laying down the law. For the two years after the still largely unexplained departure of Lévitan in the spring of 1987, the Tour was run by businessmen. This was not a successful period and culminated in the badly-handled Delgado affair. It was a relief to everyone when a journalist once more took over as director of the race. Leblanc was a one-time Tour rider, a columnist on *L'Equipe* and the editor of *Vélo*. He knows the riders and what they want from the race, and the press and their needs. Under his influence the Tour has become a more agreeable place to work, if perhaps a little less nervously exciting. And if there's tension, it comes from the riders not the administration.

At present the race seems to be going through a spell of retrenchment, trying to make things work, not make them different. The Americans and the Russians have come to the Tour without the Tour having to go to them (inspired by LeMond and Hampsten, there were said to have been 135 American amateurs riding in France in the summer of 1990, and at least as many East Europeans). And although it could come up again, there is no more far-fetched talk at present of the Tour starting in New York or Tokyo. It seems as much of an anachronism as that Paris-Moscow pro-am race passing through the Berlin Wall which very nearly went ahead a few seasons ago. Events have submerged it. There may still be a place for a regular global competition, but the World Cup series is a more appropriate framework than a national tour for developing that.

Whatever the shape of things to come, the 1991 Tour, as outlined, is very much the shape of things as they are. It strikes a decent balance between sport and pure theatre (which often in the past has been the theatre of cruelty, anyway). No gimmicks, no megalomania, no obvious bias towards any speciality, but a straightfoward contest to find the *courer complet*. A new Giant of the Road might not emerge from it, but it should be more than hard enough to force another protracted struggle out of half-a-dozen riders of closely matched talents. And in the end, with all respect to Hinault and Merckx, the public will probably find that more absorbing than a foregone victory for Superman.

When in doubt I often try to see the Tour through the eyes of the late Robert Dutein, a grumpy, humorous bear of a man, an 'homme-du-Midi' as he liked to call himself, with genial but explosive prejudices. He had once been a trackman, and in his day had ridden against 'Reg 'arris at 'erne 'ill'. In 1968 he was the cycling correspondent of the *Sud-Ouest* of Bordeaux, a provincial paper of similar status, I suppose, to the *Yorkshire Post* or the *Western Mail*. That year I followed the Tour in Dutein's car along with his driver and a younger reporter who wrote up the interviews and news stories. In another car was a driver and a telex operator (the only sense in which the paper did things by halves was that it also took a half-share in an aeroplane to photograph the race passing through its home territory).

My rented place in the car had been arranged between the Tour and the newspaper management, and the team at first seemed as pleased to take me in as a quiet-living country couple would be if they had an uncouth evacuee billeted upon them. But relations eased once they discovered that I didn't dally over my copy and wasn't faddy with my food – he wouldn't miss his *musette*, as they put it approvingly – and after a month we were getting on famously.

The trip was a revelation. Dutein's daily article was entitled 'From the Heart of the Peloton', and to live up to that billing he had to forgo his mid-day meal and travel in that small press column which follows the race wing-mirror-to-wing-mirror with the team cars. There you began to appreciate that even when Radio Tour said they had nothing to report there was constant activity back there. *Domestiques* fetching water-bottles for their teams, exhausted riders losing contact with the peloton or straining to regain their place after punctures, doctors leaning out of their cars applying dressings to wounded limbs. There was a lot of naked panic and desperation even at the quietest times.

More important, though, was sharing a French view of the race. To Dutein the Tour de France should be literally what it said. Straying outside the frontiers was not only asking for trouble, it was a betrayal. Belgium wasn't too bad; at least the people there spoke French. But when a Spanish stage finished in Seo del Urgel, Dutein saw no reason to stay there overnight. He didn't trust the food or the telephone system. There was nothing for it but to recross the Pyrenees before sending our copy and sitting at table. 'It is better to do these things in France,' he said, and that was that.

So what would he think of the modern Tour? I don't believe that he would have anything against the success of Roche or LeMond (except the latter's preference for Mexican food, ice-cream and US medical treatment). He had admired 'arris and described Tom Simpson as 'un grand champion'. But he would have been exasperated by the failure of the French to produce a great champion of their own. Not that he was a hero worshipper. When Poulidor was brought down by a press photographer's motorbike and was forced to abandon next morning at Albi, Dutein felt he had brought the misfortune on himself by not leading the chase against his supposed ally, Roger Pingeon. And when Poulidor grandly announced that in spite of his absence the Tour would go on, Dutein could only scoff.

It's not, I believe, the foreign riders that Dutein would have disliked (though he might have got a bit restless about their numbers), but what he would have seen as the encroachment of alien television. The enlargement of the cavalcade. The priority given to cameras. The separation of press and press room from the race. The crush, the traffic jams, the babel. In a word (and it's one which he would have detested), mondialisation, and the dilution of much that was distinctively and attractively French about the Tour de France.

Yet, if it's only natural to regret these changes, what would the Tour have become without them? In all probability, a piece of folklore played out each July in memory of more heroic days, its cast and its audience diminishing with every passing year. Instead, the Tour's position as one of the sporting wonders of the world is more secure than it has ever been.

Past Masters

Year	Starters	Finishers	Distance in kms	No. of stages	Avge speed	Winner
1903	60	21	2,428	6	25.28	Maurice Garin (Fr)
1904	88	23	2,428	6	24.29	Henri Cornet (Fr)
1905	60	24	2,975	11	27.28	Louis Trousselier (Fr)
1906	82	14	4,637	13	24.46	René Pottier (Fr)
1907	93	33	4,488	14	28.47	Lucien Petit-Breton (Fr)
1908	114	36	4,487	14	28.74	Lucien Petit-Breton (Fr)
1909	150	55	4,507	14	28.65	François Faber (Lux)
1910	110	41	4,474	15	28.68	Octave Lapize (Fr)
1911	84	28	5,344	15	27.32	Gustave Garrigou (Fr)
1912	131	41	5,319	15	27.89	Odile Defraye (Belg)
1913	140	25	5,387	15	27.62	Philippe Thys (Belg)
1914	145	54	5,405	15	27.02	Philippe Thys (Belg)
1919	69	10	5,560	15	24.95	Firmin Lambot (Belg)
1920	113	22	5,519	15	24.13	Philippe Thys (Belg)
1921	123	38	5,484	15	24.72	Léon Scieur (Belg)
1922	120	38	5,375	15	24.20	Firmin Lambot (Belg)
1923	139	48	5,394	15	24.42	Henri Pelissier (Fr)
1924	157	60	5,425	15	23.95	Ottavio Bottecchia (It)
1925	130	49	5,430	18	24.77	Ottavio Bottecchia (It)
1926	126	41	5,745	17	24.06	Lucien Buysse (Belg)
1927	142	39	5,320	24	26.83	Nicolas Frantz (Lux)
1928	162	41	5,377	22	27.83	Nicolas Frantz (Lux)
1929	155	60	5,286	22	28.32	Maurice Dewaele (Belg)
1930	100	59	4,818	21	27.97	André Leducq (Fr)
1931	81	35	5,095	24	28.75	Antonin Magne (Fr)
1932	80	57	4,520	21	29.21	André Leducq (Fr)
1933	80	40	4,395	23	29.69	Georges Speicher (Fr)
1934	60	39	4,363	23	29.46	Antonin Magne (Fr)
1935	93	46	4,338	21	30.62	Romain Maes (Belg)
1936	90	43	4,442	21	31.07	Sylvère Maes (Belg)
1937	98	46	4,415	20	31.74	Roger Lapébie (Fr)
1938	96	55	4,694	21	31.56	Gino Bartali (It)
1939	79	49	4,224	18	31.96	Sylvère Maes (Belg)
1947	100	53	4,640	21	31.37	Jean Robic (Fr)
1948	120	44	4,922	21	33.40	Gino Bartali (It)
1949	120	55	4,775	21	32.11	Fausto Coppi (It)
1950	116	51	4,808	22	32.78	Ferdinand Kubler (Switz)
1951	123	66	4,697	24	32.97	Hugo Koblet (Switz)
1952	122	78	4,807	23	31.60	Fausto Coppi (It)

Winning margin	Second	Third	Fourth
2h 49′	R Pothier (Fr)	Augereau (Fr)	Muller (It)
2h 16′14″	Dortignacq (Fr)	Jousselin (Fr)	Catteau (Fr)
26pts*	Aucouturier (Fr)	Dortignac (Fr)	L Georget (Fr)
28pts	Passerieu (Fr)	Trousselier (Fr)	Petit-Breton (Fr)
19pts	Garrigou (Fr)	E Georget (Fr)	Passerieu (Fr)
32pts	Faber (Lux)	Passerieu (Fr)	Garrigou (Fr)
20pts	Garrigou (Fr)	J Alavoine (Fr)	Duboc (Fr)
4pts	Faber (Lux)	Garrigou (Fr)	Van Hauwaert (Belg)
41pts	Duboc (Fr)	E Georget (Fr)	Crupelandt (Fr)
59.5pts	Christophe (Fr)	Garrigou (Fr)	Buysse (Belg)
8′37″	Garrigou (Fr)	L Buysse (Belg)	Lambot (Belg)
1′49″	H Pélissier (Fr)	J Alavoine (Fr)	Rossius (Belg)
1h 42′45″	J Alavoine (Fr)	Christophe (Fr)	Scieur (Belg)
57′00″	Heusghem (Belg)	Lambot (Belg)	Scieur (Belg)
19′02″	Heusghem (Belg)	Barthélémy (Fr)	Lucotti (It)
41′15″	J Alavoine (Fr)	Sellier (Belg)	Heusghem (Belg)
30′41″	Bottecchia (It)	Bellenger (Fr)	Tiberghien (Belg)
35′36″	N Frantz (Lux)	L Buysse (Belg)	Aymo (It)
54′20″	L Buysse (Belg)	Aymo (It)	N Frantz (Lux)
1h 22′25″	N Frantz (Lux)	Aymo (It)	Beeckman (Belg)
1h 48′21″	Dewaele (Belg)	J Vervaecke (Belg)	Leducq (Fr)
50′07″	Leducq (Fr)	Dewaele (Belg)	Maertens (Belg)
32′07″	Demuysère (Belg)	Pancera (It)	Cardona (Sp)
14′19″	Guerra (It)	A Magne (Fr)	Demuysère (Belg)
12′56″	Demuysère (Belg)	Pesenti (It)	Rebry (Belg)
24′03″	Stoepel (Ger)	Camusso (It)	Pesenti (It)
4′01″	Guerra (It)	Martano (It)	Lemaire (Belg)
27′31″	Martano (It)	R Lapébie (Fr)	Vervaecke (Belg)
17′52″	Morelli (It)	Vervaecke (Belg)	S Maes (Belg)
26′55″	A Magne (Fr)	Vervaecke (Belg)	Clemens (Lux)
7′17″	Vicini (It)	Amberg (Switz)	Camusso (It)
18′27″	Vervaecke (Belg)	Cosson (Fr)	E Vissers (Belg)
30′38″	Vietto (Fr)	Vlaemynck (Belg)	Clemens (Lux)
3′58″	Fachleitner (Fr)	Brambilla (It)	Ronconi (It)
26′16″	Schotte (Belg)	G Lapébie (Fr)	L Bobet (Fr)
10′55″	Bartali (It)	Marinelli (Fr)	Robic (Fr)
9′30″	Ockers (Belg)	L Bobet (Fr)	Géminiani (Fr)
22′00″	Géminiani (Fr)	L Lazaridès (Fr)	Bartali (It)
28′17″	Ockers (Belg)	B Ruiz (Sp)	Bartali (It)

* During the eight Tours of 1905–12, results were based not upon accumulated time but on a flexible system of points. These were based on finishing positions at the end of each stage modified by the time-gaps between riders.   237

Year	Starters	Finishers	Distance in kms	No. of stages	Avge speed	Winner
1953	119	76	4,479	22	34.60	Louison Bobet (Fr)
1954	110	69	4,855	23	34.63	Louison Bobet (Fr)
1955	130	69	4,495	22	34.43	Louison Bobet (Fr)
1956	120	88	4,528	22	36.51	Roger Walkowiak (Fr)
1957	120	56	4,686	22	34.50	Jacques Anquetil (Fr)
1958	120	78	4,319	24	36.90	Charly Gaul (Lux)
1959	120	65	4,363	22	35.24	Federico Bahamontes (Sp)
1960	128	81	4,173	21	37.21	Gastone Nencini (It)
1961	136	72	4,397	21	36.28	Jacques Anquetil (Fr)
1962	147	94	4,274	22	37.56	Jacques Anquetil (Fr)
1963	130	76	4,137	21	36.66	Jacques Anquetil (Fr)
1964	132	81	4,504	22	35.58	Jacques Anquetil (Fr)
1965	130	96	4,188	22	36.08	Félice Gimondi (It)
1966	130	82	4,303	22	36.74	Lucien Aimar (Fr)
1967	130	88	4,696	22	35.01	Roger Pingeon (Fr)
1968	110	63	4,684	22	35.18	Jan Janssen (Neth)
1969	129	86	4,110	22	35.44	Eddy Merckx (Belg)
1970	150	100	4,359	23	36.56	Eddy Merckx (Belg)
1971	130	94	3,578	20	37.15	Eddy Merckx (Belg)
1972	132	88	3,730	20	35.48	Eddy Merckx (Belg)
1973	132	87	4,150	20	33.93	Luis Ocana (Sp)
1974	130	105	4,098	22	35.66	Eddy Merckx (Belg)
1975	140	86	4,000	22	34.90	Bernard Thévenet (Fr)
1976	130	87	4,017	22	34.51	Lucien Van Impe (Belg)
1977	100	53	4,096	22	35.41	Bernard Thévenet (Fr)
1978	110	78	3,908	22	36.08	Bernard Hinault (Fr)
1979	150	90	3,765	24	36.51	Bernard Hinault (Fr)
1980	130	85	3,842	22	35.14	Joop Zoetemelk (Neth)
1981	150	121	3,753	24	38.96	Bernard Hinault (Fr)
1982	169	125	3,507	21	38.05	Bernard Hinault (Fr)
1983	140	88	3,809	22	36.23	Laurent Fignon (Fr)
1984	170	124	4,021	23	35.88	Laurent Fignon (Fr)
1985	179	144	4,109	22	36.23	Bernard Hinault (Fr)
1986	210	132	4,094	23	37.2	Greg LeMond (USA)
1987	207	135	4,231	25	36.64	Stephen Roche (Ire)
1988	198	151	3,284	22	38.90	Pedro Delgado (Sp)
1989	198	138	3,257	21	37.81	Greg LeMond (USA)
1990	198	156	3,400	21	37.48	Greg LeMond (USA)

Winning margin	Second	Third	Fourth
14'18"	Malléjac (Fr)	Astrua (It)	Close (Belg)
15'49"	Kubler (Switz)	Schaer (Switz)	Dotto (Fr)
4'53"	Brankart (Belg)	Gaul (Lux)	Fornara (It)
1'25"	Bauvin (Fr)	Adriaenssens (Belg)	Bahamontes (Sp)
14'56"	M Janssens (Belg)	Christian (Austria)	Forestier (Fr)
3'10"	Favero (It)	Géminiani (Fr)	Adriaenssens (Belg)
4'01"	Anglade (Fr)	Anquetil (Fr)	Rivière (Fr)
5'02"	Battistini (It)	Adriaenssens (Belg)	Junkermann (W Ger)
12'14"	Carlesi (It)	Gaul (Lux)	Massignan (It)
4'59"	Planckaert (Belg)	Poulidor (Fr)	G Desmet (Belg)
3'35"	Bahamontes (Sp)	Perez-Frances (Sp)	Lebaube (Fr)
55"	Poulidor (Fr)	Bahamontes (Sp)	Anglade (Fr)
2'40"	Poulidor (Fr)	Motta (It)	Anglade (Fr)
1'07"	Janssen (Neth)	Poulidor (Fr)	Momene (Sp)
3'40"	Jimenez (Sp)	Balmamion (It)	Letort (Fr)
38"	Van Springel (Belg)	Bracke (Belg)	San Miguel (Sp)
17'54"	Pingeon (Fr)	Poulidor (Fr)	Gimondo (It)
12'41"	Zoetemelk (Neth)	G Petterson (Sweden)	V d Bossche (Belg)
9'51"	Zoetemelk (Neth)	Van Impe (Belg)	Thévenet (Fr)
10'41"	Gimondi (It)	Poulidor (Fr)	Van Impe (Belg)
15'51"	Thévenet (Fr)	Fuente (Sp)	Zoetemelk (Neth)
8'04"	Poulidor (Fr)	Lopez-Carrill (Sp)	Panizza (It)
2'47"	Merckx (Belg)	Van Impe (Belg)	Zoetemelk (Neth)
4'14"	Zoetemelk (Neth)	Poulidor (Fr)	Delisle (Fr)
48"	Kuiper (Neth)	Van Impe (Belg)	Galdos (Sp)
3'56"	Zoetemelk (Neth)	Agostinho (Port)	Bruyère (Belg)
13'57"	Zoetemelk (Neth)	Agostinho (Port)	Kuiper (Neth)
6'55"	Kuiper (Neth)	Martin (Fr)	De Muynck (Belg)
14'34"	Van Impe (Belg)	Alban (Fr)	Zoetemelk (Neth)
6'21"	Zoetemelk (Neth)	Van der Velde (Neth)	Winnen (Neth)
4'04"	Arroyo (Sp)	Winnen (Neth)	Van Impe (Belg)
10'32"	Hinault (Fr)	LeMond (USA)	Millar (GB)
1'42"	LeMond (USA)	Roche (Ire)	Kelly (Ire)
3'10"	Hinault (Fr)	Zimmermann (Switz)	Hampsten (USA)
40"	Delgado (Sp)	Bernard (Fr)	Mottet (Fr)
7'13"	Rooks (Neth)	Parra (Col)	Bauer (Can)
08"	Fignon (Fr)	Delgado (Sp)	Theunisse (Neth)
2'	Chiappucci (It)	Breukink (Neth)	Delgado (Sp)

Landmarks

Victories and places
Three men have won the Tour five times: Jacques Anquetil
(Fr), Eddy Merckx (Belg) – who also share the record of four
consecutive wins – and Bernard Hinault (Fr). Philippe Thys
(Belg) and Louison Bobet (Fr) won three times, the latter in
successive years. Merckx wore the race leader's yellow jersey
most often – 96 days – followed by Hinault, 75, and Anquetil,
49.

Raymond Poulidor (Fr), who never won the Tour, finished
most often among the first three, with three second places and
five third. Hinault was placed seven times, with five wins and
two seconds. So was the remarkable Zoop Zoetemelk (Neth),
who was runner-up six times and scored his only victory in
1980 at the age of thirty-three. Zoetemelk also holds the record
of having ridden 16 Tours from start to finish. Lucien Van
Impe (Belg) entered and completed 14. André Darrigade (Fr)
finished 13 of his 14, Poulidor 12 of 14, and Joaquim
Agostinho (Port) 12 of 13.

By 1990 after 77 Tours, France had provided 36 winners,
Belgium 18, Italy 8, Luxemburg 4, and Spain and the United
States 3. Switzerland and the Netherlands had each won 2,
and Ireland one.

Youngest and oldest winners
The youngest winner was twenty-year-old Henri Cornet (Fr) in
1904, though he owed his place in the records to the disqualification of the first four finishers. Otherwise the youngest
winners, all twenty-two, were Octave Lapize (Fr) in 1910,
François Faber (Lux) 1909, Romain Maes (Belg) 1935, Félice
Gimondi (It) 1965 and Laurent Fignon (Fr) 1984. The oldest
was Firmin Lambot (Belg), thirty-six, in 1922, followed by
Henri Pelissier (Fr) 1923 and Gino Bartali (It) 1948, both
thirty-four.

Bartali had previously won in 1938, making his the longest time-span between victories, although, because of the war, the Tour had meanwhile been run only twice. Eugène Christophe (Fr), '*le vieux Gaullois*', rode only eight Tours, but he achieved the record span of 19 years between first (1906) and last (1925). His best result was runner-up in 1912.

Biggest and smallest winning margins
The biggest winning margin, 2hr 49min, was achieved by Maurice Garin (Fr) in the first Tour, 1903, and the fifth and last over the hour was in 1927. The biggest since the war was 26min 16sec by Gino Bartali (It) in 1948. The closest call came in 1989 when Greg LeMond (USA) beat Laurent Fignon (Fr) by 8sec. Next was the 38sec victory of Jan Janssen (Neth) over Herman Van Springel (Belg) in 1968.

Yellow jersey from first to last
Four riders since 1919 have taken the lead on the opening day and held it to the end, although only one, Nicolas Frantz of Luxemburg in 1928, was literally in the yellow jersey throughout the race. As the previous year's winner he was entitled to wear it from the start in Paris, and secured it by winning that day at Caen. He was never overtaken, and his five stage wins included the last from Dieppe back to Paris.

Ottavio Bottecchia won his jersey on the first stage to Le Havre in 1924 and kept it by taking half an hour's lead in the Pyrenees and winning three more stages, among them the final sprint in Paris. It was Italy's first Tour success.

Romain Maes, a Belgian outsider, made his own luck in 1935 by escaping alone when a level crossing closed on his pursuers at Bruay on the Paris-Lille stage. He had only one further stage win before he, too, capped his unexpected rise to fame by taking the final stage from Caen to Paris.

Jacques Anquetil owes his inclusion in this list to the fact that the 1961 Tour began with two half-stages. He lost the first, Rouen-Versailles, which went to André Darrigade, but comfortably won the afternoon time trial to qualify as leader at the end of the opening day. He wasn't seriously challenged after that, reinforcing his position, as usual, in the second time trial.

Winners on the final stage

Two post-war riders have won the Tour on the final day without having previously held the lead, receiving their only yellow jersey on the podium in Paris.

In 1947 the Frenchman, Jean Robic, was 2min 58sec down on the Italian, Pierre Brambilla, before the start of the Caen-Paris stage. Breaking with the tradition that this should be treated as a triumphal march to the capital, Robic attacked on a hill at Rouen when he noticed that Brambilla had dropped back. With help from some other opportunists he maintained the breakaway for 140km to win the Tour by 3min 58sec. One of his companions, Fachleitner, moved up to second place overall, while Brambilla dropped to third, more than ten minutes down.

Before the concluding 54.5km time trial from Melun to Paris in 1968 the Dutchman, Jan Janssen, was lying third, 16sec behind the Belgian race leader, Herman Van Springel. But in this speciality their comparative skills were well known, and there was no great surprise when Janssen beat Van Springel by 54sec to win the Tour by 38sec.

The American, Greg LeMond, also came from behind to snatch the 1989 Tour, though he had worn the yellow jersey for seven days earlier in the race. In a more dramatic conclusion than that of 1968, and over less than half the time trial distance, LeMond wiped out Laurent Fignon's 50sec race lead with 8sec to spare.

Most stage wins

Eddy Merckx (Belg) heads the list with a career total of 34 stage wins. Bernard Hinault (Fr) had 27, André Leducq (Fr) 25, André Darrigade (Fr) 22 and Nicolas Frantz (Lux) 20. This order seems likely to remain undisturbed for some time since at the end of the 1990 Tour the most successful contemporary stage winner, Laurent Fignon, aged 29, had eight to his credit.

Merckx also shares the record of eight stage victories in a single Tour with Charles Pelissier (Fr) in 1930 and Freddy Maertens (Belg) in 1976 – but Merckx did it twice, in 1970 and 1974. Gino Bartali (It) in 1948 and Hinault in 1979 won seven stages. In 1909 François Faber (Lux) had the distinction of winning five stages in succession.

The long escapes
Before tactical racing gradually evolved, stages of the Tour were more like the marathon races of athletics. The small fields tended to break up from the start as the strong men, the potential Tour winners, eased away from the weaker riders, and there was little organised counter-attack from behind. In this period François Faber (Lux) made the two most imposing attacks to win the 1909 Tour, taking stage 2 at Metz and stage 3 at Belfort by the same margins of 33min. A lead of 25min 48sec on a glacial stage to Luchon also gave Lucien Buysse the 1926 Tour.

Since the war, because of the ability of the peloton to organ-ise a pursuit, attacks by the favourites, even in the mountains, have generally been shorter and more carefully calculated. The long escapes have been by relatively minor characters profiting from the indulgence of the leaders. They come in two categories.

In distance the longest post-war solo escape was by Berrichon Bourlon (Fr) in 1947. He attacked at the start of the Carcassonne-Luchon stage and covered the entire distance of 253km to win by 16min 30sec. In 1965 José Perez-Frances (Sp) led for 223km of the 240km stage from Ax-les-Thermes to Barcelona, gaining 4min 23sec. Third longest, in 1950, was by Maurice Blomme (Belg) with a solitary 214km of the 233km between Saint-Gaudens and Perpignan; he earned 7min 9sec.

In terms of time gained the palm goes to José-Luis Viejo (Sp) who won the 1976 stage from Montgenèvre to Manosque by 22min 50sec after 160km alone. Next were P Baffi (It) with 21min 48sec at Bordeaux in 1957 (145km), D De Groot (Neth) with 20min 31sec (150km) at Albi in 1955 and the Yorkshire-man Brian Robinson with 20min 06sec at Châlon-sur-Sâone (140km) in 1959.

Winning combinations
Five riders have won both the Tours of Italy and France in the same year: Fausto Coppi (It) in 1949 and 1952; Jacques Anquetil (Fr) 1964; Eddy Merckx (Belg) 1970, 1972 and 1974; Bernard Hinault (Fr) 1982, 1985; Stephen Roche (Ire) 1987. Two have doubled the Tours of Spain and France: Anquetil

(1963) and Hinault (1978). Nobody has won all three major tours in the same year, and only four riders – Anquetil, Félice Gimondi (It), Merckx and Hinault – have won all of them at some time. Five riders have won the Tour de France and World Championship road race in the same year: Georges Speicher (Fr) 1933; Louison Bobet (Fr) 1954; Merckx 1971 and 1974; Roche 1987; Greg LeMond (USA) 1989. Only Merckx (1974) and Roche did so in the year that they also won the Tour of Italy.

Winners of the Mountain prize
(with finishing positions)

1933 V Trueba (Sp): 6th
1934 R Vietto (Fr): 5th
1935 F Vervaecke (Belg): 3rd
1936 J Berrendero (Sp): 11th
1937 F Vervaecke (Belg): aban
1938 G Bartali (It): 1st
1939 S Maes (Belg): 1st
1947 P Brambilla (It): 3rd
1948 G Bartali (It): 1st
1949 F Coppi (It): 1st
1950 L Bobet (Fr): 3rd
1951 R Géminiani (Fr): 2nd
1952 F Coppi (It): 1st
1953 J Lorono (Sp): 50th
1954 F Bahamontes (Sp): 25th
1955 C Gaul (Lux): 3rd
1956 C Gaul (Lux): 13th
1957 G Nencini (It): 6th
1958 F Bahamontes (Sp): 8th
1959 F Bahamontes (Sp): 1st
1960 I Massignan (It): 10th
1961 I Massignan (It): 4th
1962 F Bahamontes (Sp): 14th
1963 F Bahamontes (Sp): 2nd
1964 F Bahamontes (Sp): 3rd

1965 J Jimenez (Sp): 23rd
1966 J Jimenez (Sp): 13th
1967 J Jimenez (Sp): 2nd
1968 A Gonzales (Sp): 13th
1969 E Merckx (Belg): 1st
1970 E Merckx (Belg): 1st
1971 L Van Impe (Belg): 3rd
1972 L Van Impe (Belg): 4th
1973 P Torres (Sp): 13th
1974 D Perurena (Sp): 44th
1975 L Van Impe (Belg): 3rd
1976 G Bellini (It): 16th
1977 L Van Impe (Belg): 3rd
1978 M Martinez (Fr): 10th
1979 G Battaglin (It): 6th
1980 R Martin (Fr): 3rd
1981 L Van Impe (Belg): 2nd
1982 B Vallet (Fr): 12th
1983 L Van Impe (Belg): 4th
1984 R Millar (GB): 4th
1985 L Herrera (Col): 7th
1986 B Hinault (Fr): 2nd
1987 L Herrera (Col): 5th
1988 S Rooks (Neth): 2nd
1989 G-J Theunisse (Neth): 4th

1990 T Claveyrolat (Fr): 21st

Winners of the Points prize

1953 F Schaer (Switz)	1972 E Merckx (Belg)
1954 F Kubler (Switz)	1973 H Van Springel (Belg)
1955 S Ockers (Belg)	1974 P Sercu (Belg)
1956 S Ockers (Belg)	1975 R Van Linden (Belg)
1957 J Forestier (Fr)	1976 F Maertens (Belg)
1958 J Graczyk (Fr)	1977 J Esclassan (Fr)
1959 A Darrigade (Fr)	1978 F Maertens (Belg)
1960 J Graczyk (Fr)	1979 B Hinault (Fr)
1961 A Darrigade (Fr)	1980 R Pevenage (Belg)
1962 R Altig (W Ger)	1981 F Maertens (Belg)
1963 R Van Looy (Belg)	1982 S Kelly (Ire)
1964 J Janssen (Neth)	1983 S Kelly (Ire)
1965 J Janssen (Neth)	1984 F Hoste (Belg)
1966 W Planckaert (Belg)	1985 S Kelly (Ire)
1967 J Janssen (Neth)	1986 E Vanderaerden (Belg)
1968 F Bitossi (It)	1987 J-P Van Poppel (Neth)
1969 E Merckx (Belg)	1988 E Planckaert (Belg)
1970 W Godefroot (Belg)	1989 S Kelly (Ire)
1971 E Merckx (Belg)	1990 O Ludwig (E Ger)

Climbers and sprinters

Five riders on eight occasions have won both the mountain prize and the Tour: Gino Bartali (It) 1938 and 1948; Fausto Coppi (It) 1949 and 1952; Eddy Merckx (Belg) 1969 and 1970; Sylvère Maes (Belg) 1939; Federico Bahamontes (Sp) 1959. Only two riders on four occasions have won both points prize and Tour: Merckx in 1969, 1971 and 1972, and Bernard Hinault (Fr) 1979. Only Merckx (1969) has won all three competitions in the same year.

Bahamontes and Lucien Van Impe (Belg) hold the record with 6 mountain wins each; next comes Julio Jimenez (Sp) with 3. The top nations are Spain with 15 wins, Belgium with 11, Italy 10 and France 8. The Dutch had never won the prize until Steven Rooks took it in 1988; then Gert-Jan Theunisse won it for them again the following year.

Sean Kelly (Ire) holds the points record with 4 wins, followed by Jan Janssen (Neth), Merckx and Freddy Maertens (Belg) with 3. Belgium has dominated the competition with 18 wins to 7 for second-placed France, and 4 for Ireland, lying third.

Starting points
The Tour has always ended in Paris. Until 1951 it also started there every year except 1926, when it set off to cover a record distance of 5,745km from the spa town of Evian. Since 1951 it has begun in the Paris area just four times – in 1963, 1983, 1984 and 1986 (for commercial reasons, Paris was given as the point of departure only in 1963; for the rest emphasis was put on the district which provided sponsorship). Otherwise the start has been in the provinces or, on ten occasions, in neighbouring countries.

The Tour crossed the French frontier as early as 1906, when it briefly entered Alsace-Lorraine at Auboué. The first stage finish in Belgium was at Brussels in 1947, the first in Spain, San Sebastian, two years later. The Tour's only visit to the British Isles came in 1974 when stage 2 was a 164km circuit race on Plympton bypass near Plymouth.

1951 Metz	1971 Mulhouse
1952 Brest	1972 Angers
1953 Strasbourg	1973 SCHEVENINGEN
1954 AMSTERDAM	1974 Brest
1955 Le Havre	1975 CHARLEROI
1956 Reims	1976 Saint-Jean-de-Monts
1957 Nantes	1977 Fleurance
1958 BRUSSELS	1978 LEIDEN
1959 Mulhouse	1979 Fleurance
1960 Lille	1980 FRANKFURT
1961 Rouen	1981 Nice
1962 Nancy	1982 BASLE
1963 Paris (Nogent-sur-Marne)	1983 Fontenay-sous-Bois (Paris)
1964 Rennes	1984 Montreuil (Paris)
1965 COLOGNE	1985 Vannes
1966 Nancy	1986 Boulogne-Billancourt (Paris)
1967 Angers	1987 WEST BERLIN
1968 Vittel	1988 Pontchâteau
1969 Roubaix	1989 LUXEMBURG
1970 Limoges	1990 Futuroscope (nr Poitiers)

In 1991 the Tour is due to start in Lyons.

Landmarks

1903: First Tour, devised by Henri Desgrange and composed of six stages separated by four rest days, starts from Paris on 1 July. Sixty riders take part.

1905: Number of stages increased to 11 to eliminate night riding. Only one rest day in between. Race judged on points instead of overall time, a system which survives until 1913. First mountain stages include the Ballon d'Alsace in the Vosges and the côte de Laffrey and col Bayard in the Alps.

1906: First frontier crossing into Lorraine, then German territory.

1907: Experimental use, for one Tour only, of pace-makers on certain sections of two stages.

1910: First inclusion of Pyrenees, with ascents of Aspin, Aubisque, Peyresourde and Tourmalet. Broom wagon introduced.

1911: First ascent of Galibier (Alps).

1913: Return to classification based on overall time, not points.

1919: Yellow jersey for race leader introduced in latter part of Tour. First worn by Eugène Christophe (Fr) on departure from Grenoble.

1922: First ascent of Izoard (Alps).

1923: Time bonuses of 2min awarded to stage winners.

1926: For the first time Tour starts in the provinces, at Evian.

1927: On flat stages teams are sent off at 15min intervals – the beginnings of the team time trial.

1929: Tour enters Italy, the first post-war frontier crossing.

1930: National teams introduced. Tour provides standard yellow bicycles for all riders. First appearance of publicity caravan.

1932: Time bonuses awarded to first three at stage finish, and additional bonus to rider winning stage by more than 3min.

1933: Vincente Trueba (Sp) first to be acknowledged as best climber.

1934: Introduction of prize for best climber, judged on the order of passage over 14 cols; won by René Vietto (Fr). Time bonuses also awarded on mountain summits. First individual time trial held as 90km half-stage from La-Roche-sur-Yon to Nantes.

1936: Illness forces Henri Desgrange, founder of Tour, to leave the race. At Charleville Jacques Goddet takes over as director.

1937: Use of *derailleur* gears accepted.

1939: First mountain individual time trial. Elimination of last rider on general classification.

1947: First foreign stage finish (Lille-Brussels) and first wholly foreign stage (Brussels-Luxemburg).

1949: First entries into Spain (finish San Sebastian) and Italy (finish Aosta).

1950: Elimination for finishing outside stage time limit introduced.

1951: Twenty-five years after Evian, the Tour sets off from Metz, abandoning Paris as its regular starting point.

1952: First stage finishes at mountain summits – l'Alpe-d'Huez, Sestrières and Puy-de-Dôme.

1953: Introduction of the points competition to reward consistently high stage placings, and the green jersey for its leader.

1954: For the first time Tour starts outside France, at Amsterdam.

1955: The continuous thread of the Tour is broken, with transfers by team car from one stage finish to the next stage start.

1960: Tour makes the first transfer by train.

1961: Birth of Tour de l'Avenir, an amateur (later open) race run over an abridged version of the Tour route.

1962: Return of trade teams after thirty-two years. Félix Lévitan appointed deputy director of Tour.

1964: First post-war crossing into Germany. For the first time final stage into Paris takes the form of a time trial.

1967: Introduction of the time trial prologue. Return, for two-year period, to national teams. Parc des Princes, Paris, where the Tour had finished every year since 1904, used for the last time. For next seven years the finish is at the Stade Municipale de Vincennes.

1968: The so-called Tour of Health, with daily drug tests imposed for first time.

1970: Félix Lévitan becomes co-director of Tour with Jacques Goddet.

1971: First transfer by air between stages.

1972: After eight years as a time trial, the final stage into Paris becomes a conventional massed-start race once more.

1974: First transfer by sea as Tour pays its only visit to the British Isles for a stage at Plymouth.

1975: Tour finishes on Champs-Elysées for the first time.

1983: Tour is made an open race; Colombia is the only amateur team to take part.

1984: Introduction of the Tour Féminin.

1987: Departure of Félix Lévitan; Xavier Louy becomes race director with Jacques Goddet as managing director.

1989: Jean-Marie Leblanc takes over as race director. For the first time since 1971 the final stage to Paris is a time trial.

Glossary

Cycle racing has its own particular language, and I don't just mean everyday French. Since dictionaries misleadingly translate *commissaire* as commissioner, steward or ship's purser, and *musette* as bagpipe, nosebag or haversack, it might be useful to explain what special meaning these, and some other unclear terms, have for riders and followers of the Tour.

bidon Plastic drinking bottle usually carried in a holder on the down-tube, sometimes additionally on the seat-tube. In the cap is a valve which the rider can prise out with his teeth and so take small quantities of liquid. Although the bottle currently issued on the Tour bears the Coca-Cola logo, the contents, according to the rider's taste, are more typically water with lemon juice, cold tea or liquefied cereals.

bonification Bonus of so many seconds deducted from the rider's overall time, generally as a reward for finishing in the first three on a flat stage. Bonuses go in and out of fashion, so do the formulae on which they are based, as the organisers try to trim the balance of advantage between sprinters and climbers. They were dropped at the stage finish after 1985, but in 1990 were reinstated for the period up to the Alps. The stage winner received 20sec, the second man 12sec, the third 8sec. Smaller bonuses of 6sec, 4sec and 2sec were retained at the intermediate sprints.

casque Safety helmet.

casquette Light racing cap with stiffened peak.

classement général General classification or, as it's chummily known in Britain, gen class: the ranking list of riders, revised and published at the end of each stage, which shows their accumulated time so far (taking any bonuses into account) and their current standing in the race. The rider at the head of the list in the Tour wears the leader's yellow jersey. In 1990 the prize for the eventual winner was £200,000.

classement par équipes Ranking order of teams in the race, on the day and overall. It is based on the times of the three fastest riders from each team on each stage (and as far as the overall classification is concerned, of course, those riders contributing to the team time will vary from day to day). In 1990 the winners of the team time trial received £5,000, the team winning other stages £1,200, the team leading the competition (who wore a yellow *casquette*) £500 per day, and the eventual overall winners, £12,000. A similar competition based on points was discontinued.

classement par points Points classification. A separate ranking based not on finishing times but on finishing positions in the stages. It was introduced as a contest in its own right in 1953, jubilee of the Tour, when it was known as the Grand Prix du Cinquantenaire, and was afterwards retained as a special incentive for the sprinters. Its leader wears a green jersey. The points have been attributed in various ways. In 1990 the system was this: on flat stages 35 points went to the winner, 30 to the runner-up, and so on down to one point for the rider in 25th place; on moderate mountain stages it was 25 for the winner down to one for the 20th; on high mountain stages the scale was 20-1 for the first 15, and in time trials 15-1 for the first ten. The wearer of the green jersey received £250 per day, and the overall winner £15,000.

commissaire One of a number of officials responsible for enforcing the rules of the sport; in effect, a referee.

contre la montre Against the watch; see *étape contre la montre.*

contrôle de ravitaillement Feeding station: a predetermined stretch of road where team officials are allowed to hand up *musettes* of food and drink to their passing riders.

contrôle médical Euphemistic term for the centre where selected riders are required to give urine samples for drug tests.

Coupe du Monde World Cup competition for individual riders and teams introduced in 1989 and based on finishing positions in certain one-day races held in the earlier and later months of the season. In 1990 there were 12 races in the series, some new, others established classics; only one was staged outside Europe, the Canadian GP des Amériques.

critérium In English, criterium (simply without the accent): a race held over repeated laps of a short road circuit, so allowing spectators to see the riders frequently and watch the contest develop. This type of event, particularly popular in Belgium, is more widely staged on the continent in the month or so after the Tour, often as the centrepiece of town and village fêtes. The *critérium* principle is also used on certain Tour stages which have a circuit finish.

délai d'arrivée Time limit for finishing a stage, beyond which a rider faces elimination from the race. The limit is calculated as a percentage of the stage winner's time – this percentage varying from 7 per cent to 25 per cent according to the average speed and the difficulty of the stage. In short, riders are treated more leniently in time trials, and in fast or mountainous stages.

démarrage An escape or breakaway.

directeur-sportif Racing manager of a team.

domestique The humblest member of the team. His job is to sacrifice his own interests to those of the leader or to the two or three "protected" riders. He will fetch *bidons* for them, surrender his bicycle or a wheel to them if they have mechanical trouble, pace them back to the field if they stop for service, shadow their opponents and lead them out in the sprints. It's a dog's life, but occasionally he has his day, and is let off the leash to try to win on his own account.

dossard Rider's individual racing number, generally printed on a plastic panel and worn on either hip.

équipe de marque Trade team, one which bears the name of its commercial sponsor.

équipier May mean simply team-mate, but more often implies a member of the other ranks, not a leader.

étape Stage: any of the separately numbered sections of the Tour, whether or not it takes the race further along its route (some stages finish where they begin). Only the prologue is not counted as a stage – except by the fastest man who, by custom, claims it as a stage win.

étape contre la montre Time trial; literally, a stage raced against the stopwatch in which riders start at set intervals – usually of one minute in a short trial, but up to three minutes in a long one – and are individually timed over the course. In a team time trial (*contre la montre par équipes*) the members of each team start and, as far as is practicable, cover the course together. There is a longer interval between the teams, often of four minutes. The time of the fourth or fifth member to cross the finishing line is credited to each team-mate who finishes with or ahead of him. Any rider who falls behind is individually timed.

étape en ligne The typical stage in which all the riders start together.

extra-sportif Of a sponsor, from outside the cycle industry. The early professional teams were financed almost entirely by the manufacturers of cycles, tyres and accessories. Rising costs forced them to look for co-sponsors from unrelated fields who would link their names with the sport to build good-will and brand recognition. These have now taken over as the main, and very often the sole, sponsors.

FICP Fédération Internationale de Cyclisme Professionel, the governing body of professional cycle racing based in Brussels. The *classement FICP* is an individual and team ranking list based on results in international one-day and stage races. It is increasingly used to qualify for entry into major events.

fringale Sudden loss of strength and energy which a rider may suffer through inadequate feeding (though serious enough in its consequences it can often be quickly cured by eating a piece of cake or a sandwich). In English, hunger knock, or the bonk.

Grand Prix de la Montagne Special prize for climbers introduced into the Tour in 1933, and based on points gained in the order of arrival at certain summits along the route. The points system varies from Tour to Tour, but in 1990 the climbs were placed in one of four catagories or in the case of the most severe (l'Alpe-d'Huez, col du Tourmalet, for instance) were classed *hors-catégorie*. The first rider to the top of an H.C. climb was awarded 40 points and £500, and the points went down to one for the 15th man. Climbs in the lowest category, the fourth – simple hillsides described as *côtes* rather than *cols* – were worth only 5 points and £50 to the winner and one point to the third man. The current leader of the competition now wears the *maillot aux pois*. In 1990 it was worth £100 a day to wear the jersey, and the overall winner's prize was £15,000.

grimpeur Climber, in particular a climbing specialist.

jour sans A day when a rider is inexplicably drained of energy and suffers in consequence.

lanterne rouge The last rider on general classification. He was once made much of since, for all his struggles, he had at least finished the race, and was often presented with a red lamp. Latterly this sentiment has faded.

maillot à pois Jersey worn by the leader in the *Grand Prix de la Montagne*, decorated with red 'peas' the size of cricket balls on a white background.

maillot arc en ciel Rainbow jersey – white with blue, red, black, yellow and green horizontal stripes across the chest – which is awarded to winners of world championship events.

maillot jaune Yellow jersey introduced in 1919 to identify the current Tour leader to spectators (the colour was chosen because *L'Auto*, the newspaper which then promoted the race, was printed on yellow paper). The wearer used to receive a daily payment, but this practice was discontinued in 1990. Other tours have borrowed the idea: in the Tour of Spain the leader also wears yellow (the *maillot amarillo*), but in the Tour of Italy the jersey is pink (the *maglia rosa*).

maillot vert Green jersey worn by the leader of the points competition.

musette Light cloth bag with shoulder strap in which food and drink are handed up to the rider at the feeding station. Once he has stowed these rations away in a rear pouch on his racing jersey, the rider normally throws the musette to the side of the road where it becomes another souvenir for the first spectator to pounce on it.

neutralisation Period during which the riders pedal on together but racing is officially suspended. It occurs whenever there is a ceremonial stage start (*départ fictif*) in the centre of town, but the riders have to reach the outskirts before the true start (*départ réal*) is given. The race may also be neutralised in cases of emergency – obstruction of the road, extreme weather, for instance.

peloton Literally platoon: the main cluster of riders at any time during the race. If the field divides into two or more large groups these may also be called the first and second *pelotons*, etc, or referred to by the name of the most prominent rider in them, the *peloton maillot jaune, peloton Delgado*, for instance. The term isn't properly applied to groups of, say, fewer than twenty riders.

prime Prize awarded to the first rider to cross a particular point along the route – whether a mountain top or a sprint line. Most *primes* are part of the official prize structure, but towns and villages often put up sums of money for their own sprint, simply announcing it to the riders on a roadside placard.

prologue Individual time trial, usually of 5-7km (the longest was of 11km at Mulhouse in 1971) held on the eve of the opening stage. It was first introduced into the Tour at Angers in 1967, and has since been retained, except in 1988 when it was dropped to meet new regulations restricting the Tour to twenty-one days. Its purpose is to present the riders to the public in a brief, dramatic fashion, and to give the race a genuine leader right from the start.

rouleur A strong rider who, without being a specialist climber or sprinter, is capable of exerting pressure over a long and difficult stage.

routier-sprinter A sprint specialist on the road as distinct from the track.

soigneur/soigneuse Person attached to the team primarily to give massage, but usually practised in treating minor injuries and disorders.

sprint intermédiaire Flying sprint held at certain predetermined points along the route – indicated by a line on the road and a banner above it – without interruption to the race. The first three riders placed win a cash prize, points which count towards the green jersey competition, and in certain cases a small time bonus (see *bonification*). In the past the sprint has carried the name of its sponsor – e.g. *Point Chaud Michaud* or *Catch* – and its points have also counted in a separate classification whose leader wore a red jersey. But in 1990 the classification and jersey were dropped, and the sprints, reduced in number from 53 to 40, were simply absorbed into the points contest.

UCI Union Cycliste Internationale, world governing body for cycle racing. It is based in Geneva, which explains why some fines for racing misdemeanours are levied in Swiss francs.

voiture balai Broom wagon: vehicle bearing a symbolic besom or witch's broom as decoration which drives behind the last rider on the road to sweep up anyone who abandons the race.

Acknowledgments

In preparing *Le Tour* I gathered information, in 1990 and over previous years, from a number of sources beside official channels and the riders themselves – from colleagues, newspapers and magazines, and books. Cycling writers are unusually generous in sharing what they know, and I would like to acknowledge help received at various times from Stephen Bierley, Samuel Abt, Phil Ligget, Mike Price, François Tomaso, William Fotheringham, Rupert Guinness, Alan Fraser, Susan Bickelhaupt, John Wilcockson, John Pierce and Graham Watson; from Graham Jones, Paul Sherwen and Paul Kimmage, who had actually ridden the thing; and in the recent past from David Walsh, Bob Zeller, Keith Bingham, Dennis Donovan, David Taylor and Charles Burgess. *L'Equipe* and *Cycling Weekly* were indispensable. I also referred to the monthlies, *Vélo*, *Miroir du Cyclisme* and *Winning* and, during the Tour, to various French provincial papers whose coverage of the race is exhaustive, not to say sometimes exhausting.

Books which I have consulted and recommend are listed in the bibliography.

Bibliography

The Tour de France, Peter Clifford (Stanley Paul, 1965)

Le Tour a 75 ans, ed. Noel Coudel & Roger Lemoine (L'Equipe,1978)

Tour de France, the 75th anniversary cycle race, Robin Magowan (Stanley Paul, 1979)

Breakaway: On the road with the Tour de France (Random House, 1985), *In High Gear* (Bicycle Books, 1989), *Greg LeMond, The Incredible Comeback* (Stanley Paul, 1990), all by Samuel Abt

A Rough Ride, Paul Kimmage (Stanley Paul, 1990)

Wide-Eyed and Legless, Inside the Tour de France, Jeff Connor (Simon & Schuster/Sportspages, 1988)

The Agony and the Ecstasy, Stephen Roche with David Walsh (Stanley Paul, 1988)

Continental Cycle Racing, N. G. Henderson (Pelham Books, 1970)

Vélo, an annual book of results and records ed. Harry Van Den Bremt & René Jacobs (Editions Velo)

Le Guide du Tour, Daniel Pautrat (published annually since 1987, latterly by Editions de l'Aurore)

King of the Road, Andrew Ritchie (Wildwood House, 1985)

Bicycling, A History, Frederick Alderson (David & Charles, 1972)

The Penguin Book of the Bicycle, Roderick Watson & Martin Gray (Penguin Books, 1978)

Index